SEVEN CHURCHES FOUR HORSEMEN ONE LORD

SEVEN
CHURCHES
FOUR
HORSEMEN
ONE
LORD

LESSONS FROM THE APOCALYPSE

JAMES MONTGOMERY BOICE

EDITED BY PHILIP GRAHAM RYKEN

P&R
PUBLISHING
P.O. BOX 817 • PHILLIPSBURG • NEW JERSEY 08865-0817

Unless otherwise indicated, Scripture quotations are from the ESV® Bible (The Holy Bible, English Standard Version®), copyright © 2001 by Crossway, a publishing ministry of Good News Publishers. Used by permission. All rights reserved.

Scripture quotations marked (NIV) are from the HOLY BIBLE, NEW INTERNATIONAL VERSION®. NIV®. Copyright © 1973, 1978, 1984 by International Bible Society. Used by permission of Zondervan Publishing House. All rights reserved.

Italics within Scripture quotations indicate emphasis added.

Excerpt from *Genesis* Vol. 1 by James Montgomery Boice, copyright © 1982, 1998. Used and adapted for this work by permission of Baker Books, a division of Baker Publishing Group.

Excerpts from *More Than Conquerors* by William Hendriksen, copyright © 1940, 1967. Used by permission of Baker Books, a division of Baker Publishing Group.

Printed in the United States of America

Library of Congress Cataloging-in-Publication Data

Names: Boice, James Montgomery, 1938-2000, author. | Ryken, Philip Graham, 1966- editor.
Title: Seven churches, four horsemen, one Lord : lessons from the apocalypse / James Montgomery Boice ; edited by Philip Graham Ryken.
Description: Phillipsburg, New Jersey : P&R Publishing, 2020. | Includes index. | Summary: "Never before published, Boice's dynamic work on Revelation 1-6 instructs us on worship and the church. As you look to Christ's return, learn how to live for his glory"-- Provided by publisher.
Identifiers: LCCN 2019046074 | ISBN 9781629957647 (hardcover) | ISBN 9781629957654 (epub) | ISBN 9781629957661 (mobi)
Subjects: LCSH: Bible. Revelation, I-VI--Sermons.
Classification: LCC BS2825.54 .B65 2020 | DDC 228.07/7--dc23
LC record available at https://lccn.loc.gov/2019046074

CONTENTS

FOREWORD

No one knew it at the time, but these were the last sermons that James Montgomery Boice ever preached—his last regular weekly Bible expositions from the historic pulpit of Philadelphia's Tenth Presbyterian Church.

As he neared the end of a long series of sermons on the book of Matthew, Dr. Boice had begun to think about tackling what is perhaps a preacher's greatest challenge: the profound mysteries of the book of Revelation. When he casually mentioned to colleagues on Tenth's pastoral staff that he was "thinking about preaching Revelation," we urged him to ignore every possible alternative and preach the series that we knew would electrify the congregation.

Any Christian who has ever turned to the back of the Bible to "see how the story ends" or has puzzled over the bizarre and sometimes disturbing images in its final pages knows how strange Revelation is—and how deeply our hearts desire to know what it means. Dr. Boice's clear and compelling expositions of the Bible's famous last book became one of his last gifts to his beloved congregation before he died. He began his sermons on Revelation in November of 1999 and concluded them on April 16 of the following year, shortly after receiving the difficult diagnosis of liver cancer. Now, for the first time, these marvelous messages are appearing in print for the blessing of the wider church.

If you look through the table of contents, you will notice immediately that Dr. Boice never made it to the end of Revelation. Sadly, the rapid progression of his disease compelled him to cut his series short, which is one of the obstacles we faced as we considered publication: would people really be interested in reading a commentary on Revelation that ended at chapter 6?

There were other challenges as well. Although Dr. Boice completed his customary first edit of the manuscript—we have the handwritten notes to prove it—he never had the opportunity to prepare it for publication. So, inevitably, some important decisions needed to be made without the benefit of consulting with the author.

I have worked closely with Linda McNamara Boice throughout the editorial process. Like me, Mrs. Boice believed strongly that her late husband's sermons on Revelation deserved a wider audience. We are both deeply grateful to David Almack and other friends at P&R Publishing and also to Bob Brady at the Alliance of Confessing Evangelicals for their strong partnership in bringing this book to print, as well as to Lydia Brownback for kindly preparing the indexes.

The entire manuscript has been carefully reviewed for accuracy. The Scripture passages have been updated to the English Standard Version—a more recent, literal, and accurate translation than the one that Dr. Boice typically used for preaching. In various places, Mrs. Boice, the editorial team at P&R, and I agreed that a word was missing or a phrase was redundant, that a pronoun needed to identify its antecedent, that an anachronism ought to be updated, or that the manuscript should be clarified in some other way. But the expositions in this book are essentially the messages that Dr. Boice preached, in a form that he might have approved for publication.

Although the following commentary is incomplete, it stands as an unfinished masterpiece. In the opening chapters, Dr. Boice covers the full range of introductory topics, providing an orientation to the main themes of Revelation. His expositions of the seven letters to the seven churches show how those epistles are fully integrated into the symbols and significance of the book as a whole. His manuscript ends before the opening of the seventh seal, leaving readers to anticipate the coming judgment of God and the consummation of his kingdom. We stand in the same position today—waiting for Christ's return. Thus, in God's sovereign providence, the book ends precisely where it should end: with a warning to us to repent of our sin before the final judgment and an invitation to believe in Jesus Christ before his second coming.

James Boice believed that "the purpose of Revelation is to get Christians from all periods of history and in all circumstances to look at things from God's perspective rather than from man's and to draw comfort and strength from that perspective" (p. 42). His last Bible expositions have the same purpose: to give us the comfort and strength that come when we see life and eternity from God's point of view.

Philip Graham Ryken
President
Wheaton College

1

THE REVELATION
OF JESUS CHRIST

Revelation 1:1–3

In his commentary on Revelation, J. Ramsey Michaels quotes this tongue-in-cheek definition of *Revelation* by Ambrose Bierce in *The Devil's Dictionary*: "REVELATION, *n.* A famous book in which St. John the Divine concealed all that he knew. The revealing is done by the commentators, who know nothing."[1]

It is not entirely true that John concealed what he knew, because the ending of the book records these words from John's angelic guide: "Do not seal up the words of the prophecy of this book, for the time is near" (Rev. 22:10), meaning that the book was written to be read and understood. Indeed, the very first paragraph contains a blessing for those who read and heed it: "Blessed is the one who reads aloud the words of this prophecy, and blessed are those who hear, and who keep what is written in it, for the time is near" (Rev. 1:3). But Revelation is still obscure to most, if not all, readers, and even the most diligent and persistent scholars are divided over what John is saying. More books have been written about Revelation than about any other book in the Bible. G. K. Beale's commentary on the book has 852 items in its bibliography, and even the more "selected

---

1. J. Ramsey Michaels, *Revelation*, The IVP New Testament Commentary Series (Downers Grove, IL: InterVarsity Press, 1997), 13.

bibliography" of Robert H. Mounce contains 278 commentaries, articles, or reference volumes.

St. Jerome stood in awe of Revelation. He said, "The Apocalypse of John has as many secrets as words."[2] Martin Luther did not like Revelation—he wrote, "My spirit cannot accommodate itself to this book." Why not? He explained, though with sad misunderstanding, "There is one sufficient reason for the small esteem in which I hold it—that Christ is neither taught in it nor recognized."[3] Ulrich Zwingli, another Protestant Reformer, did not like Revelation either, saying that "it is not a biblical book."[4]

Yet how can we avoid studying Revelation? Its words and images have made their way into popular culture. We speak of the new millennium, using a concept that is drawn from Revelation 20. The title of the popular movie *Armageddon* came from the name of the place where the final battle between the forces of God and the forces of Antichrist will be fought, according to Revelation 16. And what of the word *Antichrist* itself? Or the mystical number 666? Or the "seventh seal"? Or the "new Jerusalem"? Or the "four horsemen of the apocalypse"? The list is almost endless.

The real reason for studying Revelation, however, is not its use in popular culture but the fact that it is part of the Bible—and the Bible tells us,

> *All* Scripture is breathed out by God and profitable for teaching, for reproof, for correction, and for training in righteousness, that the man of God may be complete, equipped for every good work. (2 Tim. 3:16–17)

If we study this book carefully, we will find that it is as edifying as any other portion of God's Word and will be used by God to equip us for obeying him and doing good works.

---

2. *Epistle*, letter 53, sec. 9, quoted in G. B. Caird, *A Commentary on the Revelation of St. John the Divine* (New York: Harper & Row, 1966), 2.

3. Quoted in Caird, 2.

4. Quoted in William Barclay, *The Revelation of John*, vol. 1, *Chapters 1 to 5*, rev. ed. (Philadelphia: The Westminster Press, 1976), 1.

A BOOK LIKE NO OTHER

The first three verses of this book speak of John in the third person, suggesting that they were added by some official church body as an introduction to and endorsement of the prophecy. This is similar to a verse at the end of the gospel of John (21:24)—which may indicate that both books are by the same author and authenticated by the same church body.[5] But what kind of book did he write? We have to consider what Revelation is like before starting to study it, because it is unlike any other book of the Bible. The technical word that is used to classify various types of literature is *genre*. What we need to do is determine Revelation's genre. We do not have to do that for Paul's letters or the Gospels, because we know what those types of literature are like—but Revelation is different.

So what is Revelation? It is not a theological treatise or a poem or a history or a gospel. Actually, it is three things all at the same time: (1) a *letter*, which is addressed to "the seven churches that are in Asia" (v. 4); (2) a *prophecy*, which is how the author chiefly identifies his book, beginning as early as verse 3 (see also Rev. 22:7, 10, 18–19); and (3) a unique type of writing from this period of history that is known as an *apocalypse*. We meet references to two of these three types of literature in Revelation 1:1–3 and then to the third type in verse 4.

Let's begin with the strangest of these literary genres.

APOCALYPSE

The word *apocalypse* has come into English as a transliteration of the Greek word for "revelation." It has two parts: *apo*, meaning "away from," and *kalupsis*, meaning a "covering" or "veiling." Thus, *apokalupsis* means "an unveiling" or "a revelation," and this is how the word is translated in Revelation 1:1: "the revelation of Jesus Christ." Interestingly enough, it is because of Revelation's use

---

5. However, Robert Mounce says that "there is no reason to believe that the prologue is the work of some later redactor. It appears to have been added by the author himself after completing the book." Robert H. Mounce, *The Book of Revelation* (Grand Rapids: Wm. B. Eerdmans, 1977), 63.

of *apokalupsis* in this verse that scholars describe this type of literature as apocalyptic—the entire genre took its name from the wording of this verse.

This literary genre encompasses a body of Jewish writings that flourished in the Near East between roughly 200 BC and AD 100—or, we might say, between the fierce persecution of the Jews by Antiochus Epiphanes in 167 BC and the destruction of the Jewish nation by Hadrian in AD 135. These books are filled with vivid images, such as one might see in a dream or vision, and the chief idea throughout them is that history is the working out of a struggle between good and evil on a cosmic scale. They often have angelic guides or interpreters and use symbolic numbers, such as John's 666. Examples of apocalyptic literature are the book of Enoch, which one writer called "one of the world's six worst books," and the Ezra Apocalypse, which is responsible for some of the worst features of medieval theology.[6]

Revelation is like such literature in some ways, but it is different too. For one thing, Revelation identifies its author. It says it was written by a man named John. Apocalyptic literature usually claims to have been written by a well-known historical figure (like Ezra) when it is actually written later by someone who does not identify who he really is. Revelation, in contrast, is identified as having been written by a living person—not by someone who was claiming to be a historical figure. The book also claims to be a prophecy, which apocalyptic literature generally does not.

This leads us to the second of these three genres.

PROPHECY

This is the word John himself uses to describe his work, with its earliest occurrence coming in verse 3: "Blessed is the one who reads aloud the words of this prophecy, and blessed are those who hear, and who keep what is written in it, for the time is near." Its mention of prophecy puts Revelation in the same category as many Old Testament books, such as Isaiah, Jeremiah, Ezekiel, Daniel, and the Minor Prophets. These books predict the future, but that is only one

---

6. See Caird, *Commentary on the Revelation of St. John,* 10.

(and not necessarily the most important) thing that they do. Prophets speak to the present, in light of what is soon to come, and they call for repentance, faith, and changes in lifestyle from those who hear or read the prophecy. The conclusions of the letters to the seven churches of Asia Minor in Revelation 2 and 3 are examples of this feature of prophecy.

LETTER

Revelation is also a letter. It begins in a customary letter format, with the name of the author followed by the name of those to whom he is writing, which is followed in turn by a greeting (see 1:4–5), and it ends as a letter too (see 22:8–21). Elsewhere in my writings I have referred to Romans as a doctrinal treatise wrapped up in a letter. In a similar way, we might call Revelation an apocalyptic prophecy wrapped up in a letter. G. K. Beale, the scholar whom I mentioned having 852 items in his bibliography, lifts a sentence from a large *Introduction to the New Testament* by D. A. Carson, Douglas Moo, and Leon Morris to conclude that "the most preferable view is that Revelation is 'a prophecy cast in an apocalyptic mold and written down in a letter form.'"[7] But, J. Ramsey Michaels says, "If a letter, it is like no other early Christian letter we possess. If an apocalypse, it is like no other apocalypse. If a prophecy, it is unique among prophecies."[8]

FOUR APPROACHES TO REVELATION

There is another matter that we have to consider in this first introductory study, and that is the period of history to which John's prophecy should be applied. This is a problem that confronts us early on, because as early as the first paragraph of the book, John refers to his visions as "the things that must soon take place" (v. 1) and

---

7. D. A. Carson, Douglas J. Moo, and Leon Morris, *An Introduction to the New Testament* (Grand Rapids: Zondervan, 1992), 479, quoted in G. K. Beale, *The Book of Revelation: A Commentary on the Greek Text* (Grand Rapids: William B. Eerdmans, 1999), 39.

8. J. Ramsey Michaels, *Interpreting the Book of Revelation* (Grand Rapids: Baker, 1992), 30, quoted in Beale, *The Book of Revelation*, 39.

pronounces a blessing on those who read his prophecy and take it to heart, "for the time is near" (v. 3). Really? More than nineteen hundred years have passed since John wrote these words, and the end times do not seem to have come yet. Or have they? The question leads us to think about the four main approaches that scholars have taken to John's prophecy.[9]

THE HISTORICIST APPROACH

This is the historic Protestant interpretation of the book. It sees Revelation as a pre-written record of the course of the world from the time of the writer to the end. There is much to commend this view. For one thing, much if not all prophecy is about what is to come. For another, numerous phrases in the book suggest an unfolding future outlook, such as Revelation 1:19, in which John is told to write down "the things that you have seen, those that are and those that are to take place after this," or Revelation 4:1, in which a voice from heaven calls to him, saying, "Come up here, and I will show you what must take place after this." Proponents of this view have generally understood the seals, trumpets, and bowls as foretelling such successive historical events as the invasion of the Christianized Roman Empire by the Goths and the Muslims, the corruption of the medieval papacy, the founding of the Holy Roman Empire under Charlemagne, the Protestant Reformation, and even the age of Napoleon or the Nazi era or the collapse of the Soviet Union.

The main problem with this view is its subjectivity. Its proponents invariably see the events of Revelation reaching a culmination in their own time and the second coming of Jesus as virtually around the corner. Besides the fact that there has been little agreement among those who hold this view, Jesus has obviously not yet returned. These interpretations also usually ignore what has taken place in lands other than those in the Christianized West.

---

9. These four approaches are discussed in most of the major commentaries. For a sampling, see Beale, *The Book of Revelation*, 44–49; Mounce, *The Book of Revelation*, 39–45; Steve Gregg, ed., *Revelation: Four Views; A Parallel Commentary* (Nashville: Thomas Nelson, 1997), 34–46; and Leon Morris, *The Book of Revelation: An Introduction and Commentary*, rev. ed. (Grand Rapids: Wm. B. Eerdmans, 1988), 18–24.

THE PRETERIST APPROACH

The word *preterist* comes from the Latin verb *praeterire*, which means "to go before" or "to have happened in the past." Used in regard to Revelation, this term means that the events prophesied in the book (and in such other New Testament passages as Matthew 24) have already occurred. Preterists are concerned with taking references to time, such as "soon" (Rev. 1:1), "the time is near" (Rev. 1:3), and "this generation will not pass away until all these things take place" (Matt. 24:34), literally. How? By maintaining that the fulfillment of these prophecies has already occurred as a result of God's judgment on Jerusalem, through its destruction by the Romans in AD 70. It is true that some preterists believe that the final chapters of Revelation look forward to the second coming of Christ, but even these see the bulk of John's prophecies as having been fulfilled in the fall of Jerusalem.

There are several problems with this view. For one thing, if Revelation and other prophetic passages are about the past, then we are left with no real words about the future. The disciples' question "When will these things be, and what will be the sign of your coming and of the end of the age?" (Matt. 24:3) is not answered. Another problem is that the decisive victory described in Revelation's last chapters did not occur during the destruction of Jerusalem, which is why some preterists break with the pattern and see these chapters as pertaining to the future.

THE FUTURIST APPROACH

The easiest way to solve these difficulties is to defer the fulfillment of the prophecies of Revelation to the future—to a time shortly before Christ's return. This is the approach of dispensationalism, but dispensationalists are not the only futurists. This is probably the dominant broad evangelical view. In this approach, chapters 2 and 3 of the book, which contain the letters to the seven churches, are usually seen as a description of the things that are happening now (see Rev. 1:19), while chapter 4 through verse 5 of chapter 22—the bulk of the book—is seen as referring to the end times exclusively. These chapters are understood to teach the following: the restoration of ethnic Israel to its own land, the church's rapture into heaven, a seven-year tribulation period, the appearance of the Antichrist, the battle of Armageddon, Christ's second coming, the subsequent millennium, and the establishing of a new heaven and new earth. Futurists tend to take the prophecies more literally than other views do, which is easy for them since, none of these events having occurred, their interpretations cannot be falsified.

The major weakness of this position is that it leaves the book without any real significance for those to whom it is addressed— and Revelation is meant to be significant. "Blessed are those who hear [this prophecy], and who keep what is written in it," John says (Rev. 1:3).

THE IDEALIST APPROACH

This fourth approach is sometimes also called the *symbolic* or *spiritual* approach. It affirms that the prophecies do not describe actual historical events, whether past or future, but instead use symbols to portray transcendent spiritual realities, such as the conflict between Christ and Satan or good and evil. The strength of this position lies in the fact that Revelation obviously does employ symbols as a literary device and that such symbols can and do have present significance. The weakness of the view is that it denies the book any specific historical fulfillment.

NOW, BUT ALSO NOT YET!

In one way or another, each of these views has been with us for centuries—and in many cases the positions of their adherents have hardened. This might suggest that there is no way to resolve these matters—that we simply have to take one and get on with it, whether it is right or not. I do not think that such pessimism is warranted. On the contrary, what I observe is a maturing approach to Revelation in many recent commentaries, which can perhaps be best understood as a conservative attempt to recognize and include the best features of each of these four views while rejecting the most problematic aspects of each.

Let me explain how I want to approach Revelation. I have two main guidelines. First, I believe that Jesus himself gives the overall framework for all New Testament prophecy (which the New Testament writers consciously follow) in Matthew 24. In that chapter, he recognizes and prophesies the imminent destruction of Jerusalem but indicates that, as shattering as that event will be, it is not a sign of his immediate coming. There will be many "signs" in history—wars, famines, earthquakes, persecutions, apostasy in the church, and false prophets—but none of these will be genuine signs of his return. This is because his actual coming will be without warning. It will be sudden—like lightning flashing from the east to the west. The conclusion to this discourse is that, since we do not know when Jesus will return, we need to "keep watch" and "be ready." Jesus uses no fewer than seven illustrations, images, or parables to make this point (see Matt. 24:36–25:46).

My second guideline is from 1 John 2:18, where the same John who, in my opinion, wrote Revelation declares, "Children, it is the last hour, and as you have heard that antichrist is coming, so now many antichrists have come." This means that a biblical prophecy can have a genuine fulfillment in history without that fulfillment necessarily being the prophecy's final or full fulfillment.

There are examples of what I mean in Revelation itself. For example, John refers in verse 14 of chapter 2 to people who "hold the teaching of Balaam" and in verse 20 to "that woman Jezebel." These are not reincarnations of that ancient mercenary prophet or that particularly wicked queen. They are examples of what we might call a recurring biblical pattern. You have heard of Balaam; even now there are many Balaams. You have heard of Jezebel, but even now there are many Jezebels. In a similar way, John the Baptist not only was like but in a sense actually was Elijah (see Matt. 11:14).

Let me put it another way. When the Reformers of the sixteenth century identified the pope of their day as the Antichrist and the papacy as the great prostitute of Babylon, that was literally the case for them and for their time. Rome was proclaiming a false gospel. She was the enemy of Christ. This was a true fulfillment. But this does not exclude an even more complete or literal fulfillment of the

9

prophecies concerning the Antichrist and the prostitute of Babylon in the last days. Are there antichrists today? False prophets? There certainly are. But we can also believe that a final Antichrist and a final false prophet will appear before Jesus Christ returns.

Earlier I wrote that I detect a maturing approach to Revelation along these lines in several recent writers. Let me give two examples. The first is Robert Mounce, who writes,

> It is important to see with the preterist that the book must be interpreted in light of the immediate historical crisis in which the first-century church found itself. The author employs a literary genre that grew out of his own cultural and linguistic milieu. His figures of speech and imagery are to be interpreted in the context of his own historical setting. They are not esoteric and enigmatic references to some future culture totally foreign to first century readers (e.g., cobalt bombs, Telstar, the European Common Market, etc.).
>
> With the *historicist* it is important to notice that the philosophy of history revealed in the Apocalypse has found specific fulfillment in all the major crises of human history up to the present day.
>
> With the *futurist* we must agree that the central message of the book is eschatological, and to whatever extent the End has been anticipated in the course of history, it remains as the one great climactic point toward which all history moves. This age will come to an end. Satan and his hosts will be destroyed and the righteous will be vindicated. These are historical events which will take place in time. And they are future.
>
> With the *idealist* one must agree that the events of history give expression to basic underlying principles. God is at work behind the scenes to bring to pass his sovereign intention for man. To whatever extent the idealist rules out a consummation, it is difficult to see from history alone any cause for optimism. It is the end that gives meaning to the process.[10]

10. Mounce, *The Book of Revelation*, 43–44.

My second example represents an idealist or symbolic approach, but it is still a combination of the different views. J. Ramsey Michaels writes,

> Just as chapters 2–3 are now read (much like Paul's letters) as pastoral messages to first-century congregations with implications for other churches in many different times and places, so chapters 4–22 should be read as a series of first-century visions containing promises and warnings to Christian believers always and everywhere. They remind us, for example, that the world we live in is a battleground between good and evil, that in heaven the battle is already won, and that Jesus Christ, the Lamb of God, is now in control (chap. 5). Troubles and disasters on earth are actually part of the divine plan. . . . The devil is active on earth deceiving the nations because he was defeated and thrown out of heaven (chap. 12), not because he ever prevailed over God. Christians will confront the devil's futile anger in the form of an oppressive state that calls them to worship a human being rather than God (chap. 13).[11]

Michaels believes that, although in John's situation "the oppressive state was Rome," even after Rome has been destroyed, the devil will deceive the nations again, and the conflict will repeat itself.

THE KINGDOM HAS COME

I want us to see one more thing before I end this study. It comes from the fact that (although this is difficult to notice in our English translations) the first verse of Revelation is probably a deliberate echo of Daniel 2:28, but with one important change. (We are going to notice many deliberate echoes of Daniel as we proceed). Daniel told Nebuchadnezzar that God had "made known" to him (the word is "revealed," just as in Revelation 1:1) "what will be in the latter days." When we remember that this is said in regard to Nebuchadnezzar's dream of a great statue representing four successive world empires,

---

11. Michaels, *Revelation*, 25–26.

and that the climax of the vision is about a stone that will strike and destroy the statue and then grow up to become a mountain that will fill the whole earth, we recognize this as a prophecy that the kingdom of Jesus will one day fill the earth. But here is the significant thing: John's opening echo of Daniel's words replaces the phrase "in the latter days" with "soon." In other words, John is saying that, unlike Daniel who was told to seal up the words of his prophecy "until the time of the end" (Dan. 12:9), John's own words are for now, for our time, because Jesus has come and is building his kingdom in our days.

Years ago, when I wrote a book on Daniel, I was unsure about how to interpret this statue vision. I recognized the destruction of the statue's iron legs to be the destruction of the Roman Empire, but I did not know whether the growth of the mountain was a picture of what we would call the church age or a preview of the final kingdom of Christ in the very last days. I said at the time that I probably favored the latter.[12]

I do not see it that way now. I still believe in a future fulfillment of the vision. The kingdom of Christ will be a real, literal kingdom in the last days. I believe in a literal future millennium. But I also see the fulfillment in the present, for it is also now, in this age, that Jesus is doing these things. Daniel looked forward to the coming of the Messiah in the future. John is saying that his prophecies are for now—but also for every age of history until the final culmination in the second coming of Jesus and the last judgment. Which is why the opening paragraph ends with a blessing for those who read, hear, and take to heart what is written (see Rev. 1:3). This beatitude is the first of seven in the book (the others are found in Rev. 14:13; 16:15; 19:9; 20:6; 22:7, 14)—nearly everything in Revelation seems to happen in series of sevens. This first beatitude almost perfectly reproduces the words of Jesus from Luke 11:28 ("Blessed rather are those who hear the word of God and keep it") and is matched at the end of the prophecy by a curse on those who do not obey the instruction (Rev.

---

12. See James Montgomery Boice, *Daniel: An Expositional Commentary* (Grand Rapids: Zondervan, 1989), 41–43.

22:18–19). It is also the only blessing in the Bible that is attached to the reading of a particular book.

The words of this blessing show that Revelation was written not primarily to give information for the mind, as if its goal were only to enable us to figure out what might happen at the end of time or even merely to look back at the past and understand it. It was written to enable Christian people to live for Jesus today. And it requires that they do! The book imparts a moral obligation. Revelation teaches us that the kingdom of the world has become the kingdom of our Lord and of his Christ (see Rev. 11:15). Therefore, although the kingdoms of this world seem powerful and sometimes even glorious from our point of view, we must know that the world is destined for destruction and that the kingdom of Christ will triumph—and we must live like we believe it. The empire of Babylon collapsed. Rome was overrun by the Huns and the Goths. But the kingdom of our God is forever. Hallelujah!

2

JOHN TO THE SEVEN CHURCHES

Revelation 1:4—5

The book of Revelation has two beginnings: the paragraph that we looked at in the previous study (Rev. 1:1–3) and the verses that follow (vv. 4–8), part of which we are going to look at now. This double beginning is fortunate, because it provides us with two opportunities to examine the complex introductory matters that we need to think about before we plunge into the prophecies that comprise the bulk of the book.

If Revelation is a letter (among other things), as we saw in the previous study, then its formal beginning is in verse 4. But how commonplace this beginning is! It seems strange for a book that is going to become so wild and imaginative and puzzling later. Most of the letters in the New Testament begin like this. First, there is the name of the author; second, the name of those to whom he is writing; third, a greeting; and fourth, a blessing or doxology. In this case the author identifies himself as John. He is writing "to the seven churches that are in Asia." His greeting is "grace . . . and peace." The doxology follows from verses 5 through 7; we will look at it in the next study.

WHO IS JOHN?

The author of this mysterious book identifies himself as John—not only in verse 4 but also three other times (see Rev. 1:1, 9; 22:8). But who is John? There are differences of opinion on the matter.

15

Most of the early church fathers identified the author of Revelation as the Lord's disciple. Examples are Justin Martyr, Irenaeus, Clement of Alexandria, and Tertullian. Justin Martyr referred to him as "a certain man . . . whose name was John, one of the apostles of Christ."[1] Irenaeus called him "John, the disciple of the Lord."[2] Another early witness to the authorship of Revelation is a Gnostic document known as the *Apocryphon of John*, which was discovered in upper Egypt in 1945. It says that Revelation was written by "John, the brother of James, these who are the sons of Zebedee." Yet Dionysius, the head of the Christian school at Alexandria in the mid–third century, was the first to ascribe Revelation to "another John"—a presbyter thought to have been mentioned in an ambiguous statement by Papias in the second century. This view was taken up later by Eusebius, the early Christian historian.[3]

One reason for assigning Revelation to another John is the fact that the book is so different from the traditional Johannine writings: the gospel of John and the three letters (1, 2, and 3 John). Most of these differences can be explained by the different subject matter. After all, a dream is usually a good bit different from real life. But there is a more serious difference, and that is the difference in grammar between Revelation and the other four books. The gospel of John is written in flawless, even elegant, Greek. Any scholar of Greek can see that. Yet the Greek of Revelation, according to the view that assigns Revelation to an author other than John the Evangelist, is deficient. R. H. Charles, one of the great students of Revelation, said it has a veritable grammar of its own. He even wrote a textbook for the "barbarous" grammar of Revelation, as he called it.[4]

We have an example of what bothered Charles in our passage for

---

1. Justin Martyr, "Dialogue with Trypho, a Jew," chap. 81, available in *The Ante-Nicene Fathers: Translations of the Writings of the Fathers Down to A.D. 325*, vol. 1, *The Apostolic Fathers—Justin Martyr—Irenaeus*, ed. Alexander Roberts and James Donaldson (repr., New York: Charles Scribner's Sons, 1903), 240.

2. "Irenaeus against Heresies," bk. 3, chap. 11, par. 1, available in Roberts and Donaldson, *The Ante-Nicene Fathers*, 426.

3. See Eusebius, *Ecclesiastical History*, bk. 7, chap. 25, par. 7–16.

4. See R. H. Charles, *A Critical and Exegetical Commentary on The Revelation of Saint John* (Edinburgh: T. & T. Clark, 1920), 1:cxvii–clix.

this study, in which John sends blessings "from him who is and who was and who is to come" (v. 4). In Greek, the preposition "from" is *apo*, and *apo* needs to be followed by an object. We have a similar construction in English. When a pronoun is the subject of a sentence, we use a different grammatical form—we say "he" (for example, "He did it!"). But when the pronoun follows "from," we alter its form and say "him" (for example, "The gift is from him"). If John had been writing proper Greek, he should have followed the preposition *apo* with the correct pronoun, writing "from *him* who is, and who was, and who is to come"—which is how most translators have rendered the sentence to make it sound right in English. But this is not what John actually wrote. He wrote, "from *he* who is, and *he* was, and *he* is to come."

Is there an explanation for this other than an ignorance of correct Greek grammar, which would suggest that the author of Revelation is someone other than the author of the gospel that bears his name? Actually, there is a good explanation. John is not making up this wording. He is drawing on Exodus 3:14, where God revealed his name to Moses as "I AM WHO I AM." This is all in the nominative case, and the majority opinion among today's commentators is that John keeps the name of God in the nominative case to make clear that he is alluding to this defining passage from Exodus. Commentator G. K. Beale says, "It is possible that John employs such kinds of constructions here and elsewhere as Hebraisms in order to create a 'biblical' effect and so to show the solidarity of his work with that of God's revelation in the Old Testament."[5] In other words, John's alleged grammatical "mistakes" are intentional.

William Barclay defends John even more strongly: "John has such an immense reverence for God that he refuses to alter the form of his name even when the rules of grammar demand it."[6]

There are other reasons why some scholars seek an author for Revelation other than John the apostle. They point out that John

---

5. G. K. Beale, *The Book of Revelation: A Commentary on the Greek Text* (Grand Rapids: William B. Eerdmans, 1999), 189.

6. William Barclay, *The Revelation of John*, vol. 1, *Chapters 1 to 5*, rev. ed. (Philadelphia: The Westminster Press, 1976), 30.

repeatedly calls himself a prophet but nowhere calls himself an apostle or appeals to his apostolic authority, for example. But this is a formal objection only. Perhaps the best answer to this is that even if John does not style himself as an apostle, he nevertheless seems to exercise an authoritative apostolic role in writing to the churches. On the whole, an identification of John the apostle, the son of Zebedee, as the author of Revelation seems the best option—if for no other reason than the unlikelihood that any person in the early church *other* than the apostle was so well-known that he could refer to himself simply as "John" without any additional identification. We would do well to side with Justin Martyr, Irenaeus, and the other early witnesses on the matter of Revelation's authorship.

A CHAIN OF REVELATION

One thing that points to a Johannine authorship is the way that John includes himself in the chain of revelation that is outlined in these opening verses. This is a fulfillment of something Jesus said to the disciples, as recorded by John (significantly enough) in his gospel. Jesus said, "When the Spirit of truth comes, he will guide you into all the truth, for he will not speak on his own authority, but whatever he hears he will speak, and he will declare to you the things that are to come" (John 16:13). John is writing to the seven churches of Asia. But he is not writing the things that he says on his own. He is writing what has been revealed to him by God.

The chain of revelation goes like this: First, according to verse 1 of Revelation, God the Father gave the revelation to Jesus Christ. Second, also according to verse 1, Jesus imparted it to "his angel"—who, third, made it known to John. In this book, John is now making known to the churches what he has received—namely, "the word of God" and "the testimony of Jesus Christ" (v. 2). "The testimony of Jesus Christ" could mean God's words about Jesus, but the context indicates that they are actually the words that Jesus gave. In other words, "the word of God" and "the testimony of Jesus Christ" are the same thing. John sees himself as the communicator of this important revelation.

When John says that God gave him these visions to "show to his servants the things that must soon take place" (v. 1), he is also conscious of being a link in the chain of revelation by which God spoke through other servants (the prophets) in the past. This is especially true since John explicitly calls himself a prophet (see Rev. 1:3; 22:7, 10, 18–19). He is conscious of belonging to that older prophetic tradition. Unlike most other New Testament books, Revelation does not have even one direct quotation from the Old Testament. But it does contain hundreds of allusions to familiar passages and phrases from the Old (and even from the New) Testament. Steve Gregg maintains that there are 79 references to Isaiah, 54 to Daniel, 48 to Ezekiel, 43 to the Psalms, 27 to Exodus, 22 to Jeremiah, 15 to Zechariah, 9 to Amos, and 8 to Joel.[7] Bruce M. Metzger reckons that of the 404 verses that comprise the 22 chapters of the book of Revelation, 278 contain one or more allusions to an Old Testament passage.[8]

WHEN DID JOHN WRITE?

There is one more introductory matter that we need to consider before going further in our study, because it has bearing on how we will interpret some passages later on. It is the question of dating. When did John write Revelation? There are two main theories about the dating of the book. Some writers hold to a late date—from the reign of the Roman emperor Domitian (AD 81–96). Others hold to an early date—from the reign of Nero (AD 54–68).

THE REIGN OF DOMITIAN (AD 81–96)

This is the traditional dating because, like the testimony to John the apostle's authorship, it has been affirmed from the earliest days of the church. The first hard evidence for this date comes from Irenaeus, who wrote, concerning the identity of the Antichrist, "We will not . . .

---

7. See Steve Gregg, ed., *Revelation: Four Views; A Parallel Commentary* (Nashville: Thomas Nelson, 1997), 20.

8. See Bruce M. Metzger, *Breaking the Code: Understanding the Book of Revelation* (Nashville: Abingdon Press, 1993), 13.

incur the risk of pronouncing positively as to the name of Antichrist; for if it were necessary that his name should be distinctly revealed in this present time, it would have been announced by him who beheld the apocalyptic vision. For that was seen no very long time since, but almost in our day, towards the end of Domitian's reign."[9]

This is also the general consensus among scholars today, most of whom would date the book to about AD 95—though they hold this view not primarily because of such early Christian writers as Irenaeus but because Revelation seems to be concerned with times of persecution for Christians related to their refusal to accept emperor worship (see 13:4, 15, 17; 14:9; 16:2; 19:20), and this problem seems to have arisen during the reign of Domitian. Nero blamed Christians for the fire that destroyed much of Rome, and he condemned many to die in the arena, but there is no evidence that his persecution extended beyond the capital. By contrast, Domitian demanded Caesar worship. He informed the provincial governors that official pronouncements must begin "Our Lord and God Domitian commands . . ." Anyone who spoke to him directly had to begin by calling him "Lord and God."[10] It is true that the evidence for widespread persecution under Domitian is not particularly strong, but there is no other period in the first century in which it would have been more likely.

The decline of the churches that is described in chapters 2 and 3 also seems to fit a later date for Revelation. For example, the Laodicean church is called "wealthy," but Laodicea was destroyed by an earthquake in AD 60–61. The natural assumption is that it took longer than three or four years to rebuild it.

THE REIGN OF NERO (AD 54–68)

This date is favored by preterists, because they see the entire book as predicting the destruction of Jerusalem in AD 70, and if it predicted the city's fall, it obviously had to be written before that time. Preterists think of *Babylon* as being a disguised reference to

---

9. "Irenaeus against Heresies," bk. 5, chap. 30, par. 3, available in Roberts and Donaldson, *The Ante-Nicene Fathers*, 559–60.

10. See Barclay, *The Revelation of John*, 19.

Jerusalem, though John probably uses it of Rome—and *Babylon* became a term for Rome only in Jewish circles and only after (and because of) the destruction of Jerusalem in AD 70.

One argument for an early date for Revelation is that the temple is mentioned in Revelation 11:1–2, but with no indication of its destruction. But this assumes a literal reading of these verses, which is probably not right. Another argument is drawn from Revelation 17:9–10, which speaks of "seven mountains" (probably a reference to Rome) followed by a reference to "seven kings"—five of whom are fallen, the sixth of whom is reigning, and the seventh of whom is yet to come. Some work out the sixth king to be Nero. But everything depends on where one starts, of course, and a great deal of juggling seems to be needed in order to get this to work. The first actual emperor was Augustus. If we start with him, the emperors were as follows: Augustus (27 BC–AD 14), Tiberius (AD 14–37), Caligula (AD 37–41), Claudius (AD 41–54), Nero (AD 54–68), Galba, Otto, and Vitellius (who reigned for only eighteen months together), Vespasian (AD 69–79), Titus (AD 79–81), and Domitian (AD 81–96). This makes Nero—the reigning emperor when Revelation was written, according to this view—the fifth of these seven kings, and therefore he should already have died. If we arbitrarily move back one emperor and start with Julius Caesar (even though he was not an emperor), Nero becomes the sixth; but then the eighth, dreaded king who is also described as "the beast" (v. 11) is Otto, who hardly deserves that title. Or, if we skip over the short reigns of Galba, Otto, and Vitellius, then the eighth is Titus, who was not a persecutor. It is a difficult problem that leaves us without a sound basis for dating the book of Revelation.

A further reason for believing that the book was written in the reign of Nero is the number 666, which is said to be "the number of the beast" in Revelation 13:18. This is said to stand for "Neron Caesar," based on assigning numerical equivalents to the Hebrew letters that make up that name. We will discuss this puzzle when we get to chapter 13, but it is worth noting here that the identification of the number with Nero is based on the Hebrew spelling of his name and on the Hebrew system of *gematria*—a method of interpretation that is based on calculating the numerical value of Hebrew words—and who among John's Greek readers would have known what that meant? The first person even to suggest it was a scholar named Fritzsche in 1831.[11] In the quote from him that was presented earlier, Irenaeus discussed the conjectures that were known to him in his day, but he did not even mention Nero as a possibility.

As in the matter of deciding who wrote Revelation, we are probably correct if we stick to the traditional dating and conclude that the prophecy was given to John for a time in history when the churches were beginning to feel pressure to bow to the Roman emperor in worship and was written to prepare them for standing firm in such extremities.

THE SEVEN CHURCHES OF ASIA

Revelation 1:4 tells us that John is writing to "the seven churches that are in Asia." These were actual churches established in the principal cities of the Roman province, and they lay on a more or less circular route that might well have been traveled by a postal clerk who was bearing the book for all seven. Ephesus is the first church mentioned in verse 11 as well as the first to be addressed in chapter 2, and it was the church that lay closest to Patmos, where John was imprisoned (see 1:9).

Yet there is probably more to John's reference to "seven churches" than mere geography. For one thing, there were more than seven churches in Asia at this time. We know, for example, of the churches that were in Troas (see Acts 20:5–6), Colossae (Col. 1:2), and Hierapolis (Col. 4:13), and there were probably others. Why does John address his letter to these seven only? When we think about the frequency of the number seven in Revelation (seven candlesticks, seven stars, seven lamps, seven seals, seven horns, seven eyes, seven angels, seven plagues, seven bowls), we suspect that the number

11. See Theodor Zahn, *Introduction to the New Testament*, trans. John Moore Trout et al. (New York: Charles Scribner's Sons, 1909), 3:447n4.

has been chosen in Revelation 1:4 for a symbolic purpose. If that is the case, it undoubtedly stands for completeness or fullness here, as it does in other places. In other words, the seven churches are to be thought of as being representative of the church universal—of that day as well as of ours. Were they real churches? Of course. The book was sent to and was to be read by each one. But we are to read it as well. The letters of chapters 2 and 3 contain John's charge "He who has an ear, let him hear what the Spirit says to the churches" (Rev. 2:7, 11, 17, 29; 3:6, 13, 22)—and this charge includes us as well as the churches John was originally writing to.

BLESSING FROM THE TRIUNE GOD

I said at the start of this study that Revelation 1:4–7 is in the form of an ancient opening to a letter and that the identification of the author (John) and the identification of those to whom he was writing (the seven churches in the province of Asia) are followed by a blessing: "Grace to you and peace from him who is and who was and who is to come, and from the seven spirits who are before his throne, and from Jesus Christ the faithful witness, the firstborn of the dead, and the ruler of kings on earth" (vv. 4–5).

In spite of the fact that John speaks of "the seven spirits who are before his throne," which is puzzling, this seems to be a deliberately Trinitarian greeting.

GOD THE FATHER

I have already written about John's identification of God as "him who is and who was and who is to come." It is imprecise grammar, but an intentional reference to the name of God that was given to Moses at the burning bush, as recorded in Exodus 3:14. This name is echoed in other places in the Bible, too. In Isaiah, God declares, "I am the first and I am the last" (Isa. 44:6; 48:12)—a sentence that Jesus applies to himself in Revelation 1:17. In Revelation 1:8, God refers to himself, saying, "I am the Alpha and the Omega . . . who is and who was and who is to come, the Almighty." At the end of Revelation, Jesus puts a number of these titles together, declaring,

"I am the Alpha and the Omega, the first and the last, the beginning and the end" (22:13).

Have you noticed the order of the tenses in Revelation 1:4? Under normal circumstances, we would start with the past, revert to the present, and end with the future: "him who *was* and *is* and *is to come*." John begins with the present and then moves to the past and the future: "him who *is* and who *was* and who *is to come*." Is there a reason for this? Of course. There is always a reason for the specific words and order of words in the Bible. When John begins with the present, he is emphasizing that God is the eternally present one—or, as we might say, that the past and the future are embraced in the present for him. We are going to look at the meaning of this more closely in another study, because God claims this title for himself again in verse 8.

THE HOLY SPIRIT

On one hand, the words "the seven spirits who are before his throne" are unusual and may mean that this is not a Trinitarian passage after all—especially since John refers to "the seven spirits" in three other places in Revelation (3:1; 4:5; 5:6) and the words do not seem to mean the Holy Spirit there. On the other hand, this phrase is probably drawn from Isaiah 11:2, where the prophet says that the sevenfold Spirit will equip the Messiah for his end-time reign. He is the Spirit (1) of "the LORD," (2) of "wisdom," (3) of "understanding," (4) of "counsel," (5) of "might," (6) of "knowledge," and (7) of "the fear of the LORD."

JESUS CHRIST

The most important titles in these verses are those that are given to Jesus. Before we discuss them, however, there is a question for us to consider: why is Jesus mentioned last, since the usual way of referring to the Trinity is to speak of the Father, the Son, and the Holy Spirit? The answer is very simple. John mentions Jesus last because he wants to amplify Jesus as the central figure in the book—in fact, even in this chapter. In the following verses he utters a doxology in praise of Jesus and reminds us of his second coming (see vv. 5–7), and in the remainder of the chapter he provides a vision of Christ standing among the lampstands that represent the seven churches (see vv. 9–20). But first, here in verse 5, he lists three of Christ's titles.

"The faithful witness." Jesus was a faithful witness to all that God instructed him to teach—which is how Jesus speaks of himself (in conjunction with the Old Testament agents of revelation) in John 3: "Truly, truly, I say to you, we speak of what we know, and bear witness to what we have seen, but you do not receive our testimony" (v. 11). John's gospel goes on to place a special emphasis on Jesus's testimony before Pilate at the time of his trial: "For this purpose I was born and for this purpose I have come into the world—to bear witness to the truth" (John 18:37). Paul refers to this testimony specifically in his charge to Timothy:

> I charge you in the presence of God, who gives life to all things, and of Christ Jesus, who in his testimony before Pontius Pilate made the good confession, to keep the commandment unstained and free from reproach until the appearing of our Lord Jesus Christ. (1 Tim. 6:13–14)

When we remember that Revelation was written to Christians who might soon be facing persecution and even death for the sake of their testimony to Christ, we can understand how John's description of Jesus as a "faithful witness" would be a source of encouragement for them. Jesus bore a faithful witness before the rulers of this world and suffered for it. John's readers should do the same even though persecution or death might be the consequence. Indeed, the letter to the church at Pergamum acknowledges the death of Antipas—"my faithful witness, who was killed among you" (Rev. 2:13). The Greek word for "witness" is the same as the word for "martyr" (*martus*). The Christians to whom John was writing would need to remember that although Jesus died once, he also triumphed over death by the resurrection—which is the reason for the next important title that this verse gives us.

"The firstborn of the dead." Jesus bore his witness and died for it, but he was also raised from the dead by the Father—and so would the believers in Asia be, if they would also remain faithful. They needed to persevere in their faith, for, as Jesus himself said, it is the one who "endures to the end" who "will be saved" (Matt. 10:22).

Do we endure? Not many in western lands are in danger of direct physical persecution for their testimony to Christ, but we are under constant pressure to compromise in less obvious ways. Sin is treated lightly today. In fact, it is almost a nonexistent category. *Whatever Became of Sin?* asked Karl Menninger.[12] We are pressured to adopt the politically correct stance on moral issues and to treat as normal behavior sins that the Bible says will bring the unrepentant to judgment. As far as the name of Jesus is concerned, well, Jesus may be tolerated (as most other religions and pseudo religions are tolerated), but woe to us if we bring him off the reservation and proclaim him as a true and relevant figure for our times. Woe upon woe if we faithfully proclaim him to be the only source of truth, the only way to God, and the sole basis for living a full, wholesome, and God-pleasing life (see John 14:6). It is precisely with such affirmations and in the face of such people as your family, neighbors, and colleagues at work that a faithful testimony like this must be rendered.

"The ruler of kings on earth." John is probably drawing from Psalm 89:27–37 when he describes Jesus as "the ruler of kings on earth." In fact, this is probably also where he got the idea of Jesus being "the firstborn"—though it may also have been from Paul, who was the first to use that full phrase (see Col. 1:18). In Psalm 89, the One who is appointed by the Father to be the firstborn is also appointed to be the King of Kings.

> And I will make him the firstborn,
>> the highest of the kings of the earth.

. . . .

12. (New York: Hawthorn Books, 1973.)

> I will establish his offspring forever
> > and his throne as the days of the heavens. (vv. 27, 29)

When we consider this psalm in a New Testament context, which reminds us of Jesus's trial before Pilate and his triumph through the resurrection, we cannot help but contrast what is ascribed to Jesus in this last phrase with the offer that the devil made to him at the time of his wilderness temptation. Satan offered him "all the kingdoms of the world and their glory"—if only Jesus would bow down and worship him (Matt. 4:8–9; see also Luke 4:5–7). Jesus was not uninterested in the kingdoms of this world. They are his, and he was promised a thorough and everlasting possession of them. But he would not take them on the devil's terms. He would not rule with Satan. Jesus knew that the way to the kingdoms of this world was the cross, followed by the resurrection, and that only if he pursued that path would he reign with the blessing of the Father and with those whom the Father had given to him before the creation of the earth.

This is also the path that is set before us. Many want to have the kingdoms of the world without suffering. They want this treasure through the world's own means—through political manipulation and compromise. It does not come that way. It comes through the faithful testimony and suffering of those who are the disciples of the Lamb.

3

SOLI DEO GLORIA

Revelation 1:5–7

Any proper theology of Jesus Christ develops its ideas in two categories: (1) who Jesus is and (2) what Jesus did. This is because the value of what Jesus did depends on who he was and also, at the same time, it is because of who he is that he did what he did. We can hardly miss noticing that John develops both ideas in these opening verses of his prophecy. Verse 5 reminded us of who Jesus is—he is "the faithful witness, the firstborn of the dead, and the ruler of kings on earth." Those phrases refer to the witness Jesus gave before Pilate, his resurrection, and his present and future rule over kings and all other persons. The second half of verse 5 through verse 7 reminds us of what he did—chiefly regarding his work of redemption—and how we are affected by it.

Thinking of Jesus as "the faithful witness, the firstborn of the dead, and the ruler of kings on earth" seems to have brought John so much joy that immediately he broke into a doxology, exclaiming, "To him be glory and dominion forever and ever. Amen" (v. 6). This is the first of many doxologies in Revelation. Does thinking about Jesus and his work draw praise from you, as it did from John? Does Jesus's love awaken your dormant affection and lead you to praise him more?

WHAT HAS JESUS DONE?

We already looked at what John has to say about the person of Jesus when we examined, in the previous study, the titles he attributes to him in the first half of verse 5. Here we need to ponder what Jesus has done for us and for our salvation. The apostle reminds us of three important things: Jesus (1) "loves us," (2) "has freed us from our sins by his blood," and (3) "made us a kingdom, priests to his God and Father."

1. JESUS LOVES US

John puts "love" in the present tense because love is an eternal attribute of God. And it is because Jesus *is* love that he did what John mentions next: he "freed us from our sins by his blood." We can hardly read these words without thinking of John 3:16—probably the best-known verse in the Bible and one that was written, interestingly enough, by this same human author: "For God so loved the world, that he gave his only Son, that whoever believes in him should not perish but have eternal life." Here in Revelation, however, John ascribes this eternal saving love to Jesus rather than to God the Father.

Can any words by mere human beings do justice to God's love? Can we describe it adequately? We cannot. The love of God the Father and of Jesus the Son is a love so great, so giving, so winsome, so victorious, so infinite that we can only marvel at it. It is a love that reaches from the heights of divine holiness to the pit of human depravity in order to save us and keep us from sin. Frederick Lehman wrote a wonderful hymn about God's love, called simply "The Love of God";[1] but the final stanza—the best, in my opinion—was one that he added only later. It was written instead by a man who had been confined in an asylum and was found written on the wall of his room after he had died. It reads,

> Could we with ink the ocean fill
> And were the skies of parchment made;
> Were every stalk on earth a quill
> And every man a scribe by trade,
> To write the love of God above

1. Frederick M. Lehman, "The Love of God," 1917.

Would drain the ocean dry,
Nor could the scroll contain the whole
Though stretched from sky to sky.

2. JESUS FREED US FROM OUR SINS BY HIS DEATH

This is the only place in the New Testament where the words "freed us" (*lusanti hemas*) occur. The Authorized Version says "*washed* us from our sins," but this is based on a textual variant (*lousanti*) that is a copyist's error. The word is significant, as is the contrast in tenses between "loves us" and "has freed us."

Jesus loves us (an eternal present), but his work of redemption (past tense) has been done once and for ever. Since John's words echo many Old Testament passages, it may be that he is thinking of Isaiah 40:2 here—"her sin has been paid for" (NIV).

In any case, the doctrine that he has in mind is redemption. There are three Greek words for redemption: *agorazo, exagorazo,* and *luo. Agorazo* means "to buy in the market." *Exagorazo* means "to buy out of the market," as one might buy a slave in order to set the slave free. The third word—the one that occurs here—has more to do with "loosing," "unshackling," or "untying" in order to set a slave or some other imprisoned person free. All these words involve the payment of a price.

We can see this connection to the payment of a price especially in the way that various words for redemption developed from the root verb *luo*. At the beginning of the word's history, *luo* itself meant only "to loose or loosen"—as in taking off a suit of clothes or unbuckling one's armor. When used of persons, it could also signify loosening bonds so that, as I said above, a prisoner might be set free. However, it was usually necessary to pay a ransom price in order to free a prisoner. So in time a noun was created from *luo* to signify this specific "ransom price": the noun *lutron*. In time this word produced another verb of its own—*lutroo*—which, like *luo*, meant "to loose" or "to set free" but, unlike *luo*, always meant to free through the payment of a price. At last, from these two words, the technical Greek words for redemption came about: *lutrosis* and its cognate *apolutrosis*—words that mean freeing a slave by paying the ransom price for him. In

Christian vocabulary, these words describe what Jesus did when he freed us from sin's slavery by his death.

Charles Wesley described the deliverance aspect of our salvation beautifully in the fourth verse of one of his greatest hymns, which reads,

> Long my imprisoned spirit lay
> Fast bound in sin and nature's night;
> Thine eye diffused a quick'ning ray—
> I woke, the dungeon flamed with light:
> My chains fell off, my heart was free,
> I rose, went forth and followed thee.[2]

We must never forget that this deliverance was accomplished by Jesus at the cost of his life, since it was "by his blood" that he freed us. As long as we remember that amazing cost, we will always love Jesus deeply for being our Redeemer.

3. JESUS MADE US INTO A KINGDOM OF PRIESTS WHOSE WORK IS TO SERVE GOD

We have already been told that Jesus is a king, for he is "the ruler of kings on earth" (Rev. 1:5). Kings have kingdoms—and now, in striking language, John adds that we who have been saved by him and have believed in him *are* that kingdom. In other words, the kingdom of the Lord Jesus Christ is not a territorial kingdom but a kingdom of those who have come to know and begun to live by God's truth. This is precisely how Jesus described his kingdom when he was on trial before Pilate. He said, "You say that I am a king. For this purpose I was born and for this purpose I have come into the world—to bear witness to the truth" (John 18:37). It is interesting that John, the author of Revelation, is also the gospel writer who records this specific bit of Jesus's teaching.

The other thing John says that Jesus has done for us is to make us priests. In the Old Testament period, only the male members of the

---

2. Charles Wesley, "And Can It Be That I Should Gain?" 1738.

tribe of Levi were priests. They alone had access to the temple; all other Jews had to approach God and the temple through them. However, way back in the book of Exodus, God had told the people through Moses, "All the earth is mine; and you shall be to me a kingdom of priests and a holy nation" (Ex. 19:5–6), and Isaiah repeats the promise that one day all God's people would be priests: "You shall be called the priests of the LORD; they shall speak of you as the ministers of our God" (Isa. 61:6). That day was long in coming. But here in Revelation John says that it has come, and the reason is that Jesus has opened a new and living way for us into the presence of God through his death on the cross (see Heb. 10:19–22). God made this clear when he tore the veil of the temple in two from top to bottom at the time of Jesus's death. Because the way has been opened, all who believe on Christ can now come boldly to the throne of God's grace (see Heb. 4:16).

This truth must have meant a great deal to the apostle Peter, as well, because he repeated it several times in the first of his own letters. Peter wrote,

> As you come to him, a living stone rejected by men but in the sight of God chosen and precious, you yourselves like living stones are being built up as a spiritual house, to be a holy priesthood, to offer spiritual sacrifices acceptable to God through Jesus Christ. (1 Peter 2:4–5)

And again,

> But you are a chosen race, a royal priesthood, a holy nation, a people for his own possession, that you may proclaim the excellencies of him who called you out of darkness into his marvelous light. (1 Peter 2:9)

Why has Jesus done all this? The answer, according to John, is so that we might serve God the Father (v. 6). If we ask *how* we are to serve him, Peter has told us. It is by declaring the praises of him who called us out of darkness into his light.

This is a reality for all believers now. Unfortunately, even after knowing all that we know about the kingly and priestly ministry of Jesus (after whom our own ministries are patterned), many evangelicals still instinctively relegate this promise to a final kingly reign on earth—perhaps in the millennium. But this is not what John is saying. He is saying that we are to function as kings and priests right now. I believe that we will reign in a future day as well. But far more important is the fact that we are to fulfill our roles as faithful witnesses to the Lord Jesus Christ and his kingdom precisely where we are now. We are to do this by living for him, in opposition to the values and standards of this world; by proclaiming our Lord's spiritual rule over all peoples and nations; and by interceding for others before the throne of God's grace. The rest of Revelation is going to explain exactly how we are to do this in our turbulent and hostile world.

THE FIRST DOXOLOGY

"To him be glory and dominion forever and ever. Amen." This is the shortest of the seven doxologies in Revelation, but it is a great one, since it flows so spontaneously and strongly from John's summary of Jesus's person and work. John is teaching that it is because of who Jesus is and what he has done that all power and glory must be given to him forever. The other doxologies ascribe the following to either the Father or the Son or both: "glory and honor and thanks" (4:9); "glory and honor and power" (4:11); "power and wealth and wisdom and might and honor and glory and blessing" (5:12); "blessing and honor and glory and might" (5:13); "blessing and glory and wisdom and thanksgiving and honor and power and might" (7:12); and "salvation and glory and power" (19:1). At this point we might want to add the words of the "Gloria Patri," which was written in the second century: "As it was in the beginning, is now, and ever shall be: world without end. Amen."

LOOKING UP

What do most Christians think of when they think about the future? I would argue that it is not the resurrection of believers or the final judgment or the millennium or the Antichrist, or any of the other fascinating details of this fascinating book, but the second coming of our Lord. This is as it should be. For Jesus is the Lord and focal point of history. He stands at the beginning, as the Creator; he stands at the center, as the Savior hanging on the cross; and he stands at history's culmination, as the one who is coming again to receive his people to himself and to execute a final judgment on the nations. John knows this, and it is why he calls his readers to look up and look forward expectantly to Christ's coming: "Behold, he is coming with the clouds, and every eye will see him, even those who pierced him, and all tribes of the earth will wail on account of him. Even so. Amen" (Rev. 1:7).

This is the first time John has mentioned the second coming of Jesus in this book, but it is a theme that permeates Revelation and grows throughout, until it reaches a great, soaring climax at the end. "Surely I am coming soon," says Jesus. To which the church replies, "Amen. Come, Lord Jesus!" (Rev. 22:20).

This first reference to the Lord's return in Revelation is put together from two Old Testament verses: Daniel 7:13 and Zechariah 12:10. Daniel 7:13 is part of an amazing passage, which continues into the next verse, in which the prophet describes "one like a son of man" who comes "with the clouds of heaven." This individual approaches the Ancient of Days, is led into his presence, and is given "dominion and glory and a kingdom." "All peoples, nations, and languages" worship him. In Daniel this is a judgment scene. The point John makes here is that Jesus is this awesome individual. Jesus is the Judge.

The second reference is from an equally amazing section of Zechariah, which is part of what the prophet calls an "oracle." In this oracle, Zechariah is describing a time of blessing on Israel in the last days. It is a time when the enemies of the people will be defeated and the inhabitants of Jerusalem will be cleansed of their sin. This will happen because of God's grace, through the people's repentance and by their faith in the One they had pierced. The text says, "I will pour out on the house of David and the inhabitants of Jerusalem a spirit of grace and pleas for mercy, so that, when they look on me, on him whom they have pierced, they shall mourn for him, as one mourns for an only child, and weep bitterly over him, as one weeps over a firstborn" (Zech. 12:10).

John understands this oracle to be about Jesus, which it clearly is—but he also broadens it by adding that "every eye" will see him and "all tribes of the earth" will mourn because of him. In other words, John is not thinking only of the Jews, who pierced him, but of all who have rejected him. As in the passage in Daniel, John is presenting Jesus as the Lord of all peoples, nations, and languages. He is the Lord to whom every person who has ever lived must one day give an account.

Was John aware of the other gospels when he was writing Revelation? Quite likely. He seems at least to have known Matthew's gospel, because the words in Revelation 1:7 seem to echo those of Matthew 24:30, where Jesus says, "Then will appear in heaven the sign of the Son of Man, and then all the tribes of the earth will mourn, and they will see the Son of Man coming on the clouds of heaven with power and great glory."

When is this coming? Or has Christ already come? Here is where the various approaches that I outlined in the first study in this book affect the interpretation of Revelation.

Futurists see this as a final coming at the end of time. This has been the dominant view throughout most of church history, even among those who have differed on other, more minor points of prophecy. Jesus said that he would return—"If I go and prepare a place for you, I will come again and will take you to myself, that where I am you may be also" (John 14:3). And he has not returned yet. Therefore, the coming of which he spoke is still future.

Idealists interpret this as referring to many comings of Christ throughout history. Whenever something significant occurs, whether a historical judgment or a period of great spiritual blessing, there Christ has come. Idealists do not look forward to a literal, bodily return of Jesus at some future date. Rousas Rushdoony interprets Revelation 1:7 by saying, "Christ comes continually in the clouds of judgment over history."[3]

---

3. Rousas John Rushdoony, *Thy Kingdom Come: Studies in Daniel and Revelation* (Fairfax, VA: Thoburn Press, 1978), 87.

Preterists see Jesus's return as something that has already occurred—that is, as the destruction of Jerusalem by Roman armies under Titus in AD 70, though some preterists also look forward to a different second coming at history's end. Revelation 1:7 could then be a description of that first-century destruction. "Coming with the clouds" might be an Old Testament way of referring to any cataclysmic event. Mourning, particularly by those "who pierced him," might apply to the anguish of those terrible days.[4] But the preterist view depends on dating Revelation before the fall of Jerusalem, which most scholars do not believe is right; and if passages like this are all referring to the events of AD 70, where are those that tell us about the Lord's future coming? Or is there no future coming? Where is the Christian's "blessed hope" (Titus 2:13)?

I have already indicated how I intend to interpret these passages. In line with John's reference to the "many antichrists" who are already here as well as to the Antichrist who is coming (1 John 2:18), I acknowledge many "comings" of Christ, including in the destruction of Jerusalem. There are comings of Jesus in this age. His coming to judge the seven churches is an example (see Rev. 2:5; 3:20). But he is also coming at the end of history, and that is the important thing. It is this to which we must be looking. "Surely I am coming soon," Jesus says. We should reply, "Amen. Come, Lord Jesus!" (Rev. 22:20).

John makes the same reply. He does it emphatically in the very last words of our text: "Even so. Amen." This response combines the Greek (*nai*) and Hebrew (*Amen*) forms of solemn affirmation, as if John were saying, "So shall it be! So shall it be!" or "Amen and Amen."

A PERVASIVE BIBLE DOCTRINE

Let me note, as I close this study, how unfortunate it is that the second coming of Christ has faded into a remote and sometimes even irrelevant doctrine in the view of many Christians, and even within

4. A summary of the preterist arguments for interpreting this verse as referring to the destruction of Jerusalem may be found in Steve Gregg, ed., *Revelation: Four Views; A Parallel Commentary* (Nashville: Thomas Nelson, 1997), 34–46, 57.

large segments of the evangelical church. This may be true because so many foolish and unscriptural teachings have been linked to it by bad teachers. But that has been true of almost all doctrines at some point in history, and it should not keep us from appreciating and learning from a truth that has blessed so many through the ages and is so prominent in the Bible. Commentators have pointed out that in the New Testament one verse in twenty-five deals with the Lord's return in some way. It is mentioned 318 times in the 260 chapters of the New Testament, and it occupies a prominent place in the Old Testament too—inasmuch as the greater part of its prophecies concerning the coming of Christ deal not with his first advent, in which he died as our Sin-Bearer, but with his second coming, in which he is to reign over all peoples and nations as their King. The return of Jesus is mentioned in every one of the New Testament books except for Galatians, which deals with a particular problem that had emerged in the churches of that region, and for the very short books such as 2 and 3 John and Philemon.

Jesus spoke of his return quite often. Mark records him as saying, "Whoever is ashamed of me and of my words in this adulterous and sinful generation, of him will the Son of Man also be ashamed when he comes in the glory of his Father with the holy angels" (Mark 8:38), and "Then they will see the Son of Man coming in clouds with great power and glory. And then he will send out the angels and gather his elect from the four winds, from the ends of the earth to the ends of heaven" (Mark 13:26–27).

Paul's letters are also full of the doctrine of the second coming. To the believers at Thessalonica he wrote,

> For the Lord himself will descend from heaven with a cry of command, with the voice of an archangel, and with the sound of the trumpet of God. And the dead in Christ will rise first. Then we who are alive, who are left, will be caught up together with them in the clouds to meet the Lord in the air, and so we will always be with the Lord. (1 Thess. 4:16–17)

And he told the Philippians,

But our citizenship is in heaven, and from it we await a Savior, the Lord Jesus Christ, who will transform our lowly body to be like his glorious body, by the power that enables him even to subject all things to himself. (Phil. 3:20–21)

When this doctrine does appear throughout Scripture, it is portrayed as a source of hope for waiting believers. Peter called the return of Jesus our "living hope" (1 Peter 1:3). Paul called it our "blessed hope" (Titus 2:13). In these verses and many others, the early Christians expressed their belief in Jesus's personal return, encouraged one another with this hope during trials and temptations, and acknowledged that their lives should be lived on a higher plane because of it.

Is belief in the personal return of Jesus a practical doctrine? It certainly is. The great English social reformer Lord Shaftesbury supposedly said, near the end of his life, "I do not think that in the last forty years I have lived one conscious hour that was not influenced by the thought of our Lord's return." It was the awareness that he would meet Jesus face-to-face and give an accounting to him that motivated Shaftesbury's social reforms.

Thoughts of the imminent return of Jesus comfort those who are suffering. They certainly did so for the earliest Christians. We can imagine that as some of them lay in prison, beaten and facing death, they looked for Jesus's coming and thought that perhaps in an instant and without warning he would appear and call them home. As they entered the arena to face the lions or looked up from their cells to face their executioners, many would have thought, "Perhaps this is the moment Jesus will return; even now before the beasts can spring or the ax can fall, I shall be raised to meet him." After Paul had written to the Thessalonians about Christ's return, he admonished them, "Therefore encourage one another with these words" (1 Thess. 4:18).

A HYMN FOR GOD'S PEOPLE

Earlier in this study I referred to the last words of verse 6 as a doxology, which they are. But in a broader sense everything in verses 5 through 7 is a doxology—or, to put it differently, a hymn to be sung joyfully by God's people. J. Ramsey Michaels, in his fine commentary on Revelation, points out that although there are many hymns found throughout the book, including those elaborate ones that are sung before God's throne by the four living creatures, the twenty-four elders, and the angels,[5] this hymn in the first chapter is "a song to be sung on earth, one that the public readers of John's letter can lead their congregations in singing."[6] He adds rightly that it is a communal hymn, for its repetition of "us" and "our" draws John and his readers together as a confessing community of faith.

This is what hymns are meant to do. They are a means God gives us for confessing our beliefs, lifting up our flagging spirits, encouraging our hearts, and worshiping God together. Can anything be more joyful and uplifting than that? Nothing at all—until we sing perfectly in the presence of our Savior and God.

5. See Revelation 4:8–11; 5:9–14; 7:10–12; 11:15–18; 12:10–12; 15:3–4; 16:5–7; 18:2–8, 21–24; 19:1–8.
6. J. Ramsey Michaels, *Revelation*, The IVP New Testament Commentary Series (Downers Grove, IL: InterVarsity Press, 1997), 56.

4

JEHOVAH SPEAKS

Revelation 1:8

This is our fourth study on the first part of the book of Revelation (Rev. 1:1–8), but we have not yet answered the question as to John's purpose for writing this amazing composition. We have considered what kind of a book Revelation is, who wrote it when, and to whom it was written, but we have not yet thought about its purpose. Some would say that John's purpose for writing Revelation is obvious: to unveil the future—to let Christians know what is going to happen in the world's final days. Others (who are much closer to the truth, in my opinion) would say that Revelation was written to encourage Christians who were going through or might soon be going through times of terrible persecution by the Roman government. Yet I suggest that it is none of these. As I see it, the primary purpose of Revelation is to enable Christians from every age and in every possible circumstance to view what is happening in history from God's point of view, rather than from man's, and to be comforted and strengthened by this perspective to live for Christ and his glory at all times.

I can put it differently. The purpose of Revelation is to give Christians a heavenly perspective on earthly happenings, however terrible they may be. It was written to help us develop a heavenly world- and life-view.

This explains the overall pattern of the book, which is not primarily the recurring series of "sevens" that strikes us at first (the seven churches, seven seals, seven trumpets, seven bowls of wrath, and so on) but instead the repeated passing from a scene on earth to a scene in heaven and then back again. Thus, chapters 1 through 3 are about particular earthly churches. Chapters 4 and 5 lift our eyes to heaven. In chapter 6 through the first half of chapter 7 we see the judgments of God poured out on earth. In the last half of chapter 7 the scene returns to heaven, where we see the felicity of the saints as well as their worship of God. Chapter 8 through the first half of chapter 10 show us more earthly judgments. In the last half of chapter 11 we are again in heaven. And so it goes until the final scene, when we are back on earth, as we were at the beginning, and the saints are now looking upward in solemn expectation of Jesus's second coming. "Amen. Come, Lord Jesus!" is their cry (Rev. 22:20).

So let me say it again: *the purpose of Revelation is to get Christians from all periods of history and in all circumstances to look at things from God's perspective rather than from man's and to draw comfort and strength from that perspective.*

GOD ALMIGHTY SPEAKS

This is also the reason for Revelation 1:8—the verse to which we have now come in our progressing exposition. It is the last verse of John's remarkable two-part introduction, which is comprised of verses 1 through 3 and verses 4 through 8. What is remarkable about it is that here God the Father himself is speaking, which he does directly at only one other place in Revelation (see 21:5–8). Everywhere else in the book the words of God come through the chain of revealers in the first verse: (1) God the Father, (2) Jesus Christ, (3) an angel or angels, (4) John, (5) the public readers of the letter, and (6) those who hear the letter being read.

God says, "I am the Alpha and the Omega, who is and who was and who is to come, the Almighty." This sentence contains various phrases through which God identifies himself as the one who stands behind the revelation. It tells us that he is the true or genuine God and is eternal, unchanging, and sovereign.

What is the point of these self-identifying words? Beale has it right when he says, "The purpose of v[erse] 8 is to emphasize God's sovereignty over all history by repeating the threefold description of God found in v[erse] 4a and by explaining its meaning by the addition of two further phrases."[1]

This is an important matter, at least to believers who are going through persecution or hard times. Is God sovereign? Is he regulating affairs on earth, today and at all times? Or are things somehow out of control? Or in man's hands? Or even controlled by the devil? There seems to be cause for supposing that God has lost control. When Jesus was speaking about the end times in Matthew 24, he said that history would be marked by wars and rumors of wars, famines, earthquakes, persecutions, apostasy, and false prophets. Does that sound like things over which God is altogether sovereign? And what about Revelation itself? Revelation unveils all kinds of earthly evils, destructions, pain, and killings. It speaks of those who are martyred for their faith. Could God have willed that?

One person looked at the Bible's teaching, compared it with life as we know it, and expressed his observations in a limerick.

> God's plan made a hopeful beginning,
> But man spoiled his chances by sinning.
> We trust that the story
> Will end in God's glory,
> But at present the other side's winning.

This poem, which is attributed to Oliver Wendell Holmes, is funny, but its theology is not. If "the other side's winning," we are all in deep trouble. But the other side is not winning. What Revelation teaches is that God is sovereign over all things, including the ups and downs of human history, and that he is indeed working out everything according to the counsel of his own inscrutable and yet perfect will.

---

1. G. K. Beale, *The Book of Revelation: A Commentary on the Greek Text* (Grand Rapids: William B. Eerdmans, 1999), 199.

THE ETERNITY OF GOD

Revelation 1:8 contains three titles or descriptions of God the Father, just as there were three titles for God the Son in verse 5. In that verse Jesus was identified as "the faithful witness, the firstborn of the dead, and the ruler of kings on earth." In this verse God identifies himself as "the Alpha and the Omega, who is and who was and who is to come, the Almighty."

"Alpha and Omega" is a *merism*—a figure of speech that sometimes involves using the first and last items in a series to indicate that everything in between is included. *Alpha* and *omega* are the first and last letters of the Greek alphabet. The Hebrew equivalent would be "*aleph* and *tau*." When the rabbis talked about Adam's sin and Abraham's obedience, they said that Adam transgressed the law but that Abraham kept it from *aleph* to *tau*. They meant that he kept it all, just as Paul claimed he had done as a Pharisee when he told the Philippians that, with respect to "righteousness under the law," he had been "blameless" (Phil. 3:6). So being the "Alpha and Omega" means that God is the source of, and himself encompasses, all things. This is the point with which Paul ends Romans 11: "For from him and through him and to him are all things. To him be glory forever. Amen" (v. 36).

Yet there is more to the meaning of "Alpha and Omega" than this. God is the source of and himself encompasses not only all *physical* things but *all* things—which includes time as well. Therefore, his being the "Alpha and Omega" also means that God is eternal. It is what Moses meant when he wrote in Psalm 90, "Before the mountains were brought forth, or ever you had formed the earth and the world, from everlasting to everlasting you are God" (v. 2). It means that God has always existed. Before there were mountains or stars or quarks or quasars or anything else that we are aware of, God was there—not only for a day, a decade, an age, or a millennium but "from everlasting." There was never a moment when God was not.

God's eternity involves several other attributes that theologians rightly call his incommunicable attributes, meaning that they are unique to God and cannot be shared by his creatures—even man—in any way: his self-existence and his self-sufficiency.

God's *self-existence* means that he has no origins—that he has always been and that he owes his existence to no one else. When you and I speak of our existence, we have to say, "I am what I am by the grace of God." But when God revealed himself to Moses at the burning bush, he said only, "I AM WHO I AM" (Ex. 3:14). God exists in himself alone and is therefore ultimately unknowable. He can be known only to the extent that he reveals himself to us. He cannot be analyzed as created things can be.

His *self-sufficiency* means that God has no needs and therefore depends on no one. Again, we are not like that. We have countless needs—we need oxygen to breathe, food to eat, clothes to wear, houses in which to live, and more. But God does not need anything; in himself, he is and has everything.

This runs counter to ideas that many people have about God. Supposing him to be like themselves, they imagine that at one time God was lonely and thus created men and women to keep him company. They forget that God is a Trinity and that he has always had perfect and perfectly fulfilling fellowship within the Godhead.

Other people suppose that God needs worshipers. But if every individual on the face of the earth became an atheist tomorrow and refused to acknowledge God's existence, God would be no more deprived by our atheism than the sun would be deprived of light if all of us should become blind.

Other people suppose that God needs helpers, even suggesting that he created us to help him "get the job done." It is true that God has given us the privilege of doing useful and meaningful work for him. In this age of gospel proclamation, he has given us the task of being his evangelists and has even called us "fellow workers" with Jesus Christ. But this does not mean that he needs us. God can manage very well without us, and he has. That he chooses to use us is due only to his own free and utterly sovereign will.

Some might suppose that this reduces the work we are capable of doing to nothing, making it of no importance whatsoever. But that is not the case—nor is it how Moses saw things in the psalm that

I quoted earlier. Psalm 90 is full of examples of Moses's profound awareness of how little and insignificant man is and how brief is the span of his life. This awareness intensifies as Moses reflects on the eternity of God. He is forever; we are for but a moment.

But it is precisely because God is eternal, because he is God, that we have hope that our works will last and have significance. It is because God is able to establish them—which is why the psalm ends by saying, "Let the favor of the Lord our God be upon us, and establish the work of our hands upon us; yes, establish the work of our hands!" (v. 17).

One way of looking at Revelation is to see it as God's assurance that he will indeed establish the works of his downtrodden and often persecuted people. Even more, he will establish his people themselves. For they will be victorious over all their enemies and will reign with his Son, the Lord Jesus Christ, forever.

THE IMMUTABILITY OF GOD

The second of these descriptive titles of God is repeated from verse 4: "who is and who was and who is to come." When I looked at that verse in the second study in this book, I focused on the unusual grammar of this phrase, answering the criticism that John's Greek is barbarous. Here, where John repeats this title for God in verse 8, we need to look more closely at its meaning. The words "who is and who was and who is to come" are an echo of the words God spoke to Moses at the burning bush. When Moses asked for God's name, God replied, "I AM WHO I AM" (Ex. 3:14). That name is known as the *tetragrammaton*, meaning the four Hebrew letters that constitute the proper name of God: *YHWH*. They are a variation of the Hebrew verb "to be."

God is pure being, which is another way of saying that he exists in all the tenses of the Hebrew verb. He existed in the eternal past, exists now, and will exist always. We see the beginning of the drawing out of the full meaning of this verb in Isaiah 44:6, where God says, "I am the first and I am the last; besides me there is no god," and in Isaiah 48:12, where he says, similarly, "I am he; I am the first, and I am the last." The rabbis took this further, interpreting Exodus 3:14 and parallel verses to mean "I am he who is and who will be," "I am now what I always was and always will be," and "I am he who is and who was, and I am he who will be."[2]

GOD'S CHARACTER DOES NOT CHANGE

These words "who is and who was and who is to come" indicate that God is an eternal being, as the words "Alpha and Omega" also do. But the unique meaning of these words is that God is also immutable, or unchanging, in his eternal being. He is today what he always was, and what he is today he always will be. He is unchangeable in his essence and his attributes. The Shorter Catechism says rightly, "God is a Spirit, infinite, eternal, and *unchangeable*, in his being, wisdom, power, holiness, justice, goodness, and truth."[3]

This should be a great comfort for God's people, for it means that God can be counted on to be what he has revealed himself to be. This is not true of mere men and women. Human beings are in a constant state of change. They promise to be our friends forever, but they frequently change their attitudes toward us, forget us, or hurt us. Their attitudes are dictated by their own changing interests, desires, and experiences. A. W. Tozer wrote,

> What peace it brings to the Christian's heart to realize that our heavenly Father never differs from himself. In coming to him at any time we need not wonder whether we shall find him in a receptive mood. He is always receptive to misery and need, as well as to love and faith. He does not keep office hours nor set aside periods when he will see no one. Neither does he change his mind about anything. Today, this moment, he feels toward his creatures, toward babies, toward the sick, the fallen, the sinful, exactly as he did when he sent his only begotten Son into the world to die for mankind. God never changes moods or cools off in his affections or loses enthusiasm.[4]

2. For references in the Hebrew Targums and Midrashim, see Beale, 187.
3. Westminster Shorter Catechism, answer 1.
4. A. W. Tozer, *The Knowledge of the Holy: The Attributes of God; Their Meaning in the Christian Life* (New York: Harper & Brothers, 1961), 59.

GOD'S TRUTH DOES NOT CHANGE

God is the only being in the universe whose word can be always and absolutely trusted. J. I. Packer writes,

> Men sometimes say things that they do not really mean, simply because they do not know their own mind; also, because their views change, they frequently find that they can no longer stand to things that they said in the past. All of us sometimes have to recall our words, because they have ceased to express what we think; sometimes we have to eat our words, because hard facts refute them. The words of men are unstable things. But not so the words of God. They stand forever, as abidingly valid expressions of his mind and thought. No circumstances prompt him to recall them; no changes in his own thinking require him to amend them. Isaiah writes, "All flesh is grass . . . the grass withereth . . . but the word of our God shall stand for ever" (Isa. 40:6 ff.).[5]

GOD'S PURPOSES DO NOT CHANGE

It is not only God's essence, attributes, and truth that do not change. His plans do not change either. Our plans do change, because we cannot see the future or anticipate everything that might happen. We also lack the power to do all that we may plan to do. But God has perfect knowledge of all things, past, present, and future, and he has infinite power to accomplish his desires. Numbers 23:19 reads, "God is not a man, that he should lie, nor a son of man, that he should change his mind. Does he speak and then not act? Does he promise and not fulfill?" (NIV).

To change one's mind means to revise one's plan of action. But God does not need to do this, since his plans are made on the basis of his perfect knowledge, and his perfect power sees that they are accomplished.

This has several important areas of application. First, if God's purposes do not change, then his purposes for Christ will not change. His purpose is to glorify Christ. Paul told the Philippians that God

---

5. J. I. Packer, *Knowing God* (Downers Grove, IL: InterVarsity Press, 1973), 70.

has exalted Jesus to the highest place, giving him the name that is above every name, so that in days to come "every knee should bow . . . and every tongue confess that Jesus Christ is Lord, to the glory of God the Father" (Phil. 2:10–11). If this is so, then it is foolish to resist Christ and his glory. We may attempt to do so now, as many people do. But the day is coming when Jesus must be confessed as Lord even by those who would not have him as Lord in this life. The book of Revelation shows how this is to happen.

Second, if God's purposes do not change, then his purposes for his redeemed people will not change. God's plan is to make us into the image of Jesus Christ and to bring us safely into his own presence at the end of life's journey. We read about this in Hebrews.

> For when God made a promise to Abraham, since he had no one greater by whom to swear, he swore by himself, saying, "Surely I will bless you and multiply you." And thus Abraham, having patiently waited, obtained the promise. For people swear by something greater than themselves, and in all their disputes an oath is final for confirmation. So when God desired to show more convincingly to the heirs of the promise the unchangeable character of his purpose, he guaranteed it with an oath, so that by two unchangeable things, in which it is impossible for God to lie, we who have fled for refuge might have strong encouragement to hold fast to the hope set before us. (Heb. 6:13–18)

God's purpose is to bring his own into full enjoyment of their promised inheritance—into their hope. So that they can know it and be assured of it, he confirms it with an immutable oath. In Revelation he also opens our eyes to see the flow of historical events from his own perspective so that we might be reassured in that hope.

Third, if God's purposes do not change, then his purposes for the wicked will not change. We see this in Revelation as well. God's purpose is to judge the wicked, and this is what he will do. Exodus 34:7 says that God "will by no means clear the guilty." Other passages, such as those in Revelation, speak of the judgments themselves. The fact that God does not change in his determination to punish sinners should be a warning to any who have not yet turned from their sin in order to trust the Lord Jesus Christ as their Savior. Arthur Pink wrote, "Those who defy him, break his laws, have no concern for his glory, but live their lives as though he existed not, must not suppose that, when at the last they shall cry to him for mercy, he will alter his will, revoke his word, and rescind his awful threatenings. No, he has declared, 'Therefore will I also deal in fury: Mine eye shall not spare, neither will I have pity: and though they cry in mine ears with a loud voice, yet will I not hear them' (Ezek. 8:18)."[6]

The immutability of God should drive all such persons to the Savior.

THE SOVEREIGNTY OF GOD

The last words that God speaks in Revelation 1:8 to define his nature are "the Almighty." This is a translation of the Hebrew words *El Shaddai*, which occur for the first time in the Bible in Genesis 17:1, where God tells Abraham, "I am God Almighty; walk before me, and be blameless." This is the chapter in which God establishes his covenant with Abraham. The phrase "says the Lord Almighty" occurs frequently throughout Haggai, Zechariah, and Malachi to refer to God as the one who sovereignly directs his people's history. The words *the Almighty* occur frequently in other parts of the Old Testament, but strikingly only ten times in the New Testament—and nine of these are in Revelation (1:8; 4:8; 11:17; 15:3; 16:7, 14; 19:6, 15; 21:22). The only other occurrence of "says the Lord Almighty" in the New Testament is as part of a quotation from the Old Testament (see 2 Cor. 6:18).

The Greek translation of *El Shaddai* is *pantokrator*, which means "the Omnipotent." It is the word that John uses in that great text that is so familiar to us through Handel's *Messiah*: "Alleluia: for the Lord God omnipotent reigneth" (Rev. 19:6 KJV). The English

6. Arthur W. Pink, *The Attributes of God: A Solemn and Blessed Contemplation of Some of the Wondrous and Lovely Perfections of the Divine Character* (Grand Rapids: Baker Book House, n.d.), 42.

Standard Version reads, "Hallelujah! For the Lord our God the Almighty reigns."

Almighty is the word and attribute of God that John wants to leave with us as he moves into the amazing revelations that it is the purpose of the Apocalypse to unveil. What does it mean that God is "the Almighty"? It means that God is God—that he is sovereign over his creation. According to A. W. Pink, it means that because God is God and because he is almighty, he "does as He pleases, only as He pleases, always as He pleases; that His great concern is the accomplishment of His own pleasure and the promotion of His own glory; that He is the Supreme Being, and therefore Sovereign of the universe."[7]

The unbelieving world hates this doctrine, because this doctrine stands opposed to the deepest desires of the human heart, which are to do what the individual sinner wants to do and to promote the sinner's glory. It is altogether different for Christians. Knowing that God is sovereign transforms our lives.

IT DEEPENS OUR VENERATION OF THE LIVING AND TRUE GOD

What kind of a God would we have if his will were constantly being thwarted by man's disobedience or the evil designs of Satan? What kind of a God would he be if his sovereignty were restricted so that he could not invade the citadel of the human will in order to bring a rebellious sinner to repent of his or her sin and to trust Christ? A God like that would not be worthy of our worship. In fact, a God like that would not be God. But a God who rules his universe, accomplishes his will, and is never frustrated, by either human beings or the devil, is a God to be joyfully sought after, worshiped, and obeyed.

IT GIVES US COMFORT IN THE MIDST OF TRIALS, TEMPTATIONS, AND LIFE'S SORROWS

Temptations and sorrows come to everyone—to Christians as well as to those who are not Christians. How are we to meet them?

---

7. Arthur W. Pink, *The Sovereignty of God* (1930; repr., Swengel, PA: Bible Truth Depot, 1956), 21.

If we must face them with no certainty that they are controlled by God and permitted for his good purposes, then they are without meaning and life as a whole is a tragedy. That is precisely what the existentialists and others are saying. But if, by contrast, the troubles as well as the good things of life are sent and controlled by God, then we can trust that he is accomplishing a good purpose for us through them and can be both comforted and strengthened. This is what I have described as John's ultimate purpose in writing Revelation.

IT AFFORDS US A DEEP SENSE OF SECURITY

If we look to ourselves, we will have no security at all, for we are feeble creatures. If we look to the world around us, we will be utterly dismayed, for the lure of the world is stronger than even our best inclinations. But we do not look to ourselves or to the world. We look to the sovereign God, who is mighty to save us from all ills.

> For I am sure that neither death nor life, nor angels nor rulers, nor things present nor things to come, nor powers, nor height nor depth, nor anything else in all creation, will be able to separate us from the love of God in Christ Jesus our Lord. (Rom. 8:38–39)

5

WHEN JOHN SAW JESUS

Revelation 1:9—20

Most of what we have been looking at so far in our study of Revelation 1 has been introductory. However, in verse 9 we turn to the visions that form the heart of this difficult but intriguing book. The first vision is of Jesus Christ standing in the midst of seven lampstands, which represent the seven churches to whom the letters in the following two chapters are addressed. How are we to understand this vision? Or any of the following visions, for that matter? How literally should we take them?

The general rule of Bible interpretation is that a text should be taken literally unless there is a clear reason to take it some other way—as a symbol or as poetry, for instance. But Revelation is an unusual book. It is unlike any other book of the New Testament (though it is much like parts of Daniel in the Old Testament). I suggest that in the case of Revelation this general rule of Bible interpretation needs to be reversed. Revelation is not a historical narrative, as the four Gospels mostly are, nor a theological or doctrinal treatise like the New Testament Epistles. It is mostly a series of visions that point beyond themselves to realities that are greater than the visions. To say it another way, the book of Revelation is a symbolized communication.

SYMBOLIZED COMMUNICATION

John indicates at the very beginning of Revelation that this is the way his prophecy should be interpreted. In the first study in this book

I spent some time looking at the word *revelation* (or *apocalypse*) that occurs in Revelation 1:1. It is one of three descriptive terms for the book: *apocalypse*, *prophecy*, and *letter*. Yet there is another term in that verse that I did not look at carefully then, but which has bearing on what I am discussing now and needs to be considered. It is the verb *to make known* in the sentence "He made it known by sending his angel to his servant John." "Made it known" is a translation of the verb *semaino*.

Semaino means to "make known" or "communicate." But it also means "to signify or communicate by symbols"—which is how it is used here in Revelation. This is because Revelation 1:1 is a deliberate echo of words that John had read in Daniel. (There are many such echoes of Daniel in Revelation.) It is referring to something that Daniel said to King Nebuchadnezzar when he was about to explain the meaning of Nebuchadnezzar's dream about the great golden statue: "There is a God in heaven who reveals mysteries, and he has made known to King Nebuchadnezzar what will be in the latter days" (Dan. 2:28). In the Greek translation of Daniel, the verb "he has made known" is the same word that John uses in Revelation 1, and the contexts of the two uses are similar. By means of visions, God is making known what is to come. In other words, what is to be communicated to John will be made known through images, pictures, or vivid symbols. It will be a symbolized revelation—the kind of thing we might see in a dream. It has reality, but it does not necessarily exist as seen, any more than the great sheet filled with all kinds of animals was an actual sheet in the vision Peter had at Joppa.[1]

This bothers some people, because it seems to mean we are breaking with reality and ceasing to take the Bible seriously. But this is not the case. To treat a symbol as a symbol actually enables us

---

1. There is an excellent discussion of the verb *semaino* under the heading "The Symbolic Nature of the Apocalypse" in G. K. Beale, *The Book of Revelation: A Commentary on the Greek Text* (Grand Rapids: William B. Eerdmans, 1999), 50–55. Beale argues, "We are told in the book's introduction that the majority of the material in it is revelatory symbolism (1:12–20 and 4:1–22:5 at the least). Hence, the predominant manner by which to approach the material will be according to a nonliteral interpretative method" (p. 52).

to perceive what is real in a fuller way than we can achieve through mere didactic statements.

Douglas Jones and Douglas Wilson wrote a brilliant book under the imaginative title *Angels in the Architecture: A Protestant Vision for Middle Earth*. It contains a chapter on "Poetic Knowledge," which argues that for human beings, who cannot see reality directly and fully, as God does, all knowledge must in some sense be metaphorical.[2] God knows things through an immediate, thorough, and immutable cognition. We are different. Our knowledge is always mediated, which means that the language by which we speak of things is never the reality itself but always points beyond itself to what is truly and actually there—especially regarding spiritual things. For example, we call God "Father"—which we are right to do; Jesus himself told us to do it (see Matt. 6:9). But we do not mean by this that God is exactly like the fathers whom we know or even that he is the embodiment of all that is best about fatherhood. We only mean that God relates to us somewhat as a father relates to his children. To say that God is our Father is a true statement—but it is a metaphorical or poetic statement, not a literal one. Which is why an even truer statement might be one that carries the symbolism further, as does Psalm 103:13 ("As a father shows compassion to his children, so the LORD shows compassion to those who fear him") or Matthew 7:9–11:

> Which one of you, if his son asks him for bread, will give him a stone? Or if he asks for a fish, will give him a serpent? If you then, who are evil, know how to give good gifts to your children, how much more will your Father who is in heaven give good things to those who ask him!

The point that Jones and Wilson are making is that this is true of all human language. But if it is true of all language, then it is

---

2. See Douglas Wilson, "Poetic Knowledge: Learning to Be Politically Active," chap. 16 in Douglas Jones and Douglas Wilson, *Angels in the Architecture: A Protestant Vision for Middle Earth* (Moscow, ID: Canon Press, 1998).

especially true of language describing spiritual things and even more true of the visionary language of the book of Revelation. So there is a sense in which we must become poets in order to understand Revelation—starting with the vision of Jesus among the candlesticks introduced in chapter 1. Jones and Wilson demand this, arguing that "the true poet is one who has learned to think and speak of God humbly and the creation obliquely, knowing what he does."[3]

THE COMMISSIONING OF JOHN

We do not begin with such a heightened approach to reality, however. We begin in a mundane setting. John is in exile on the island of Patmos on the Lord's Day. Patmos is a rocky, crescent-shaped island about thirty-seven miles southwest of the mainland of Asia Minor that is about sixteen square miles in area. The Christian apologist Tertullian seems to have understood the words "on account of the word of God and the testimony of Jesus," in Revelation 1:9, to mean that John was banished there because of his proclamation of the Christian message,[4] and this is probably true, though we do not have any independent verification. The church historian Eusebius reports that John was later released by the emperor Nerva (who reigned AD 96–98) and that he returned to Ephesus.[5]

Verse 10's mention of "the Lord's Day" is the only use of this phrase in the New Testament, and although some take it to mean that John was carried away "in the Spirit" to behold the final day of the Lord—the last judgment—this interpretation is not necessary. John is simply saying where, when, and in what state he received this vision.

In case his readers may be thinking of Christ's kingdom as a political kingdom in which we are to exercise earthly power along with Jesus, John makes clear that the kingdom about which he is writing in verse 9 is a kingdom of suffering. Yet it is the only true

---

3. Jones and Wilson, 183.
4. See Tertullian, *Prescription Against Heretics*, chap. 36.
5. See Eusebius, *Ecclesiastical History*, bk. 3, chap. 20, par. 10–11.

kingdom. The words "tribulation" (*thlipsis*), "kingdom" (*basileia*), and "patient endurance" (*hupomone*) are introduced by a single article, which means that they belong together as part of one reality. Jesus brought the kingdom to us by means of his "faithful witness" (v. 5), John has become part of it by suffering for his "testimony" (v. 9), and the Christians to whom he is writing are suffering or will soon be suffering, too. What is about to happen in this book is that John's visions will open their eyes to see beyond their present tribulations to the wise and sovereign rule of God in and over history—even that part in which they are suffering—so that they will be encouraged to endure and triumph in their suffering for Christ's sake.

JOHN'S VISION OF JESUS

While John was "in the Spirit"—which probably means worshiping, praying, or meditating—he suddenly heard "a loud voice" that told him to write down what he was about to see and send it to the seven churches of Asia Minor: Ephesus, Smyrna, Pergamum, Thyatira, Sardis, Philadelphia, and Laodicea (see Rev. 1:10–11). These are the churches to whom the individualized letters of chapters 2 and 3 are addressed. John's words are like those that Ezekiel used to report his commissioning (see Ezek. 3:12), and the voice that is like the sound of a trumpet is like the voice that Moses heard from Mount Sinai (see Ex. 19:16, 19). This suggests that John was intentionally placing himself in the Old Testament prophetic tradition. What he heard was from the same God who gave the law from Sinai.

The first thing John noticed when he turned around was "seven golden lampstands" (Rev. 1:12). This image has roots in the instructions for making the furniture for the wilderness tabernacle, as found in Exodus 25:31–40, 37:17–24, and Numbers 8:1–4, as well as in the vision that Zechariah had of a golden lampstand in Zechariah 4:1–14. But the lampstand of the Old Testament tabernacle and, later, the temple was a single object holding seven separate lights, while the lamps of Revelation 1:12, 13, and 20 are freestanding lampstands. Jewish writings understand the seven-branched candlestick, or *menorah*, to represent Israel; but in Revelation these lamps represent the universal church. They may also have caused John to think of Jesus's well-known description, in the Sermon on the Mount, of believers as a light set upon a stand and a city on a hill (see Matt. 5:14–15).

The second and most important thing that John saw was someone "like a son of man" standing among the lampstands. This refers to the risen Lord Jesus Christ, of course, and the depiction of him in the verses that follow is well known and is based on images that are drawn from Daniel 7:9 and 10:4–6, primarily, though other texts have contributed to John's picture. What is most important about these words, more even than the individual descriptive items, is the reference to one "like a son of man." This comes directly from Daniel 7:13–14, which reads,

> I saw in the night visions,
>
> and behold, with the clouds of heaven
> > there came one like a son of man,
> and he came to the Ancient of Days
> > and was presented before him.
> And to him was given dominion
> > and glory and a kingdom,
> that all peoples, nations, and languages
> > should serve him;
> his dominion is an everlasting dominion,
> > which shall not pass away,
> and his kingdom one
> > that shall not be destroyed.

This fascinating Old Testament passage introduces a figure who is separate from the Ancient of Days and yet is given full divine honors. He has royal authority, glory, and sovereign power, and the creation worships him. This is a rare Old Testament recognition of what we would call a plurality within the Godhead, as well as a glimpse of the glory of the preincarnate Christ.

In Daniel, the figure who is "like a son of man" is described as a king who is coming to execute God's judgment on the nations. In

Revelation 1 he is more of a priest and prophet, though his kingly role becomes increasingly prominent as the book goes on. He is a priest because he is standing among the lampstands and tending them. In the Old Testament, it was the job of the priests to tend the temple lamps. He is a prophet because he has come to impart the revelation that John records.

The specific features of John's description of the risen Christ are drawn from the Old Testament—particularly from Daniel 7 and 10.

"Clothed with a long robe and with a golden sash around his chest" (Rev. 1:13). This is close to the description of the clothing of the angel who appears to Daniel in chapter 10, but the significance of the clothing is that it is what Old Testament priests wore. Thus Jesus is being presented as our faithful and only High Priest—the one who offered himself as a sacrifice for our sins, thereby making atonement for them before God the Father, and who is now ministering in the heavenly temple on behalf of his people and making intercession for them.

"The hairs of his head were white, like white wool, like snow" (Rev. 1:14). This description is an obvious way of identifying Jesus with the Ancient of Days, since it is how God himself is described in Daniel 7:9: "His clothing was white as snow, and the hair of his head like pure wool."

"His eyes were like a flame of fire" (Rev. 1:14). This image appears in Revelation 19:12 also. It is a judicial image, for these are eyes that see through and disclose everything. Fire is associated with God's appearance to Moses at the burning bush (see Ex. 3:2) and on Mount Sinai (see Ex. 19:18), and Deuteronomy 4:24 says, "For the LORD your God is a consuming fire, a jealous God" (see also Heb. 12:29).

"His feet were like burnished bronze, refined in a furnace" (Rev. 1:15). This image is found in Daniel 10:6. It suggests moral purity, but it may also speak of the force and irresistibility of Christ's

judgment, for these are the feet with which he will tread out the "great winepress of the wrath of God" (Rev. 14:19).

"His voice was like the roar of many waters" (Rev. 1:15). This is also how Ezekiel describes the sound of the Almighty (Ezek. 43:2).

"In his right hand he held seven stars" (Rev. 1:16). Daniel 12:3 also mentions stars, likening them to the wise among Israel, which is also a good way to describe those who have believed on Christ from among both the Jews and Gentiles—that is, the church. Differing from Daniel, Revelation 1:20 identifies the stars as "the angels of the seven churches." The same verse also identifies the lampstands as the seven churches themselves.

"From his mouth came a sharp two-edged sword" (Rev. 1:16). This is a clear symbol for the power of Jesus's spoken word. The author of Hebrews uses the same image when he writes that "the word of God is living and active, sharper than any two-edged sword, piercing to the division of soul and of spirit, of joints and of marrow, and discerning the thoughts and intentions of the heart" (Heb. 4:12; see also Eph. 6:17). The same figure of speech reappears in Revelation 2:16 and 19:15, 21.

"His face was like the sun shining in full strength" (Rev. 1:16). This is similar to the description of the angel in Daniel 10:6, though the actual wording is from the Greek translation of Judges 5:31. It is interesting to remember that this is not the first time John had seen the face of Jesus shining like the sun in its brilliance. He had seen it this way once before, on the Mount of Transfiguration (see Matt. 17:2).

We are going to encounter Jesus's titles and the descriptive elements of this vision again. They are not just thrown out and then forgotten in order for John to move on to something else. They reappear later—particularly in the letters to the seven churches. But remember what I wrote earlier about symbolic communication. These images are not to be analyzed to death or scientifically catalogued. They are meant to paint a mentally stimulating but essentially imaginary picture. G. B. Caird writes,

> To compile such a catalogue is to unweave the rainbow. John uses his allusions not as a code in which each symbol requires separate and exact translation, but rather for their evocative and emotive power. This is not photographic art. His aim is to set the echoes of memory and association ringing. The humbling sense of the sublime and the majestic which men experience at the sight of a roaring cataract or the midday sun is the nearest equivalent to the awe evoked by a vision of the divine. John has seen the risen Christ . . . and he wishes to call forth from his readers the same response of overwhelming and annihilating wonder which he experienced in his prophetic trance.[6]

JOHN'S REACTION

Even the words of that quote may be too mild a way of describing John's response to seeing this vision of Christ. In the Bible it is almost universally the case that when a prophet receives a vision, he falls on his face in fear and must be raised up by a heavenly being—somewhat like experiencing a resurrection. This was Isaiah's response when he saw the Lord sitting on his glorious throne (see Isa. 6:5). There are even closer parallels in Daniel 8 and 10, which John is probably following. In these passages, Daniel received further revelations after he was raised up. Here in Revelation, when John heard the voice and saw the risen Christ, he "fell at his feet as though dead" (Rev. 1:17). But then Jesus reached out, raised him up, and gave him the revelation that concludes the chapter (see vv. 17–20). This revelation contains Jesus's self-identification, his commissioning of John, and the first explanation of what John has seen.

These verses give us a new set of titles for Jesus in addition to

---

6. G. B. Caird, *A Commentary on the Revelation of St. John the Divine* (New York: Harper & Row, 1966), 25–26.

those in verse 3: "the first and the last" (v. 17), "the living one," and the one who holds "the keys of Death and Hades" (v. 18). The first title is similar to the way that God identifies himself in verse 8. Thus it identifies the Jesus of John's vision as God. "The living one" emphasizes Jesus's eternal victory over death ("I died, and behold I am alive forevermore"). The reference to holding "the keys of Death and Hades" emphasizes Christ's present rule and power. Jesus tells John, "Fear not" (v. 17)—words that may also be applied to those to whom John is writing. They also need not fear, regardless of what the future may hold or what may come into their lives, because Jesus is the living one who holds the keys to everything.[7]

VERSE 19: A CRUX INTERPRETUM

What about verse 19? Many commentators see this verse as the key to interpreting Revelation—and it is, in some ways; though how we interpret it will depend on how we are prepared to interpret the entire book. There are four main views of this verse.

1. IT PROVIDES A THREE-PART CHRONOLOGICAL SEQUENCE

At first glance this seems to be the obvious way to think of the verse. "The things that you have seen" would be the vision of Christ among the lampstands described earlier in Revelation 1. "Those that are" would be the state of the seven churches, as portrayed in chapters 2 and 3. "Those that are to take place after this" would be the bulk of Revelation, projected to the final days, as seen in chapters 4 through 22. The main problem with this view is that both chapters 2 and 3 and chapters 4 through 22 contain repeated references to both the past and the future. In fact, as I wrote in the previous study in this book, Revelation 4 through 22 seems to move back and forth between earth and heaven—that is, between the way that things seem to be now and the way that they actually are when viewed from

---

7. Jesus's reference to the keys in this verse throws light on Matthew 16:18, where Jesus tells Peter that "the gates of hell shall not prevail against" the church.

God's perspective. If this is the case, then Revelation as a whole does not present a historical sequence at all.

Again, the phrase "those that are to take place after this" is drawn from Daniel 2:28 ("what will be in the latter days") and should be interpreted to mean not the distant future but the "latter days" that the coming of the Messiah would inaugurate. Beale says, "Accordingly, 'what is to happen after these things' must refer to the eschatological period, which includes inauguration in the past, present, and future."[8] If this is true, then "the things that you have seen" probably does not refer only to the vision of Jesus among the lampstands but to the whole of the prophecy. It is what John was to write down after he had seen it all.

2. IT PROVIDES A TWO-PART SEQUENCE

This view understands "the things that you have seen" to refer to the entire vision, which is then broken down into both a present and a future reference to it. Robert Mounce holds to this view: "The proper division . . . is twofold, not three. The first statement ('Write therefore the things which thou sawest') is the essential unit and parallels the earlier command in v. 11 ('What thou seest, write in a book'). . . . Translate, 'Write, therefore, the things you are about to see, that is, both what now is and what lies yet in the future.'"[9] This is a better treatment of "the things that you have seen," because it links this phrase to verse 11. But it suffers from the same criticism as the chronological or historical-sequence view. It is not easy to divide John's material into what has happened and what is yet to happen.

3. IT REFERS TO HISTORY AS A WHOLE

This is the idealist's interpretation. This view sees the formula in verse 19 as referring to the whole of history and indicating that the book is stating truths that transcend any historical time period. This is a valid interpretation of the words "those that are and those that

---

8. Beale, *The Book of Revelation*, 162.

9. Robert H. Mounce, *The Book of Revelation* (Grand Rapids: Wm. B. Eerdmans, 1977), 81–82.

are to take place after this," because it takes them as a *merism*—that is, a phrase embracing the totality of all that happens. The problem is that it leaves the prophecy without any genuinely prophetic parts. Revelation would be telling us what history is like, but it would be giving us no specific information about anything that lies in the future.

4. IT REFERS TO THINGS THAT EXIST NOW BUT ARE ALSO NOT YET ENTIRELY FULFILLED

This view recognizes that the words "those that are to take place after this" are a deliberate reference to Daniel and that they indicate that what John was prophesying for the latter days is already here and happening because of the life, death, and resurrection of Jesus, who is ruling now in his churches—although the things "that are" also anticipate what will "take place after this" in the very last days. This is the general approach that I have taken and that I explained in the first study in this book. Nearly everything in Revelation (the things that John saw) is happening now, because the book describes the nature of this corrupt age and its repeated cycles of rebellion. But specific parts of Revelation also point forward to a literal, historical fulfillment to take place in the days preceding the return of Jesus and the final judgment.[10]

John was still on Patmos when he had this vision, but "in the Spirit" he was able to see beyond Patmos to a larger, heavenly reality. We need to see that larger reality, too. Here we are often bogged down with mere earthly trivia. But we need to see that beyond this lies the heavenly "city that has foundations, whose designer and builder is God" (Heb. 11:10).

[handwritten margin notes: "No ."; "and earthly reality"; "Our future is on earth;"]

10. There is a defense of this view, which G. K. Beale calls "the new view," in Beale, *The Book of Revelation*, 152–70. He says, "The allusions to Daniel 2 in 1:1, 19; 4:1; and 22:6 all make use of Daniel 2 contextually and understand the prophecy to have an 'already-and-not-yet' end-time sense, referring to the 'latter days,' which had begun but were not yet consummated" (p. 159).

6

TO THE CHURCH IN EPHESUS

Revelation 2:1–7

It is not unusual for the officers of a local church to meet periodi-
cally in order to evaluate the church's ministry. At Tenth Presbyterian
Church, I have sometimes wondered what it would be like if Jesus
were present with us to guide these evaluations. It would be helpful,
certainly, but I suspect that the experience would not be entirely com-
fortable. It would probably be painful. Fortunately, we have Jesus's
evaluation in a gentle form in his messages to the seven churches of
Asia Minor, which are recorded in chapters 2 and 3 of Revelation.

Those who are of the *historicist* school, who see Revelation as
a prophecy of the events that have proceeded to unfold throughout
history, view these letters as a preview of the various stages of the
church, from the days of the apostles to the time of Christ's return.
J. A. Seiss is a good example of this position,[1] but there are others.
These interpreters regard Ephesus as the church of the first century,
Smyrna as the church during the period of persecution under Rome,
Pergamum as the church during the age of Constantine, Thyatira
as the church of the Middle Ages, Sardis as the church of the
Reformation, Philadelphia as the church during the age of revivals
or the modern missionary movement, and Laodicea as the apostate
church that will exist in the final days before Christ returns. This

---

1. See J. A. Seiss, *The Apocalypse: Lectures on the Book of Revelation* (1900; repr.,
Grand Rapids: Zondervan, 1970), 66–97.

view is common among dispensationalists, such as John Walvoord, who says, "The order of the messages to the churches seems to be divinely selected to give prophetically the main movement of history."[2]

The difficulty with this view is that it varies continually as those who place the letters in a historical framework readjust their ideas to accommodate ever new stages of church history. Most interpreters see their own time being reflected by the church in Philadelphia, of which nothing bad is said, and not by the church in Laodicea, of which nothing good is spoken!

Actually, the things that are said about the churches of Asia Minor in these seven letters, both good and bad, have always been true of churches and will continue to be true of them until the Lord returns. They were clearly true of those that existed in John's day, because the letters are undoubtedly addressed to seven very real churches. However, each letter is to be read by those in the other cities as well: "He who has an ear, let him hear what the Spirit says to the churches" (Rev. 2:7, 11, 17, 29; 3:6, 13, 22). This means that we should read each letter and ask if the characteristics of that church are found among us and should adjust our own church's life and ministry accordingly.

William Hendriksen calls the historicist view unsubstantiated either by other Bible passages or by the specifics of church history. He notes the "almost humorous . . . exegesis" that is required in order to make the church at Sardis (see Rev. 3:1–6), which was dead, refer to the church of the Reformation. Then he adds—rightly, to my way of thinking—"There is not one atom of evidence in all the sacred writings which in any way corroborates this thoroughly arbitrary method of cutting up the history of the Church and assigning the resulting pieces to the respective epistles of Revelation 2 and 3. The epistles describe conditions which occur not in one particular age of Church history, but again and again."[3]

---

2. John F. Walvoord, *The Revelation of Jesus Christ* (Chicago: Moody Press, 1966), 52.

3. William Hendriksen, *More Than Conquerors: An Interpretation of the Book of Revelation* (Grand Rapids: Baker Book House, 1940), 60.

THE PATTERN OF THE LETTERS

One indication that the letters are a composite picture of conditions that will go on to exist in the church throughout its history is that they fit so artfully into the pattern of Revelation. The first chapter of the book contains descriptions of Christ that then also appear at the beginning of the letters, and the promises that end the letters are unfolded in later portions of the book. So the letters are not an independent section of the prophecy (the things "that are" as opposed to "those that are to take place after this"—Rev. 1:19), as some have suggested.

Hendriksen writes,

> Do you wish to know what is meant by the words: "To him that overcomes, to him will I give to eat of the tree of life, which is in the paradise of God"? Then turn to Revelation 22:2, 14. Again, are you looking for a definition of "the second death" in view of the glorious promise: "he that overcomes (or conquers) shall not be hurt of the second death"? Revelation 20:14 offers you just what you are seeking. The "new name" which is promised to the "conquerors," 2:17, reappears again and again: 3:12; 14:1; 22:4; cf. 19:12, 13, 16. . . . The morning star of 2:28 reoccurs at 22:16; and so it is with all the other promises. The seven epistles belong to the very essence of the book.[4]

The seven letters follow a common pattern, though there are some variations across the specific churches. There are seven sections to the pattern.

1. An *address* to the church: "to the angel of the church in . . . write."
2. A *description* of the risen Lord Jesus Christ, which in each case refers back to one of the descriptive elements of him in chapter 1.

---

4. Hendriksen, 59.

3. A *statement* commending the church: "I know your works. . . ."
4. Words of *criticism*: "But I have this against you. . . ."
5. A *reminder* that Jesus is coming again, along with an exhortation to repent or an encouragement to persevere.
6. A *warning* for the reader to heed what has been said: "He who has an ear, let him hear what the Spirit says to the churches."
7. A *promise* for those who overcome.

In the case of every church but Laodicea, Jesus finds something to commend. In the case of Smyrna and Philadelphia, he finds nothing to condemn.

THE CHURCH AT EPHESUS

Ephesus was the most prominent of these seven Asian cities. It was large (with about 250,000 inhabitants), wealthy, beautiful, and famous for its shrine of Diana—also known as the Temple of Artemis—which was one of the Seven Wonders of the Ancient World. At one time Ephesus had a harbor that could accommodate the largest ancient ships. And, because it was also at a crossroads for land travel, it had become an important commercial center.

The temple of Diana was its cultural focus. It was 425 feet long and 220 feet wide, had 120 columns that were each 60 feet high, and was at once a place for worship, a museum, a treasure house, and a refuge for criminals. The temple provided work for the hundreds of silversmiths who made their living by making miniature shrines of the goddess Diana. It was also a place for cult prostitution.

Heraclitus, the famous ancient philosopher who lived at Ephesus and was known as "the weeping philosopher," explained his tears by saying that no one could live in Ephesus without weeping at its immorality.[5]

---

5. See William Barclay, *The Revelation of John*, vol. 1, *Chapters 1 to 5*, rev. ed. (Philadelphia: The Westminster Press, 1976), 60.

And in this crassly commercial and immoral city, a church had been planted. It had been founded by Paul on his second missionary journey (see Acts 18:18–21), and he had returned to the city to spend three years there on his third journey (see Acts 19:1–41). Later, on his way back to Jerusalem from his third missionary journey, he touched on the coast south of Ephesus and had a moving farewell with the Ephesian elders (see Acts 20:17–38). Paul wrote his letter to the Ephesians during his imprisonment in Rome at around AD 60–63. Timothy had been ordained in the city and had ministered there (see 1 Tim. 1:3). Aquila and Priscilla, along with Apollos and Tychicus, had labored there as well (see Acts 18:19, 24–26; Eph. 6:21–22; 2 Tim. 4:12).

John probably took up residence in Ephesus a few years after the church had been founded—perhaps about AD 66. The church would have been in existence for more than forty years when the risen Christ directed John to send this letter to it.

THE LORD'S SELF-DESIGNATION

After addressing the letter "to the angel of the church in Ephesus," the risen Lord introduces himself as the one who "holds the seven stars in his right hand, who walks among the seven golden lampstands" (Rev. 2:1). We are not left entirely in the dark about what this image means, because Jesus has already told us that the stars represent the angels of the seven churches and that the lampstands represent the seven churches themselves (see Rev. 1:20). This is obviously a picture of Jesus being always with or in the midst of his people. He knows them and is able to speak to their condition, which he does in this letter and those that follow.

"The angels of the seven churches" were probably real angels, who functioned something like guardian angels and also represented the churches. So when Jesus says that he holds them in his hand, he is saying that he is not only aware of the condition of the churches but is also upholding and protecting them. The church at Ephesus had been troubled by "false apostles" (see Rev. 2:2), but although these teachers may have seemed wise and been persuasive, Jesus had upheld the church as it had done the hard work of testing them and finding them to be false.

JESUS'S PRAISE FOR THE CHURCH IN EPHESUS

There are three qualities for which the believers in Ephesus are praised, which we can examine in the order they occur.

THEY HAD WORKED HARD

Not all Christians do work hard. There are Christians who are lazy. None of us are as diligent as we might be. It is also possible to be so caught up in our work—even our Christian work—that we neglect things that are of greater value, as Martha did by laboring over the meal while Mary chose what was better by listening to Jesus teach (see Luke 10:38–42). While these are genuine dangers, work is nevertheless a good thing. The word that is translated as "toil" in Revelation 2:2, *kopos*, appears frequently in the New Testament. It is found in 1 Corinthians 3:8, where Paul says of God's servants that "each will receive his wages according to his labor," and in 1 Corinthians 15:58, where he reminds us that "in the work of the Lord" our "labor is not in vain." The word that is translated as "patient endurance" in this verse from Revelation is *hupomone*. It appears in Romans 5:3–4, where Paul reminds us that "suffering produces endurance, and endurance produces character, and character produces hope." William Barclay calls this virtue "triumphant fortitude."[6]

THEY HAD TESTED AND REJECTED FALSE PROPHETS

This church had also preserved and protected Christian doctrine, which means that the believers there cared about truth and were willing to be thought intolerant in their defense of it. They needed to be like this, because Jesus had issued a warning in broad terms that

6. William Barclay, *Letters to the Seven Churches* (repr., Louisville: Westminster John Knox Press, 2001), 10.

false prophets would arise to trouble the church (see Matt. 24:11), and Paul had warned the elders of Ephesus in particular that wolves would arise to ravage the flock after his departure (see Acts 20:29). Were the Christians at Ephesus aware of this danger and still on guard against it forty years after the church's founding? They seemed to have been. They knew that Christians have a duty to preserve the truth and to judge and reject false teaching (see 1 John 4:1). They knew that the standard by which we are to judge teaching as true or false is God's Word (see 2 John 9–10).

Revelation 2:6 mentions one specific case of false teaching: the teaching of the Nicolaitans, which the Ephesians are said to have hated. This error is mentioned only twice in the Bible—here and in verse 15, in the letter to the church in Pergamum. Since we have no other reliable information about the Nicolaitans, no one is certain what their error was, though it would have been clear to those who read Revelation in John's day. In Greek, the word *Nicolaitans* itself has two parts: *nikos*, which means "victory," and *laos*, which means "people." This reference to "the people," or the laity, has caused some to interpret their error as clericalism—that is, the domination of the laity by priests. But most writers link it to the error of Balaam, since the two are mentioned side by side in verses 14 and 15. Balaam advised Balak, the pagan king of Moab, to entice the Israelites to sin by sharing in the idol worship of their neighbors and by immorality.

The word "also" in verse 15 ("So also you have some who hold the teaching of the Nicolaitans") may indicate that Nicolaitanism is a separate error, but there are grounds for linking the two. The best case is made by William Barclay, who argues that the name *Balaam* may mean exactly what *Nicolaitan* means. Barclay derives it from *bela* ("to conquer") and *ha'am* ("the people"). The early church father Irenaeus said that the Nicolaitans "lived lives of unrestrained indulgence."[7] An ancient document known as *The Apostolic Constitutions* calls the Nicolaitans "shameless in

---

7. "Irenaeus against Heresies," bk. 1, chap. 26, par. 3, quoted in Barclay, *The Revelation of John*, 67.

uncleanness."[8] Clement of Alexandria wrote that they "abandon themselves to pleasure like goats . . . leading a life of self-indulgence."[9] Whatever this heresy was, the Christians at Ephesus had exposed it and rejected it in their defense of the true gospel.

THEY HAD PERSEVERED IN THEIR FAITH THROUGH HARDSHIP AND HAD NOT GROWN WEARY

This too was an important reason for Christ's praise of the church. The path that had been set before the Christians at Ephesus had not been easy. It had been a long path and had involved many difficulties. Yet in spite of the difficulties, the believers at Ephesus had hung tough in their faith and had not grown weary in their work. Perhaps they had remembered Christ's warning that it is only those who stand firm to the end who will be saved (see Matt. 24:13).

When I read these words of commendation, I think naturally of many branches of the American evangelical church today. We work hard. We struggle to reject false teaching. We frequently persevere through difficulties to accomplish some agreed-upon objective. Those things are good.

However, the church at Ephesus is also criticized for having left its first love (see Rev. 2:4), and I suspect that this is true of our churches as well. Steve Gregg says, "Their present labor (v. 2), which was not lacking in quantity, differed from the first works (v. 5) by the absence of the first love which had driven the earlier works. Like Martha, a church may become so engrossed in religious work that it neglects 'the one thing needed' (Luke 10:42). No amount of religious orthodoxy, labor or loyalty can make up for a deficit in Christian love (1 Cor. 13:2–3)."[10]

What is this "first love"? Many see it as love of the brethren, so that this criticism means "You have forgotten the love for one another that you had at first." But it is far more likely that this is a

8. *The Apostolic Constitutions*, bk. 6, par. 8, quoted in Barclay, 67.
9. *Miscellanies*, bk. 2, chap. 20, quoted in Barclay, 67.
10. See Steve Gregg, ed., *Revelation: Four Views; A Parallel Commentary* (Nashville: Thomas Nelson, 1997), 65.

love for Jesus Christ, who alone is worthy of our "first" and highest love. This letter is a reminder that it is possible to labor hard at Christian work while at the same time forgetting why we are doing it. Ephesus was now a second-generation church. So Jesus's criticism means that the fervor of the first converts had not been passed on to or picked up by their children. They were doing the work, but their love for Jesus had grown cold.

THE FAILURES OF TODAY'S CHURCH

A moment ago, we saw that a loss of our "first love" may characterize many of today's churches. But how can that be? How can we who are so active in our evangelical fervor and so vigorous in our defense of right doctrine be said to have left our first love? I think it is very evident how we have.

WE HAVE FORGOTTEN GOD

This is the point that David Wells makes in his books—particularly in the second book of his trilogy that consists of *No Place for Truth, God in the Wasteland,* and *Losing Our Virtue.* In *God in the Wasteland,* Wells writes, "The fundamental problem in the evangelical world today is not inadequate technique, insufficient organization, or antiquated music, and those who want to squander the church's resources bandaging these scratches will do nothing to stanch the flow of blood that is spilling from its true wounds. The fundamental problem in the evangelical world today is that God rests too inconsequentially upon the church. His truth is too distant, his grace is too ordinary, his judgment is too benign, his gospel is too easy, and his Christ is too common."[11]

Later in the same book, Wells argues that God has become "weightless" for the masses of today's alleged believers. He says that God rests upon us "so inconsequentially as not to be noticeable."[12]

---

11. David F. Wells, *God in the Wasteland: The Reality of Truth in a World of Fading Dreams* (Grand Rapids: Wm. B. Eerdmans, 1994), 30.
12. Wells, *God in the Wasteland,* 88.

WE HAVE FORGOTTEN CHRIST

If there is anything that seems to characterize the evangelical churches of our time, it is an emphasis on Jesus. Evangelicals seem to be talking about Jesus constantly. However, the Jesus they are talking about is often only a Jesus who panders to our selfish desires and felt needs. The "gospel" of our day has a lot to do with self-esteem, good mental attitudes, and worldly success. There is almost no preaching about sin, hell, judgment, or the wrath of God and even less of it about the doctrines that are centered on the Lord of glory and his cross: grace, redemption, atonement, propitiation, justification, and even faith. In addition, since they lack a biblical and well-understood theology, evangelicals have fallen prey to the consumerism of our times. A therapeutic worldview has replaced classical Christian categories, and many have identified the gospel with such modern idols as a particular political philosophy, psychology, or sociology. To the extent that Christ and his cross are no longer central, modern evangelicalism has become a movement shaped only by popular whim and sentimentality.

In 1996 more than a hundred evangelical pastors and leaders met in Cambridge, Massachusetts, to consider the state of today's evangelical church and to draft what came to be called the Cambridge Declaration.[13] The meeting was in part a response to the analyses of the church that had been made in the first of David Wells's three theological critiques. The Cambridge Declaration warns, "As evangelical faith has become secularized, its interests have been blurred with those of the culture. The result is a loss of absolute values, permissive individualism, and a substitution of wholeness for holiness, recovery for repentance, intuition for truth, feeling for belief, chance for providence, and immediate gratification for enduring hope. Christ and his cross have moved from the center of our vision."[14]

Many evangelicals believe that man is basically good by nature and that the gospel is mostly about God helping us to help ourselves.

13. Available in *Here We Stand! A Call from Confessing Evangelicals for a Modern Reformation*, ed. James Montgomery Boice and Benjamin E. Sasse (repr., Phillipsburg, NJ: P&R Publishing, 2004), 14–20.

14. Boice and Sasse, 16.

If this is what we believe, then is it not true that in spite of our hard work and apparent worldly success, we have forgotten the gospel? Is it not true that we have forgotten Christ? That we have forsaken our first love?

THE SURE ROAD HOME

The things that are said in these letters are, of course, designed not just to critique churches but also to help them. So we rightly move on from the diagnosis to the remedy. Jesus prescribes two things for this church's spiritual cure.

"REMEMBER"

Any true church or true believer has experienced the grace of God in the past, or else that church or person would not exist today. Therefore, the first step in a genuine spiritual recovery consists of remembering what was once known and experienced. This is especially true if we have lost "our first love." The Prodigal Son had known the father's love and, at one time, had probably loved him back. But he had forgotten this love by the time he took his share of the inheritance and fled to the far country. His spiritual recovery began when he remembered his father's house. The text says, "When he came to himself, he said, 'How many of my father's hired servants have more than enough bread, but I perish here with hunger!'" (Luke 15:17). If we have forgotten the Father and Jesus Christ, we need to remember the joy of our conversion and our spiritual heritage and must recover our first love.

"REPENT"

We also need to repent, for our spiritual declension is not merely a falling away; it is a sin against God, whose love we have forsaken. In his little book *The Grace of Repentance*, Sinclair Ferguson explains how repentance has become evangelicalism's forgotten grace, meaning that we have thought of repenting as something that we did in the past, when we first believed in Jesus, but which we do not need to repeat and have now forgotten to practice. Ferguson further reminds us that when Martin Luther posted his Ninety-Five Theses on the door of the Castle Church in Wittenberg, the very first of those theses read, "When our Lord and Master, Jesus Christ, said 'repent,' he meant that the entire life of believers should be one of repentance."[15] We never cease to be sinners, even when we are justified by God's grace. Therefore, we must always be repenting—and never more so than when we have forsaken our first love for a love of the world, the world's way of doing things, and worldly success.

PARADISE REGAINED

Jesus's last word to this church is a blessing for those who heed his commands and who overcome. The blessing is that they will "eat of the tree of life, which is in the paradise of God"—an obvious reference to the garden of Eden and the loss that Adam and Eve sustained when they turned their backs on God. This tree appears again in Revelation 22:2 as part of that glorious consummation to which each of the letters points and which the book of Revelation advances.

Ever since Adam and Eve lost Paradise because of their sin, sinners have tried to build their own paradise on earth. Cain tried it first by constructing the city of Enoch in the land of Nod. Some tried to do it at Babel by building a tower that they hoped would reach to heaven. The Greeks tried to make Athens a paradise. The Romans tried to do it in Rome. We do it too, supposing that we can have our own paradise here on earth—even in our churches. But the cities of men are doomed to destruction. They will all fall away. The only true paradise is in heaven, where it has been prepared only for those who love God. For they alone are able to overcome, "by the blood of the Lamb and by the word of their testimony" (Rev. 12:11).

15. Quoted in Sinclair Ferguson, *The Grace of Repentance* (Wheaton, IL: Crossway Books, 2000), 11.

7

TO THE CHURCH IN SMYRNA

Revelation 2:8–11

Wouldn't you like to be a part of a church about which nothing bad can be said—especially by Jesus Christ? You might insist that there is no church like that. We are all sinners; there is no person or church whom Jesus could commend without reservation. And that is true, of course. But it is also true that in this collection of letters to the churches of Asia Minor, which represent varieties of churches in all times and places, there are two churches about which Jesus says nothing critical: Smyrna and Philadelphia. We come to the letter to the church in Smyrna now. It is the shortest of the seven letters, containing only four verses, and it was written to a church that was characterized by its suffering for Jesus Christ—which shows that, unlike the church in Ephesus, the church in Smyrna had not forsaken its first love.

THE CHURCH IN SMYRNA

Smyrna is one of only two cities of the seven mentioned in Revelation that is still in existence. The other cities are mostly ruins. Represented today by the Turkish city of Izmir, at the time of John's letter Smyrna was located about thirty-five miles north of Ephesus on an arm of the Aegean Sea and was a rival of Ephesus, particularly after the port of Ephesus began to silt up and the larger ships were obliged to sail further north in order to unload. Smyrna sat on the slope of a hill that inclined gently upward from the Aegean Sea, and its splendid public buildings crowned the top of the hill, which was called Mount Pagos. It was an ancient city that had long been known for its loyalty to Rome. It had erected an altar to the goddess of Rome as early as 195 BC, when Rome was still contending with Carthage for mastery of the Mediterranean Sea, and it had remained loyal to Rome ever since. This made the city a natural center for the growing cult of emperor worship.

We have no record of the beginnings of the church in Smyrna, but it was probably founded by Paul on his third missionary journey (AD 53–56). This is suggested by Acts 19:10, which tells us that while Paul was living and teaching in Ephesus, "All the residents of Asia heard the word of the Lord, both Jews and Greeks."

About twenty years after John wrote Revelation, the early church father Ignatius stayed at Smyrna and wrote four of his letters there. Later still, after he had relocated to Troas, he wrote two letters to Smyrna—one to the church and one to Polycarp, its bishop.

Polycarp's story is interesting in view of what Revelation 2:8–11 says about the persecutions that were coming to the church in Smyrna. The bishop had been a pupil of John and was probably the leader of the church at the time that John sent this letter to Smyrna. This would have made Polycarp one of its original readers.

Polycarp was martyred for his faith on February 23, 155. It happened at the time of the public games for which the city of Smyrna was famous. The streets were crowded. Excitement filled the air. Suddenly someone shouted, "Away with the atheists; let Polycarp be searched for." The old man probably could have escaped, but he remained at his post and was eventually arrested.

The leaders of the city did not want to see Polycarp die. On the way to the arena, the officer who had led the arresting party pleaded, "What harm is it to say, 'Caesar is Lord' and to offer sacrifice and be saved?" But Polycarp insisted that only Jesus Christ is Lord.

When they entered the arena, the account says, a voice came from heaven saying, "Be strong, Polycarp, and play the man." Polycarp was brought before the proconsul, the highest-ranking officer in the city, who gave him the choice of cursing Christ and making a sacrifice to Caesar, or else death. Polycarp replied, "Eighty and six years have I served him, and he has done me no wrong. How can I blaspheme my King who saved me?" The proconsul threatened the bishop with burning. Polycarp replied, "You threaten me with the fire that burns for a time and is quickly extinguished, for you do not know the fire which awaits the wicked in the judgment to come and in everlasting punishment. . . . Do what you will."

The crowds flocked around Polycarp with torches and with wood that was torn from the workshops and public baths. They bound him to a stake, where he prayed,

O Lord God Almighty, Father of thy beloved and blessed Son, Jesus Christ, through whom we have received full knowledge of thee, God of angels and powers, and of all creation, and of the whole family of the righteous, who live before thee, I bless thee that thou has granted unto me this day and hour, that I may share among the number of the martyrs in the cup of thy Christ, for the resurrection to eternal life, both of soul and body in the immortality of the Holy Spirit. And may I today be received among them before thee, as a rich and acceptable sacrifice, as thou, the God without falsehood and of truth hast prepared beforehand and shown forth and fulfilled. For this reason I also praise thee for all things. I bless thee, I glorify thee through the eternal and heavenly high priest, Jesus Christ, thy beloved Son, through whom be glory to thee with him and the Holy Spirit, both now and for the ages that are to come. Amen.

Polycarp was the "twelfth . . . [martyr] in Smyrna," according to *The Martyrdom of Polycarp*, and those who recorded it ended their account by expressing similar convictions about their Savior: "Polycarp was arrested by Herod, when Philip of Tralles was high priest, and Statius Quadratus was governor, but our Lord Jesus Christ was reigning forever. To him be glory, honor, majesty and eternal dominion from generation to generation."[1]

---

1. This story, and the quotations throughout it, can be found in William Barclay, *The Revelation of John*, vol. 1, *Chapters 1 to 5*, rev. ed. (Philadelphia: The Westminster Press,

THE MESSAGE OF THE LETTER

The message of Jesus to the church in Smyrna has a good deal to do with death—which might be expected in light of the persecutions that were coming to the church. Significantly, the name *Smyrna* sounds like, and was often associated with, the word *myrrh*—which was an ointment used in embalming. We may remember that Joseph of Arimathea and Nicodemus together brought "a mixture of myrrh and aloes, about seventy-five pounds" (John 19:39) to prepare the body of Jesus for burial, following the crucifixion.

But Christ conquered death. In fact, it is with a reminder of this great truth that the letter to the church in Smyrna begins: "The words of the first and the last, who died and came to life" (Rev. 2:8). As in the message to Ephesus, in which Jesus identified himself as the one who holds the seven stars in his right hand and walks among the seven golden lampstands, his self-identification here is also drawn from the vision of the risen Christ that is recorded in Revelation 1. There Jesus says, "Fear not, I am the first and the last, and the living one. I died, and behold I am alive forevermore, and I have the keys of Death and Hades" (Rev. 1:17–18). What all this means is to be worked out in the letter to the church in Smyrna.

Two verses later, the believers in Smyrna are challenged to be faithful even to the point of death: "Be faithful unto death, and I will give you the crown of life" (Rev. 2:10). The promise that ends the letter strikes the same note: "The one who conquers will not be hurt by the second death" (v. 11). The message to the believers is that they will suffer; in fact, some of them will suffer death for Christ's cause. But Jesus Christ has triumphed over death, and so will they if they remain faithful.

1976), 76–79. See also *The Ante-Nicene Fathers: Translations of the Writings of the Fathers Down to A.D. 325*, vol. 1, *The Apostolic Fathers—Justin Martyr—Irenaeus*, ed. Alexander Roberts and James Donaldson (repr., New York: Charles Scribner's Sons, 1903), 37–44, as well as "The Martyrdom of the Holy Polycarp, Bishop of Smyrna" in Edgar J. Goodspeed, *The Apostolic Fathers: An American Translation* (New York: Harper & Brothers, 1950), 250–55.

THE STATE OF THE CHURCH

It is important to notice that this church, about which nothing bad is said, was a poor, afflicted church—which means that being faithful and blessed by God is not to be identified with prosperity and easy times. On the contrary, since suffering is a privilege, the most favored churches—like the most favored individuals—are often those that are persecuted.

Jesus says four things about this troubled church.

JESUS KNOWS ITS TRIBULATION

The word that is translated "tribulation" in verse 9 is *thlipsis*, which describes the crushing pressure that is used to extract the juice from grapes or to separate grain from its husks at threshing time. It does not denote mere trouble; it refers to cruel, relentless, grinding pressure—which the Christians in Smyrna had certainly experienced. In this solidly pro-Roman town, the Christians would have been shunned for their refusal to go along with the emperor cult or participate in the social worship of the city's numerous tutelary gods and goddesses. It would have been hard for them even to make a living. Under pressure? Yes, very much. But Jesus knew about their tribulations, just as he knows about the suffering that many Christians in many places endure for his sake today. That is what makes the difference: Jesus knows and understands.

Jesus said in another place, when he was talking about witnessing in spite of persecution, that "even the hairs of your head are all numbered" (Matt. 10:30) and in yet another place that he will not fail to notice inconspicuous giving to the needy, private prayer, or fasting—and that the one who does these things will be rewarded (see Matt. 6:4, 6, 18). If that is so, then Jesus obviously knows about and will reward those who are persecuted for his sake.

JESUS KNOWS ITS POVERTY

There are two Greek words that mean "poverty." The first is *penia*, which has given us the English words *penury* and *penurious*. It refers to one who is not wealthy and must therefore earn his living with his own hands—a manual worker. The second word, which is stronger, is *ptrocheia*. It describes complete destitution. We might say that the first refers to a person who has nothing superfluous, while the second describes a person who has nothing at all. It is this second, stronger word that is used here in Revelation 2:9 of the believers in Smyrna. They had been cut out of the economic fabric of the city, and as a result they had nothing. They were in the most abject poverty imaginable; they could barely survive. Poor? Indeed! But they were rich in spiritual blessings. They were storing up treasure in heaven (see Matt. 6:20; 19:21; Luke 12:21; 2 Cor. 6:10; James 2:5).

The church in Smyrna is the only church in the New Testament that is described as being spiritually rich. Its condition was the exact opposite of that of the church in Laodicea, whose believers are said to have been rich in material things but poor spiritually (see Rev. 3:17).

JESUS KNOWS THAT IT HAS BEEN SLANDERED

The letter to Smyrna does not say how the believers there had been slandered, but it is not difficult to imagine what this may have been like—especially since this particular affliction is linked to hostility from the Jews. We can think of the Jewish leaders' slander of Paul, which is recorded in Acts 17:6–7, as a comparison. Paul was in Thessalonica at the time, and the leaders were jealous of his success and told the authorities that Paul and his companions were guilty of "[having] turned the world upside down" (v. 6) and "acting against the decrees of Caesar, saying that there is another king, Jesus" (v. 7). The Christians did proclaim Jesus as a King, of course. But they were not defying Caesar, nor were they causing trouble. They were actually trying to live in peace with everyone.

Slander? Yes—and of the worst kind. But Jesus knew about it. He always knows what is true as well as what is false, and he has established a day in which the truth and those who stand for it will be vindicated while those who concoct and spread lies will be condemned.

JESUS KNOWS THAT IT IS SOON TO SUFFER EVEN GREATER PERSECUTION

This tribulation would grow out of the slander that is mentioned in verse 9, but it would be worse—in two ways. First, it would lead to prison and death. People were seldom merely kept in prison in ancient times. Incarceration was not a common punishment; prisons were temporary holding centers that were used until such time as the prisoners could be tried and either released or executed. For a Christian to be imprisoned meant that he was in danger of being killed. Second, it is said that this new period of persecution would be caused by the devil and not by mere human antagonists. This is the first mention of the devil in Revelation—though he certainly comes in again many times after this, especially in the later chapters (see Rev. 2:13; 3:9; 9:11; 12:7–12; 13:4; 20:2–3, 7–10). In the grand scheme of things, the devil is seen as standing behind all the evil of the world and all the persecutions of the people of God throughout history.

Persecutions, even unto death? Yes. But there are two qualifications to this persecution. First, the time of the persecution will be limited; it will last "for ten days" (v. 10). It is hard to know how to take this mention of ten days. It might mean a short time—that is, only ten days. But ten is also a large number, and the numbers in Revelation are symbolic—it might mean a long time. However short or long it means, the time would not last forever. The persecutions would end; the people of God would be delivered, either by life or by death; and in the end it will be Satan himself who will be punished along with the beast, the false prophet, and the fallen angels.

The second qualification is that although the trial of the believers in Smyrna would be great, it would also be something ordered by God for their good—just as God orders all things for the good of those who love him (see Rom. 8:28). Suffering would be used to test or purify God's people in Smyrna. Job himself knew the crucible of suffering, but he said of God, "He knows the way that I take; when he has tried me, I shall come out as gold" (Job 23:10).

THE SUFFERING CHURCH TODAY

We have looked at the church in Smyrna as it existed toward the end of the first Christian century. What of the worldwide church today? We have to ask that question, because our guideline for studying these letters (as well as the book of Revelation as a whole) is that they are for Christians in all periods of history and describe what they will endure for the cause of Christ and how they are to triumph in the midst of tribulation.

Do we have a suffering church today? Obviously. It has been pointed out by those who are concerned with the persecuted church throughout the world that we have seen more martyrs for the cause of Christ in the twentieth century than in any previous comparable period of history. There have been countless martyrs in such countries as Kenya, South Africa, China, Colombia, and the nations of the former Soviet Union. In many Islamic countries it is a crime punishable by death for a Muslim to convert to Christianity or for a Christian to try to convert a Muslim.

We are recognizing in recent days that suffering is an authentic mark of the true church. Dietrich Bonhoeffer, drawing support from Martin Luther and the Augsburg Confession, wrote about this in *The Cost of Discipleship*. "Suffering, then, is the badge of true discipleship. The disciple is not above his master. . . . Luther reckoned suffering among the marks of the true Church, and one of the memoranda drawn up in preparation for the Augsburg Confession similarly defines the Church as the community of those 'who are persecuted and martyred for the gospel's sake.'"[2]

Is that not biblical? Did Jesus not say,

> If the world hates you, know that it has hated me before it hated you. If you were of the world, the world would love you as its own; but because you are not of the world, but I chose you out of the world, therefore the world hates you. . . . If they persecuted me, they will also persecute you. (John 15:18–20)

THE CHURCH THAT IS NOT SUFFERING

What is the problem here? The problem is not that Christians throughout the world are suffering. That is only to be expected, if

---

2. Dietrich Bonhoeffer, *The Cost of Discipleship*, rev. ed. (1959; repr. New York: Macmillan, 1979), 100–101.

Jesus is to be believed. The problem is that we ourselves are *not* suffering, nor are many other Christians who live in prosperous western lands.

Some years ago I was interviewing a former missionary to Korea on the subject of suffering, and I asked him what he had seen of suffering in America, since he had seen much of it in Korea. He replied, "I see no persecution here at all." Thank God that is the case, we might say. But is it really a cause for thanksgiving? Is it not rather evidence that we have ceased to stand for much? That we have compromised our profession of faith and way of life in order to get along with the surrounding evil culture?

In his short book on the letters to the churches of Asia Minor, *What Christ Thinks of the Church*, John R. W. Stott of All Souls Church in London speaks about many of us when he castigates his own church, the Church of England, for its compromises—especially its failure to preach the gospel clearly and to insist on church discipline. "We who are Christians of the Church of England do not suffer much," he says. "The ugly truth is that we tend to avoid suffering by compromise. Our moral standards are often not noticeably higher than the standards of the world. Our lives do not challenge and rebuke unbelievers by their integrity or purity or love. The world sees in us nothing to hate. . . . We mind our own business lest anyone should be offended. We hold our tongue so that nobody is embarrassed."[3]

That sounds embarrassingly familiar. For it is not a description of Christians in the Church of England alone. It is a description of many Christians here and of many American denominations. We want to be liked. We want to get along. We do not want to cause anybody trouble. We want to be loved and accepted by the world that at one time crucified our Lord and Master Jesus Christ.

What if we were different? What if we were the kind of Christians that Christ has unmistakably called us to be? Stott asks, "Supposing we raised our standards and stopped our compromises? Supposing we proclaimed our message and tightened our discipline with love

---

3. John R. W. Stott, *What Christ Thinks of the Church: Insights from Revelation 2–3* (Grand Rapids: Wm. B. Eerdmans, 1958), 43.

85

but without fear? I will tell you the result: the Church would suffer. There would be an outcry. We should be called puritanical, Victorian, old-fashioned, unpractical, rigid. Indeed, every imaginable derogatory epithet would be called into the service of the unbelieving world, and the Church would again find itself where it belongs—outside the gate, and in the wilderness."[4]

I ask: would we suffer any less vilification in the United States if our churches did the same?

THE CHALLENGE TO THE CHURCH

The final words of Jesus to the church in Smyrna contain a challenge and a promise, as do each of the other letters. His challenge to the believers in Smyrna is to "be faithful" (Rev. 2:10). This is a very different challenge from the command to "repent" that was given to the believers in Ephesus.

J. Ralph Grant tells about a young woman from a wealthy family who was converted to Christ during a revival. She was scolded by her father and ridiculed by her mother, and when she resisted she was told that she must either renounce her fanaticism or forfeit her inheritance. She was given several days to think it over. On the final day, when her parents asked for her answer, she replied by sitting down at the piano, where she played and sang the verses of a hymn written by Henry F. Lyte in 1824.

> Jesus, I my cross have taken,
> All to leave, and follow thee;
> Destitute, despised, forsaken,
> Thou from hence my all shalt be;
> Perish every fond ambition,
> All I've sought or hoped or known;
> Yet how rich is my condition,
> God and heaven are still my own.

4. Stott, 44–45.

By the time she had finished the last stanza her father was weeping, and he and her mother both knelt down to confess Christ. The father said, "You have won. If you love Jesus Christ that much, we cannot resist him."[5] The members of the church in Smyrna had that spirit and were praised for it. They needed to continue in it and be faithful.

THE PROMISE

The promise of Jesus to the church in Smyrna is twofold, but both its parts point to the same thing: "I will give you the crown of life" (v. 10) and "The one who conquers will not be hurt by the second death" (v. 11). The crown that is mentioned here is not a crown of royalty, such as an emperor might wear (the word for that type of crown is *diadema*). The word that is used here is *stephanos*, which refers to the crown of laurel that was awarded to victors at athletic games. Paul speaks of it as a "crown of righteousness" (2 Tim. 4:8) and a "crown that will last forever" (1 Cor. 9:25 NIV). James calls it "the crown of life" (James 1:12) and Peter "the unfading crown of glory" (1 Peter 5:4). All these expressions have to do with salvation and the blessing of eternal life that God promises to his own.

The contrast to possessing the "crown of life" is to experience the second death. The first death is physical—the separation of the soul and spirit from the body. The second death is spiritual—the separation of the spirit and soul from God. It means to be cast, body and soul, into the lake of fire at Christ's second coming. This is explained in Revelation 20, where we are told that those who have died for their testimony return to life and then reign with Christ: "Over such the second death has no power, but they will be priests of God and of Christ, and they will reign with him for a thousand years" (v. 6).

When the Italian Reformer Savonarola was burned at the stake in Florence in 1498, the presiding bishop said the words that were customary in such cases: "I separate you from the church militant and

---

5. J. Ralph Grant, *Letters to the Seven Churches and Other Sermons* (Grand Rapids: Baker Book House, 1962), 22.

from the church triumphant." Savonarola replied, "Of the church militant, yes; but of the church triumphant, no. That is beyond your powers." And it was.

There is a story, from the time of the persecution of the church by the Roman Empire, that tells of a father and his young son who were led into the arena to face death. As the gates were opened and the lions rushed into the arena, the boy asked, "Father, will it hurt?" The father placed his arm around the son and replied, thinking of this important promise from Revelation, "Yes, son; perhaps for one swift moment—but he who overcomes will not be hurt at all by the second death."

8

TO THE CHURCH
IN PERGAMUM

Revelation 2:12–17

I was reading a book called *No God but God* and came across an interesting sentence. The editors were writing about the difficulty we have trying to live as Christians in our antagonistic, secular world, and were discussing the tensions involved in this, when suddenly they suggested as an obvious solution (and certainly with humor): "We need only to lose our first love or compromise His authority for the tension to disappear."[1] It struck me at once that the weakness of the church in Ephesus was abandoning their first love, while the danger that the church in Pergamum faced was compromising the authority of Christ and his gospel.

Love for Christ and love for the truth are essential commitments for a church to have! They are both necessary, and the loss of either is soon fatal for the church.

WHERE SATAN DWELLS

Pergamum lay about sixty-five miles north of Smyrna, along the valley of the Caicus River, and about fifteen miles inland. It

---

1. Os Guinness and John Seel, eds., *No God but God: Breaking with the Idols of Our Age* (Chicago: Moody Press, 1992), 214–15.

would have been the next place that a postal clerk might have come to on a circuit of these seven cities of Asia Minor. Pergamum was an ancient city. It was the seat of the Roman government in Asia and had the second largest library in the world—second only to the famous library of Alexandria in Egypt—containing 200,000 volumes.

There is an interesting story connected with this library. About four hundred years before the writing of Revelation, the king of Pergamum tried to entice the famous librarian of Alexandria, whose name was Aristophanes (the same name as the great comic dramatist of Athens), to leave Egypt and come to Pergamum, with the goal of making his library the more important of the two. The king of Egypt was so outraged at this attempt to seduce his chief scholar that he imprisoned Aristophanes and placed an embargo on the export of papyrus to Pergamum. Since papyrus was the material that everyone used to make books, this was a serious setback for the upstart city. However, the scholars of Pergamum discovered that in place of papyrus they could use animal skins—or parchment—to make books. In fact, although the innovation did not catch on for several hundred years, parchment actually proved to be a superior material.

But here is the interesting thing: it is Pergamum that gave us the word *parchment*, for the new material was called *he pergamos charta* ("the Pergamos sheet")—which was contracted in English to "parchment."

Pergamum must have been a terrible place for Christians to try to be Christians. The city had come to prominence after the death of Alexander the Great, when it became the capital of the Attalid kingdom, and its last king had been Attalus III, who died in 133 BC and left his territory to Rome. Therefore, Roman influence was strong there. The first temple of the imperial cult to be constructed anywhere was constructed in Pergamum in 29 BC, in honor of the goddess of Rome (Roma) and the ruling emperor, who was then Augustus. By the time John wrote Revelation, there was no city in Asia in which the worship of Caesar was stronger, and therefore no place where Christians were in more immediate danger for refusing to sacrifice to the emperor and confess that "Caesar is Lord."

Antipas, the first known martyr of the seven churches, was killed in Pergamum—presumably for failing to do just that (see Rev. 2:13). Many commentators think this is the reason that John refers to Pergamum as the place "where Satan dwells" and has his throne (v. 13).

But there may be other reasons as well why John says this. The city was concentrated on a huge, rocky hill about a thousand feet high, where it overlooked the surrounding valley, and on the top of this hill there was an enormous and much revered altar to Zeus Soter ("Zeus the Savior"). The altar was ninety feet square and surrounded by a twenty-foot-high frieze that is now located in the Pergamum Museum in Berlin. I saw it in 1966. It commemorates a victory of Attalus I over the marauding Gauls in 241 BC and shows the gods of Greece defeating a race of barbarian giants. At the time of Pergamum, this altar, surrounded by the frieze, protruded from the upper face of the hill like a gigantic throne, and sacrifices were burned there continuously, twenty-four hours a day, by a constantly rotating team of pagan priests. Some think that it was this throne-like altar, and not merely the danger of Caesar worship, that caused John to call Pergamum the place "where Satan's throne is."

The city was also filled with temples—three to the emperor, as well as more to Dionysius, Athena, Demeter, and other gods. The god of healing, Aesculapius, had a temple too—in fact, Pergamum was a medical center. (Galen, the second most famous physician of the ancient world—second only to Hippocrates—was a native of Pergamum and studied there.) Aesculapius was worshiped under the figure of a serpent—a well-known biblical symbol for Satan (see Gen. 3:1; Rev. 12:9). When we put these features of the city together, we can see how appropriate it was for Jesus to call Pergamum the place "where Satan dwells" (Rev. 2:13).

Yet here was a church—a body of believers who had come to know and love Jesus Christ and who had remained true to his name. It was a good church, for it had not denied its faith—even in days of persecution. The tense of the verb "to deny," in "you did not deny my faith" in verse 13, points to a specific past crisis—perhaps the one in which Antipas was killed. He is the only martyr of any of the

91

seven churches who is specifically identified ("Antipas, my faithful witness, who was put to death in your city"—v. 13 NIV), but his death highlights the danger in which the Christians in Pergamum, especially, lived.

THE LORD'S SELF-DESCRIPTION

Jesus introduces himself in his letter to this church as the one "who has the sharp two-edged sword" (v. 12). Pergamum was ruled by a proconsul, who had been given the right of inflicting capital punishment—the symbol of which was a sword. So this is a way of saying that Jesus, rather than some earthly ruler, is the true determiner of a believer's life or death. The Christians would need to remember that if they were arrested.

Yet strikingly, although the image of a sword occurs later in Revelation in reference to Jesus's judgment on the ungodly nations of the earth—"From his mouth comes a sharp sword with which to strike down the nations" (Rev. 19:15; see also v. 21)—here in the letter to the church at Pergamum it refers to his judgment on false teachers in the church. "Therefore repent. If not, I will come to you soon and war against them with the sword of my mouth" (Rev. 2:16). This warning is not to be taken lightly, since the sword is a repeated, binding element of this letter—both introducing and concluding it. Here Jesus threatens the church with judgment because it has compromised with the culture.[2]

THE CANCER WITHIN

The danger of such compromise is what I pointed to at the beginning of this study. The church in Ephesus was criticized because it had forsaken its first love. In other words, the concern of that letter was for the person of Christ. Their doctrine was right, but their love

2. The image of Christ bearing a sword is unique to Revelation (see 1:16; 2:12, 16; 19:15, 21), though it is anticipated in Matthew 10:34 ("Do not think that I have come to bring peace to the earth. I have not come to bring peace, but a sword"), in Ephesians 6:17, where the image of a sword is used in reference to the Word of God ("the sword of

for Christ was lacking. In Pergamum, the believers may have loved Christ, but they were tolerating error—which means that the concern of this letter is for Christ's doctrine.

The unsound teaching at Pergamum came in two forms—though they may be merely different manifestations of the same error, as I wrote in my comments on the church in Ephesus.

THE TEACHING OF BALAAM

The story of Balaam is found in Numbers 22–24. Balaam was a pagan prophet who was hired by Balak, the king of Moab, to curse Israel at the time that the Jews were advancing on Canaan prior to the conquest. Balak had seen the vast numbers of these people on his borders, and he felt that it would be only a short time before he and his people were overrun. So he turned to the prophet Balaam. What had impressed him about Balaam was that his curses seemed to work. He sent messengers to Balaam saying, "Behold, a people has come out of Egypt. They cover the face of the earth, and they are dwelling opposite me. Come now, curse this people for me, since they are too mighty for me. Perhaps I shall be able to defeat them and drive them from the land, for I know that he whom you bless is blessed, and he whom you curse is cursed" (Num. 22:5–6).

Balaam wanted to do it, because the king was willing to pay him a lot of money for the job. But the Lord told him not to curse Israel—and when he tried to do it anyway, in spite of God's warning, blessings came out of his mouth instead of curses. Balam made seven utterances in all, beginning with blessings on the nation but climaxing in several wonderful prophecies concerning the Messiah who would come (see Num. 24:17, 19).

What was the king to do now? Balaam had an answer, because nine chapters after this, in a report of the death of Balaam, we are told that he had counseled Balak to get the Midianite women to seduce the Jewish men and persuade them to join them in the worship

---

the Spirit, which is the word of God"), and in Hebrews 4:12 ("For the word of God is living and active, sharper than any two-edged sword, piercing to the division of soul and of spirit, of joints and of marrow, and discerning the thoughts and intentions of the heart").

of their god, Baal, at Peor (see Num. 31:8–16; cf. 25:1–3). Balak did this, and the Jews fell into idolatry and were judged.

This diabolical counsel is referred to several times in the New Testament. Peter calls Balaam one who "loved gain from wrongdoing" (2 Peter 2:15), while Jude writes of those who "abandoned themselves for the sake of gain to Balaam's error" (Jude 11). The fullest description of this pernicious teaching is our text here in Revelation 2, which says that Balaam "taught Balak to put a stumbling block before the sons of Israel, so that they might eat food sacrificed to idols and practice sexual immorality" (v. 14).

Pergamum's error obviously lay in compromising with the debased standards of pagan Asia—particularly regarding immorality and idolatry—and the warning to them is that, if they did not repent, Jesus would himself come and fight against the false teachers.

THE TEACHING OF THE NICOLAITANS

I discussed the possible interpretations of this error earlier. It might be what we would call clericalism, since the name *Nicolaitan* is composed of *nikos*, which means "victory," and *laos*, which means "people." This might signify "victory over" or "domination of" the laity—but this is something that happened later in church history, not in the first Christian century. It is more likely that this teaching was a variation of the error of Balaam, since the two are mentioned side by side in verses 14 and 15.

The word "also" in verse 15 seems to indicate that Nicolaitanism was a separate error ("So also you have some who hold the teaching of the Nicolaitans"), but the name *Balaam* may mean exactly what *Nicolaitan* means. As I noted earlier, William Barclay derives it from *bela*, meaning "to conquer," and *ha'am*, meaning "the people."[3] If these two errors are the same, then the verse might be translated as follows: "In fact, you also have people who hold the similar teachings of the Nicolaitans."

---

3. See William Barclay, *The Revelation of John*, vol. 1, *Chapters 1 to 5*, rev. ed. (Philadelphia: The Westminster Press, 1976), 67.

THE WORLDLY "EVANGELICAL" CHURCH[4]

Does this apply to our day? Is there anything like these errors in our churches? We do not go to idol feasts, of course. But there is a great deal of immorality in our day, and everyone who observes the contemporary church seems to be saying that the church, and evangelicals in particular, are compromising shamelessly with modernity.

For years I have spoken openly of what I consider the worldliness of the mainline, liberal churches and have accused them of pursuing the world's wisdom, embracing the world's theology, following the world's agenda, and employing the world's methods. But what has hit me like a thunderbolt in recent years is the discovery that what I had been saying about the liberal churches at the end of the 1960s and in the 1970s now needs to be said about the evangelical churches too. A few years ago, Professor Martin Marty, who has always been a shrewd observer of the American church, said in a magazine interview that in his judgment, by the end of the twentieth century, evangelicals would be the worldliest people in America. He was on target when he said that. The century has ended, and we are pursuing the same things I have long been accusing liberal churches of pursuing.

THE WORLD'S WISDOM

Evangelicals are not heretics, of course—at least not consciously. If they are asked whether the Bible is the authoritative and inerrant Word of God, most will answer affirmatively. But many have abandoned the Bible all the same, simply because they do not think it is adequate for the challenges we face in a new millennium. They do not think it is sufficient for winning people to Christ, so they turn to felt-need sermons or entertainment or "signs and wonders" instead. They do not think that the Bible is sufficient for achieving Christian growth, so they turn to therapy groups.

---

4. Much of the material in this section first appeared in James Montgomery Boice, "Reformation Needed Today," *New Horizons* 22, no. 9 (October 2001), available online at https://opc.org/nh.html?article_id=93.

THE WORLD'S THEOLOGY

As the liberals did before us, evangelicals use the Bible's words but give them new meaning. Sin becomes dysfunctional behavior. Salvation becomes self-esteem or wholeness. Jesus becomes more of an example for right living than our Savior from sin. People are told how to have happy marriages and raise nice children but not how to get right with an offended God.

THE WORLD'S AGENDA

The world's major agenda (forget world hunger, racism, the redistribution of wealth, or ecology) is to be happy—with happiness being understood as the maximum amount of personal peace, as well as sufficient prosperity to enjoy it. But is that not the bottom line of much evangelical preaching today? To be happy? To be content? To be satisfied? Far be it from us to preach a gospel that would expose people's sins and drive them to the Savior.

THE WORLD'S METHODS

Evangelicals have become like liberals in this area, too. How else are we to explain the stress so many churches place on numerical growth and money? That so many pastors tone down the hard edges of the Bible's truth in order to attract greater numbers to their services? That we support a lobby group in Washington? That we have created social action groups in order to advance specific legislation?

Or consider evangelical rhetoric. Evangelicals speak of "taking back America," "fighting for the country's soul," and "reclaiming the United States for Christ." How? By electing Christian presidents, congressmen, and senators; lobbying for conservative judges; taking over power structures; and imposing our Christian standard of morality on the rest of the nation by law. Was America ever really a Christian nation? Was any nation? What about Augustine's doctrine of the two cities, which meant so much to the Reformers? Will any country ever be anything other than man's city? And what about America's soul? Is there really an American soul to be redeemed? Or fought over?[5]

5. Parts of this analysis are borrowed from James Montgomery Boice, *What Makes a Church Evangelical?* (Wheaton, IL: Crossway Books, 1999), 11–13.

Evangelicals criticized President Bill Clinton because he seemed to take his political positions from the opinion polls, believing as truth whatever was most useful to him at the moment. But do not many preachers do the same? A column in the *New Yorker* magazine once bemoaned what it called the "brave, new audience-driven preaching" of our day: "The preacher, instead of looking out upon the world, looks out upon public opinion, trying to find out what the public would like to hear. Then he tries his best to duplicate that, and bring his finished product into a marketplace in which others are trying to do the same. The public, turning from our culture to find out about the world, discovers there is nothing but its own reflection. The unexamined world, meanwhile, drifts blindly into the future."[6]

David Wells asks rightly,

Is the antithesis against God or against the world?

The evangelical Church today imagines that this choice does not have to be made, that it can be on friendly terms with both. This attitude, more than anything else, accounts for the Church's diminished spiritual stature—for why it appears as a moral pygmy among the dilemmas of the modern world, which seem to be giants. Amidst enormous pain and confusion, evangelical faith seems by comparison to be trivial, as it indulges itself with "happy clappy" praise songs, light Sunday morning dialogs or, worse yet, drama in their place. . . .

. . . What the Church needs is not more of these strategies but more faith, more confidence that God's Word is sufficient for this time, more confidence in the power of the Holy Spirit to apply it, and more integrity in proclaiming it.[7]

How is error in the church to be defeated? Only by the sword of the Spirit, which is the Word of God. John Stott picks up on this important symbol in the letter to Pergamum:

6. Quoted in *Context* magazine, 15 April, 1991, p. 4; quoted in Guinness and Seel, *No God but God*, 168.

7. David F. Wells, *Losing Our Virtue: Why the Church Must Recover Its Moral Vision* (Grand Rapids: William B. Eerdmans, 1998), 206, 208.

God's way to overcome error is the proclamation of the gospel of Christ which is God's power of salvation to everyone who believes. Falsehood will not be suppressed by the gruesome methods of the inquisition, or by the burning of heretics at the stake, or by restrictive State legislation, or even by war. Force of arms cannot conquer ideas. Only truth can defeat error. The false ideologies of the world can be overthrown only by the superior ideology of Christ. We have no other weapons but this sword. Let us use it fearlessly, and by the open manifestation of the truth storm the strongholds of Satan.[8]

THE CHALLENGE AND THE WARNING

The challenge that Jesus gives to those who have compromised with the world and its ways is to "repent"—because compromise is sin, and repentance is the only way to deal with sin. This command appears throughout the seven letters—it is given to the churches in Ephesus (see Rev. 2:5), Pergamum (see Rev. 2:16), Sardis (see Rev. 3:3), and Laodicea (see Rev. 3:19). Surely, as Luther said, "When our Lord and Master, Jesus Christ, said 'repent,' he meant that the entire life of believers should be one of repentance."[9]

What if those who are compromising with the ways of the world do not repent? In that case, the Christ who possesses the "sharp two-edged sword" (v. 12)—which signifies a ruler's authority to prescribe either life or death—will come and "war against them with the sword of [his] mouth" (v. 16). It is not often that we think of the Lord Jesus Christ as a warrior, and still less as one who would fight against his own alleged people—against apparent believers. But that is the picture that we have here. It is a picture of Jesus opposing those who hold to the teachings of Balaam and the Nicolaitans, because he "hates" their practices, knowing the danger that they pose to the church (see Rev. 2:6). If Jesus hates and opposes such false teachings and ways of life, should we not hate and oppose them too?

8. John R. W. Stott, *What Christ Thinks of the Church: Insights from Revelation 2–3* (Grand Rapids: Wm. B. Eerdmans, 1958), 63.
9. Quoted in Sinclair Ferguson, *The Grace of Repentance* (Wheaton, IL: Crossway Books, 2000), 11.

THE PROMISE

In a context that is dealing specifically with war or fighting, it is not unexpected to read about rewards that are promised to those who conquer, though the general challenge to conquer—or overcome—is found in each of the seven letters (see Rev. 2:7, 11, 17, 26; 3:5, 12, 21). The earlier words of rebuke and repentance were spoken to the church at Pergamum as a whole; all of them needed to repent of their compromise with the world and its standards. But in verse 17 Jesus speaks to individuals—to those who conquer—and he makes great promises to them. They will receive "some of the hidden manna" and will be given "a white stone, with a new name written on the stone that no one knows except the one who receives it" (v. 17).

We understand that these symbols are important. Yet few images in the entire book have received such diverse and multiple interpretations as the symbols in this verse have.

"THE HIDDEN MANNA"

Manna is the easiest to understand, because it is a clear reference to the years when the people of Israel, while wandering in the wilderness, were fed by food from heaven (see Ex. 16). Still, this symbol has multiple overtones of meaning.

For one thing, it is identified as "the hidden manna"—a cryptic reference to the fact that Moses had placed a jar of manna within the Most Holy Place of the tabernacle (see Ex. 16:33–34; Heb. 9:4). A person would be able to eat of that manna only if a way could be opened to the presence of God—which, of course, is what Jesus did for those who believe on him and trust in his atonement.

For another, Christians would know that Jesus had referred to himself as the true manna, or bread, that came down from heaven (see John 6:33, 35). Like the manna, Jesus is "hidden" to the world, which does not believe on him—but he is made known to and is available to all Christians. If the believers at Pergamum refused the food that was offered to idols, they would be given the food that, if a man eats of it, will cause him to live forever.

"A WHITE STONE, WITH A NEW NAME WRITTEN ON THE STONE"

There are many interpretations of this unusual reference—almost as many as there are commentators. However, not all of them need be taken seriously. The most common interpretations are these:

1. The stone has been understood as a *tessera*, or ticket, admitting the possessor to a king's presence or a royal feast.
2. It has been seen as a pebble that was used to register a vote of acquittal in some courts. The Greek general and politician Alcibiades said, "If I should be accused in a capital case, I would not put my trust in anyone. I would not put my trust even in my mother for fear that through error she might put in the urn a black instead of a white stone."[10]
3. It has been viewed as one of the stones in the breastplate of an Old Testament high priest, with the name of one of the twelve tribes of Israel written on it—or the Urim and Thummim, which the priest used for determining the will of God in a specific matter.
4. It has been called an amulet intended to bring the bearer good luck.
5. It has also been called a symbol of the person wearing it—the white representing his or her purity.
6. Or it has been called a symbol that represents Christ and bears *his* name.

The fact that the stone has "a new name" written on it is the best clue for understanding this symbol, in my judgment; though commentators are divided over whether this is a new name for the Christian—one that signifies a new nature, similar to the changed names of Abraham, who formerly was called Abram; Jacob, who became Israel; or Peter (which means "rock"), whose given name was Simon—or a newly disclosed name of Jesus Christ.[11]

10. Quoted in Donald Grey Barnhouse, *Revelation: An Expositional Commentary* (Grand Rapids: Zondervan, 1985), 56.
11. In the next chapter Jesus speaks of three new names specifically: "the name of my

We do not need to choose between the two. For what is the Christian's new name if not *Christian*—the name of Jesus Christ? That we are called Christians signifies that we belong to Christ, that we are his servants, that we rejoice in his fellowship and together seek his kingdom and his glory.[12] The reason that "no one knows [the name] except the one who receives it" is because the assurance that we belong to Christ is an individual matter. No one can believe or be assured of our salvation in our stead. Are you Christ's? Then you must live for him, honor his name, and keep yourself from being polluted by the world (see James 1:27).

God," "the name of the city of my God, the new Jerusalem," and "my own new name" (Rev. 3:12). So the symbol may have broad meanings.

12. This is the view of William Hendriksen, *More Than Conquerors: An Interpretation of the Book of Revelation* (Grand Rapids: Baker Book House, 1940), 70.

9

TO THE CHURCH IN THYATIRA

Revelation 2:18–29

Most church historians would say that the worst thing that happened to the church of Jesus Christ during the first millennium was its being accepted as the religion of the Roman Empire by the emperor Constantine around AD 310. Not its struggles against paganism; not the persecutions under Nero, Domitian, or Julian; but the opportunity of being accepted and popular. When that happened, the cutting edge of Christian witness was lost. Church leaders began to seek the world's honor and pursue the power and prestige that was possessed by government officials. Values were inverted, luxury was sought, morals grew lax, and believers began to match the acceptance that the world had given them with their own grateful acceptance of the world.

When we come to Jesus's message to the church in Thyatira, we discover that a similar message of accommodation had been preached in that city.

This is the longest of the seven letters, with twelve verses—as opposed to seven for Ephesus, four for Smyrna, six for Pergamum, six for Sardis, seven for Philadelphia, and nine for Laodicea. The false teachings that were taking place in Thyatira were similar to those in Pergamum, where they were called the teachings of Balaam and the teachings of the Nicolaitans. But the situation was worse in Thyatira. In Pergamum, the pernicious errors were merely present; they were not endorsed. In Thyatira, they were "tolerated"—meaning that they had been accepted as a valid expression of Christian faith, at least by the majority of those who claimed to be believers. In other words, the problem was not merely the presence of a teaching that encouraged compromise with the world; it was a compromise with that false teaching itself, by those who should have stood against it.

And there was another difference. In Pergamum, Jesus calls for repentance from such false teachings and warns that he will come to fight against those who hold to them. In Thyatira, he knows that the chief among these teachers is utterly unrepentant—as a result of which he says that he is coming to execute a judgment that will involve sickness and even death for some of its members.

THE LEAST IMPORTANT CITY

Thyatira was the least important of the cities to which Jesus addresses the letters in Revelation 2 and 3, and we do not know much about it. It lay inland about forty-five miles east of Pergamum in a long valley connecting the Hermus and Caicus rivers, which led to Pergamum. The first historical mention of Thyatira is from 290 BC, where it is referred to as a military center that was garrisoned by Macedonian troops placed there to protect Pergamum—which even then was the more important city. Thyatira had no special religious importance—no famous temples like those in Ephesus or Pergamum. However, the valley was a major route from the Asiatic coast to Byzantium, which meant that much of the commerce from the east ran through it, and that made Thyatira a commercial center.

Thyatira manufactured and traded in items made of wool, linen, dyed material, leatherwork, and bronze. One thing we do know about this city is that it had more trade guilds than any other Asian city about which we have information. There were associations for bakers, workers of bronze, clothiers, cobblers, weavers, tanners, dyers of cloth, makers of pottery, and slave dealers. These guilds were like trade unions, but they were far more important in ancient times than anything that we know today. It would have been difficult for a Christian to make a living without belonging to one of them, and belonging to a guild meant sharing in its social life and worship. Each guild had a patron god or goddess, and official functions of the guild would require that honors be given to its god.

There is one small point of contact with Thyatira in another of the New Testament books. In Acts 16, when Paul arrived in Philippi on his second missionary journey, we are told that his first convert was a woman from Thyatira. Her name was Lydia, and she was "from the city of Thyatira, a seller of purple goods" (v. 14). The dye that produced the color purple was made from the root of a plant that grew in the valley where Thyatira was located, and the cloth that was made from it was a major export of the city. Lydia may have been the one who first established the church in Thyatira, after returning there from Philippi, but we do not know. It is also possible that the city was evangelized by believers during Paul's long stay in Ephesus.

CHRIST, THE DIVINE JUDGE

Each of these letters begins with a self-description of Jesus that is drawn from the vision John had of him in Revelation 1. The elements of the specific description that begins each church's letter correspond to that church and to what Jesus has to say to it. In this case, the words have overtones of judgment.

The words "Son of God" occur only here in the book of Revelation, even though they are used throughout the rest of the New Testament to ascribe divinity to Jesus. Here, however, John is probably thinking particularly of Psalm 2, since he quotes verse 9 of that psalm near the end of this letter. Psalm 2 is a judgment psalm in which God exalts his "Son" (vv. 7, 12) as King of Zion (see v. 6) and judge of the "rulers of the earth" (v. 10). The psalm concludes with the warning "Kiss the Son, lest he be angry, and you perish in the way, for his wrath is quickly kindled. Blessed are all who take refuge in him" (v. 12). The verse that John quotes also warns of judgment: "You shall break them with a rod of iron and dash them in pieces like a potter's vessel" (v. 9).

The description "who has eyes like a flame of fire, and whose feet are like burnished bronze" (Rev. 2:18) is from the vision described in Revelation 1. The meaning of "eyes like a flame of fire" is explained later in this letter, when Jesus describes himself as "he who searches mind and heart" (v. 23).[1] Beale says, "His knowledge pierces to the core of our being and is the basis for the judgment or reward that he renders."[2] The feet that are "like burnished bronze" are those with which Jesus will tread out "the great winepress of the wrath of God" (Rev. 14:19).

WHY THE CHURCH IS COMMENDED

What does this divine, all-seeing, terrifying judge perceive as he looks at the church in Thyatira? Surprisingly, in view of the images of judgment with which the letter begins, the first thing that Jesus sees merits his praise—his commendation. The church in Thyatira is commended for its good deeds. The Greek text strings six such deeds together, which are all connected by the word "and." But the first of these is probably *epexegetic*, which means that the items that follow are not merely others in a string of six but explanations of what the first term includes. And the last item in the series probably introduces a new item. The meaning of verse 19, then, is probably something like this: "I know your deeds—that is, your love and faith, your service and patient endurance, and that you are now doing more than you did at first."

Love is what was missing in the otherwise commendable church in Ephesus—whether love for God, for Christ, or for other believers. But Ephesus was strong in its faith, for it had tested "those who call themselves apostles and are not, and found them to be false" (Rev. 2:2). Service has not been specifically mentioned yet, though it may be involved in the hard work for which Ephesus was commended in that verse. Perseverance was present in Ephesus and Pergamum and is urged for all the churches. They were to persevere and conquer.

---

1. The Greek is actually "the kidneys and the hearts," which meant then what "hearts and minds" means today.

2. G. K. Beale, *The Book of Revelation: A Commentary on the Greek Text* (Grand Rapids: William B. Eerdmans, 1999), 264.

These four elements go together nicely in pairs, as Barclay observes, for love leads to service, and faith leads to perseverance.[3]

What is unique about Christ's praise of this church is that these four important aspects of a balanced Christian life are said to have increased—the believers in Thyatira were doing more now than they had been doing at first. This means that the church was not static. It was a church that was moving forward. In Ephesus, the first works were better than the last, but here, in Thyatira, the last works are more abundant than the first. Wouldn't you like to be part of a church like that? A church that is characterized by such qualities as love, faith, service, and perseverance? A church on the move? I know I would. Yet it is to this church that Jesus speaks some of his harshest words, as his all-seeing eyes pierce to the hollow core that had been hidden by this outward show of piety and apparent church growth.

"THAT WOMAN JEZEBEL"

The problem was that the church was tolerating a dangerous false teacher, whom John called "that woman Jezebel" (v. 20). Was this a specific person in the church? She seems to have been. In the previous letter, Jesus warned against those who held to "the teaching of Balaam" and "the teaching of the Nicolaitans" (vv. 14–15), but he did not refer specifically to "that Balaam" or "that Nicolaitan," as he speaks here specifically of "that woman Jezebel." Female figures are sometimes used by John to symbolize a false religion or false philosophy. That could be all that John intends here. Jezebel might be an early example of the harlot figure who represents the corrupt world system, as found later in the book (see Rev. 18). But there were prophetesses in the early church. Anna was a prophetess (see Luke 2:36). Philip the evangelist had four daughters who were prophetesses (see Acts 21:9). These women were often highly regarded, and that seems to be what we encounter here. Jezebel seems to have been

3. See William Barclay, *The Revelation of John*, vol. 1, *Chapters 1 to 5*, rev. ed. (Philadelphia: The Westminster Press, 1976), 103.

a real person, and whoever she was, she seemed to have had a tolerated and even respected position in the church.

Jezebel was an actual Old Testament figure, too, of course. So calling the prophetess in the church of Thyatira a Jezebel is a way of saying that she was like this particularly evil ancient figure. In order to understand what was happening in Thyatira, it is necessary for us to know something about the original Jezebel.

Here is the story. When the kingdom of Israel divided after the death of Solomon, the commercial alliance that had been established between Israel and the Phoenician cities of Tyre and Sidon ended for Judah—the part of the kingdom to the south. The northern kingdom of Israel inherited the alliance, since it was closer to the Phoenician strongholds—but this was a corrupting association. The ships of Phoenicia dominated trade throughout the Mediterranean Sea and beyond. Joining with Tyre and Sidon and trading with them meant riches for Israel. But the Phoenicians worshiped Baal and his female counterpart, the fertility goddess Astarte. Astarte was the Asian form of the Greek goddess Aphrodite and the Roman goddess Venus.

Ahab was one of the most enduring of the northern kings, and he moved to cement his alliance with Phoenicia by marrying Jezebel, who was a Phoenician princess. Her father was Ethbaal, the king of Sidon and a priest of Astarte. Politically and economically, it was a brilliant move for Ahab. Trade between the kingdoms must have increased greatly. And luxury followed, as was later condemned by the prophet Amos. But with Phoenician trade came the Phoenician gods. Jezebel persuaded Ahab to build a temple to Baal in Israel's capital, Samaria. Then she imported four hundred fifty prophets of Baal and four hundred prophets of Astarte and killed off all the prophets of Jehovah she could find. Baal worship flourished in the cities of Israel, and the worship of Astarte drew many to the sacred hilltop groves, where the male sex organ (represented by an Asherah pole) was worshiped and cult prostitution thrived.

This was the situation that Elijah challenged in the dramatic scene on Mount Carmel that is described in 1 Kings 18. He challenged the prophets of Baal to a contest in order to determine whose god was able to bring down fire on his altar. The prophets of Baal cried to their god all day long, but nothing happened. Elijah soaked his altar in water and then prayed to Jehovah, who responded with fire that not only consumed the sacrifice but also consumed the wood, the stones, and even the water in the trench. The people concluded, rightly and inevitably, "The LORD, he is God; the LORD, he is God" (1 Kings 18:39), and the prophets of Baal were killed.

A great victory, certainly. But think what was involved. When Elijah called for the people to choose God rather than Baal, he was not just posing a theological alternative. His call was an economic challenge as well. E. M. Blaiklock wrote rightly, "A break with Baal meant a break with Jezebel. A break with Jezebel meant a break with Tyre. And Tyre, without much inconvenience, could strangle the economic life of Israel." And they undoubtedly did! "Converted merchants went home from Carmel and surveyed rich carpets which would never be replaced, and packed warehouses whose shelves would empty of Tyrian bales and never be filled again."[4] It was a choice of economic depression and hard times.

It is true that the rains came immediately afterwards. The land would be fertile again, because God had promised to provide for his people by supplying daily bread. But there was no disguising the economic loss. Following God always means breaking with the world, and breaking with the world usually means losing the economic and other favors that the world brings.

THE CASE FOR COMPROMISE

But how plausible the arguments for compromise are! And how apparently biblical! The prophetess of Thyatira was not a prophetess of Baal or Astarte. She was known as a Christian teacher and would have made biblical—we can even say "Christian"—arguments for compromising with idolatry by eating meat that had been offered to false gods. Professor Beale suggests a number of arguments that she might have made from various passages of the Bible.[5]

---

4. E. M. Blaiklock, *The Seven Churches: An Exposition of Revelation Chapters Two and Three* (London: Marshall, Morgan & Scott, [1951?]), 48–49.

5. See Beale, *The Book of Revelation*, 265–66.

1 CORINTHIANS 8:4

Paul had discussed the question of eating meat that had been offered to idols and had counseled that if a Christian can eat with a pure conscience he should be free to do so, since "we know that 'an idol has no real existence,' and that 'there is no God but one.'" Since an idol has no real existence at all, participating in an idol feast cannot possibly harm anyone spiritually—that may be what the prophetess of Thyatira said.

MATTHEW 22:21

When Jesus was asked whether or not it was right to pay taxes to Caesar, he replied by saying, "Render to Caesar the things that are Caesar's, and to God the things that are God's." In a world that was ruled by the Romans, Caesar required honor in the form of libations or offerings before his statue. Based on the standard that Jesus set, wouldn't the offering of such libations be considered giving to Caesar what he had a right to demand? . . . Or so the prophetess of Thyatira might have reasoned.

ROMANS 13:1

Paul discussed the relationship of Christians to the state in his letter to the Romans, arguing that the government has been established by God and rightly requires submission from its citizens: "Let every person be subject to the governing authorities." He added, echoing Jesus, "Pay to all what is owed to them: taxes to whom taxes are owed, revenue to whom revenue is owed, respect to whom respect is owed, honor to whom honor is owed" (Rom. 13:7). Paul's teaching would have been known throughout the churches of Asia Minor. Might the prophetess of Thyatira have appealed to Paul's teaching to support her case for compromising?

1 CORINTHIANS 5:9–11

And what about Paul's advice regarding associating with people who are immoral? He had counseled that Christians should not associate with sexually immoral Christians, but he had qualified this by adding that he "not at all [meant] the sexually immoral of this world, or the greedy and swindlers, or idolaters, since then you would need to go out of the world." The prophetess of Thyatira might have argued that it was not only permissible but necessary to join the guilds in Thyatira. And if that involved participating in the worship of their tutelary deities, well, what harm would be done? Thyatira was a closely knit community. How could a person make a living if he did not join a guild and participate in its practices?

All this sounds strangely modern, and so reasonable. But lest we get swept away in our own deception at this point, we must remember that the strong, consistent teaching of the early church was that a Christian can never compromise with idolatry or pagan standards of morality in order to get by or even earn a living.

The story goes that one day a Christian complained to Tertullian, the early apologist, of the need to make a living. "After all, I must live," he pleaded.

Tertullian replied, "Must you?"

The early Christians knew that neither obeying the state, nor going along to get along, nor sharing in the life of those around us justifies idolatry or immorality. And that is precisely what the prophetess of Thyatira and her followers were advocating.

When Paul argued that it was permissible to eat meat that had been offered to idols, he did not say that it was right to do so in a pagan temple as part of a pagan worship service. When Jesus told us to give to Caesar what is Caesar's, he limited that requirement by adding "and to God what is God's." When Paul argued the necessity of Christians submitting to the governing authorities, it was on the basis of the state's rightfully exercising its power, not abusing its power by requiring idolatrous worship. And when he wrote that Christians should not utterly disassociate from those who are "sexually immoral" or "the greedy and swindlers, or idolaters," he did so in a chapter in which he also demands the expulsion of an immoral Christian from church fellowship.

There is an interesting reference to "the deep things of Satan" in Revelation 2:24. This might mean that the false teacher had been arguing that in order to conquer Satan a Christian had to learn how he thinks and what he does by participating in the world's sins. But it is more likely that her teachings were presented as "the depths of God," as Paul mentioned in 1 Corinthians 2:10, but were actually, as John says, "the deep things of Satan." That is important to remember. For, however modern or plausible an effort to compromise with the world's standards may be, such a teaching is from Satan, and the end of those who follow it will be the same as his end.

Here is the way John Stott unfolds this passage:

> If it is God's purpose to make us holy, Satan is resolved to frustrate it. He is seeking ceaselessly both to entice individual Christian believers into sin, and to insinuate evil into the churches. Where he cannot muzzle the church's witness by persecution from without, he resorts to the subtler assault of pollution from within. If the dragon's two beasts fail, there is still the harlot Babylon with her loathsome charms. If the beast from the sea cannot crush the church by force, nor the beast from the earth silence the testimony of Christians by the errors of his false cult, then the Babylonian harlot's finery and jewels and pearls may seduce them and her golden cup poison them with its impure abominations (cf. 17:1–6). Or, to drop the vivid imagery of the Revelation, if the devil cannot conquer the church by the application of political pressure or the propagation of intellectual heresy, he will try the insinuation of moral evil. Such at least was the dragon's foul strategy in Thyatira.[6]

That is why Jesus's pronouncement of judgment in this letter is so harsh. It is because this was a devilish strategy and error. If the prophetess of Thyatira was an actual woman, then the sickness that is pronounced as her judgment was probably an actual sickness, as in the case of those who had profaned the Lord's Supper at Corinth (see 1 Cor. 11:27–30). Her "children," whom Jesus says he will strike dead in Revelation 2:23, would not mean literal offspring from some adulterous relationship but those who had followed her teachings.

---

6. John R. W. Stott, *What Christ Thinks of the Church: Insights from Revelation 2–3* (Grand Rapids: Wm. B. Eerdmans, 1958), 71–72.

The prophecy is that Jesus is going to destroy this heresy as well as those who embrace it.

CHRIST'S WORDS TO THE FAITHFUL

Yet even in Thyatira there were some who did not hold to the evil teachings and had not learned "the deep things of Satan" that were being proclaimed so reasonably by the prophetess. There always are. God always has his remnant. And their task, says Jesus, is simply to hold on until he comes (see v. 25)

Jesus says that he will not "lay any other burden" on them. This is an obvious reference to the decree of the Jerusalem Council that is recorded in Acts 15. The issue there had been to what extent Jewish laws should be imposed on Gentile converts, and the decision was to impose no other burden on them than what was obvious: "abstain from what has been sacrificed to idols, and from blood, and from what has been strangled, and from sexual immorality" (Acts 15:29). This was exactly the issue at Thyatira, and Jesus's judgment was the same there, too—namely, that the answer to the world's seductions is not a new set of regulations but simply a continuation in what we have been given and in the way that has been set before us. Live free in Christ, but do not compromise with the idolatry or sexual immorality of the surrounding culture. Stott calls this "the balanced, joyful, exhilarating righteousness of the Bible, the glorious liberty of the royal law."[7]

If the believers at Thyatira conquered by obeying Jesus and doing his will to the end (see Rev. 2:26), they would be made to rule with Christ—"He will rule them with a rod of iron, as when earthen pots are broken in pieces" (v. 27)—as prophesied in Psalm 2:9. They would rule with Christ because they would be in Christ and would share in his triumph over, and governance of, the nations.

The last promise is that those who conquer will be given "the morning star" (Rev. 2:28). This image has been interpreted in various ways—as a promise of the resurrection, a victory over Satan, or the

---

7. Stott, 79.

glory of the righteous. But here is a case in which Revelation itself gives the meaning. Jesus identifies himself as "the bright morning star" in Revelation 22:16, using an image that is probably drawn from Numbers 24:14–20, which predicts a "star" that would arise out of Jacob to crush God's enemies. This "star" is the Messiah. Here, the image is applied to the saints who have already been promised to rule with Jesus on the basis of Psalm 2. Through our receiving of the gift of Jesus as Messiah, we also gain final victory.

It would not have seemed this way to many in Thyatira. To them, the path to victory was the path of compromise. They wanted to maintain their prosperous trade with Phoenicia—to prosper in Asia Minor. But where are Tyre and Sidon today? All gone! Swept clean by the armies of Alexander the Great. But those who held on now rule with Christ—and will continue to rule! "He who has an ear, let him hear what the Spirit says to the churches" (Rev. 2:29).

10

TO THE CHURCH IN SARDIS

Revelation 3:1—6

A number of years ago I came across some instructions for high school English teachers that reminded them how important it is to commend a student for something in his or her essay before making a correction, even if the only positive thing they can think to say is "What an unusual color of ink you are using!" Jesus did that in his letters to the seven churches, almost always commending before critiquing. But Sardis, like Laodicea, had a church in which Jesus found nothing to commend.

The church in Sardis was a dead church. It was like the church pastored by a minister who one day penned this bit of honest doggerel:

Tell my people when I'm dead
That they should shed no tears,
For I shall be no deader then
Than they have been for years.

A dead church is not a true church, though it may appear to be so outwardly. It may be active, but it will be an example only of what we call "nominal Christianity." It will be Christian in name—but in name only. It is useful to note at the start of this study that the city of Sardis had a noted necropolis that was known as the city of a "thousand hills"—so named because of the burial mounds that could be seen on the not-too-distant skyline. This reminds us that a church can have a thousand members (or more) and still be as dead as the inhabitants of a cemetery.

THE CITY OF SARDIS

Sardis was a very old city. It had been the capital of the ancient kingdom of Lydia by at least 1200 BC and had passed through many different hands. The most striking thing about Sardis is that the original city was situated on a high hill overlooking the valley of the Hermus river. The sides of this hill soared nearly 1,500 feet upward and were so steep that the inhabitants of the acropolis considered themselves to be unconquerable. Yet the hill was scaled, and they were conquered—twice.

One of the early kings of Sardis was Croesus, the legendary ruler whose name is remembered in the byword *as rich as Croesus*. He was so wealthy for his day that Solon, the famous lawgiver of Athens, visited him and was shown the treasures of the king. Croesus boasted that his glorious wealth made him the happiest of men, but Solon was too wise for that. He saw in Croesus and his people the seeds of softness and replied that no one should call a man happy until he is dead.

Herodotus, the Greek historian, tells how Croesus wanted to go to war against King Cyrus of Persia—the same Cyrus who appears in the book of Daniel. Croesus consulted the oracle at Delphi about whether he would be successful or not and received the famous reply "If you cross the River Halys, you will destroy a great empire." The king assumed that the empire that would be destroyed was that of Cyrus—not realizing that it might just as well be his own, which turned out to be the case. Croesus was defeated and retreated to his hilltop stronghold. He wanted to raise a second army. But Cyrus followed him quickly, surrounded the city, and offered a reward to any soldier who could find a way to climb the steep sides of the apparently impregnable acropolis.

One soldier, whose name was Hyroeades, noticed a Lydian soldier lose his helmet over the edge of the rampart and then climb down

116

to retrieve it by way of an obscure fissure in the rock. Hyroeades paid close attention, marked the way, and then climbed it himself, followed by other Persian soldiers. When the Persians reached the top they found the walls unguarded, because the citizens had assumed that no one could scale the steep hillside and get into Sardis that way. The city was not watching, so it fell.

Surprisingly, the same thing happened in 218 BC. Antiochus III, a Hellenistic Greek king, was opposed by a rival king called Achaeus, who sought refuge in Sardis. Again, a soldier found a way up the steep hillside. Once more the walls were unguarded, and again the city fell.

In AD 17 an earthquake destroyed Sardis, after which the city was rebuilt. As it outgrew the hilltop plateau, it expanded to the plain beneath—but it also entered a period of decay. Sardis was a city living on a reputation from the past, but the past was long gone. The glory of the city had departed, and it never regained the wealth or reputation it had possessed in earlier days. E. M. Blaiklock wrote of Sardis, "Sardis had a name for strength, but she was weak. Sardis had a name for permanence, but her glory departed. Sardis had a name for wealth, but she was poor."[1] The great scholar of apostolic Christianity Sir William M. Ramsay wrote about Sardis, "It was the city whose history conspicuously and pre-eminently blazoned forth the uncertainty of human fortunes, the weakness of human strength, and the shortness of the step that separates over-confident might from sudden and irreparable disaster. It was the city whose name was almost synonymous with pretensions unjustified, promise unfulfilled, appearance without reality, confidence that heralded ruin."[2]

We know nothing about the origin or growth of the church in Sardis beyond what may be gathered from this letter. However, it is interesting to record that Melito, one of its early bishops, was the first known commentator on the book of Revelation.

---

1. E. M. Blaiklock, *The Seven Churches: An Exposition of Revelation Chapters Two and Three* (London: Marshall, Morgan & Scott, n.d.), 56.

2. W. M. Ramsay, *The Letters to the Seven Churches of Asia: And Their Place in the Plan of the Apocalypse* (London: Hodder and Stoughton, 1904), 376, quoted in Blaiklock, 57.

JESUS'S FIRST WORDS

The first words of Jesus to this church, "The words of him who has the seven spirits of God and the seven stars. I know your works" (Rev. 3:1), are almost the same as his first words to the believers at Ephesus: "The words of him who holds the seven stars in his right hand, who walks among the seven golden lampstands. I know your works, your toil and your patient endurance" (Rev. 2:1–2). But there is a big difference between the two introductions. The works of the Ephesians were genuinely good deeds. They were criticized only because they had lost their first love. The works of the nominal believers at Sardis were not spiritually authentic, which is what the words "I have not found your works complete in the sight of my God" mean (Rev. 3:2).

And yet, in a sense, they were good works. This was not an inactive church. We can assume that it was well attended and successful. It met its budgets. It had programs to help the poor and to build better community relations. It had a good reputation among non-Christians, too, and it was probably respected for being a lively fellowship. "You have the reputation of being alive," Jesus said. Yes, but this was only an external impression—and by unbelievers at that. In the sight of God, the church was dead.

Can this be possible? Can a church be lively and yet dead? Apparently so! For good deeds, even many good deeds, do not prove the reality of spiritual life. They can be works of the flesh. The apostle Paul reminded the Corinthians that the day of judgment would reveal each person's works for what they were and that many would be consumed by fire (see 1 Cor. 3:12–13). The deeds of the people at Sardis must have been an empty shell. George Eldon Ladd called this a good picture of nominal Christianity: "outwardly prosperous, busy with the externals of religious activity, but devoid of spiritual life and power."[3] The church was like mighty Samson, who, when he was shorn of his locks, "did not know that the LORD had left him" (Judges 16:20).

---

3. George Eldon Ladd, *A Commentary on the Revelation of John* (Grand Rapids: William B. Eerdmans, 1972), 56.

THE PROBLEM WITH THE CHURCH IN SARDIS

There are several clues in Revelation 3 about what was wrong at Sardis, though we are not told much about the church explicitly. One clue is that the faithful few are commended in verse 4 because they "have not soiled their garments." Soiled clothing is an unmistakable image of the contamination that comes from sin; the fact that only a few church members were *not* soiled means that the majority had fallen into the sinful ways of the immoral city in which they lived. They seemed to be Christians, but their actions belied their profession. These people called Jesus "Lord," but they did not obey him. They seemed to be Christians, but they were actually "dead in [their] trespasses and sins" (Eph. 2:1).

There is also a clue about what was wrong in the absence of any mention of the church opposing heresy or suffering persecution. The church in Ephesus had left its first love, but at least it had been opposing false teaching and exposing false teachers. The church in Smyrna had been persecuted by Jews and by the Roman state—it stood for something. The churches in Pergamum and Thyatira were accommodating the false counsel of Balaam, the Nicolaitans, and "that woman Jezebel," but at least the believers there were warned against those teachings and urged to persevere. What seems to be the case in Sardis is that the church was not involved in or struggling against any heresy, nor was it being attacked from without by either the pagans or the Jews. The largest synagogue from the ancient world that has yet been found was in Sardis, which suggests that thousands of Jews lived in that city. Yet the "Christians" at Sardis were so at home in their culture that there did not seem to be anything about them that was worth attacking. The church was at peace, but "it was the peace of the cemetery," as William Hendriksen states.[4] It was dead. It had forfeited its spiritual life.

We have a description of what a church like this might look like

---

4. William Hendriksen, *More Than Conquerors: An Interpretation of the Book of Revelation* (Grand Rapids: Baker Book House, 1940), 73.

in 2 Timothy 3, where Paul is warning his young protégé against the terrible times to come in the last days—days in which people will be

> lovers of self, lovers of money, proud, arrogant, abusive, disobedient to their parents, ungrateful, unholy, heartless, unappeasable, slanderous, without self-control, brutal, not loving good, treacherous, reckless, swollen with conceit, lovers of pleasure rather than lovers of God. (vv. 2–4)

This could be referring to what we might call the *very* last days—that is, the days just before the second coming of Jesus Christ, when he returns in judgment. But since Paul is instructing Timothy about what to do in the challenges that he will face in his ministry, it seems instead like it must be referring to the entire time between the Lord's first and second comings. In other words, this is a frightening description of the world in which we live—not only of the very end times. And, of course, it does describe our world. It describes it perfectly. We live in a time when people are lovers of themselves and of money, are boastful, are rash, and so on.

But here is the shocking thing. Having described this evil worldly culture by its vices, Paul further describes its members in verse 5 as "having the appearance of godliness, but denying its power." This cannot be referring to pagans. Paul would never have described the pagans of his day as having "an appearance of godliness." He would have referred to their religions as being multiple forms of ungodliness, as he does in the first chapter of Romans. So if this cannot be a description of the pagan world, then it must be describing the church. In other words, the problem that Paul saw is not that the world will be wicked in the final days before Christ's return but that the church will be like the world—as it is today. The church will be indistinguishable from the world and will be equally corrupt—at least when you look beneath the surface.

That is what the church in Sardis was like. And Jesus evaluates it as being spiritually moribund—which we all are, apart from God's grace. An *appearance* of godliness means nothing if the power of God is not present.

Paul told Timothy what to do, and what to depend on, when such evil days come. He offered no new weapon—no new trick or novel evangelistic method. Instead of something novel, we find him recommending what Timothy had possessed all along: the Word of God—because the Bible alone is sufficient even for terrible times like these.

> But as for you, continue in what you have learned and have firmly believed, knowing from whom you learned it and how from child-hood you have been acquainted with the sacred writings, which are able to make you wise for salvation through faith in Christ Jesus. (2 Tim. 3:14–15)

The church at Sardis needed the same divine wisdom.

THE COMMANDS

The first thing Jesus urges the church in Sardis to do is to "wake up" (Rev. 3:2)—or become watchfully alert, as some other trans-lations suggest. They are to wake up in order to "strengthen what remains and is about to die." Moreover, they are to "remember" what they have received and heard, "keep it," and "repent" (v. 3). Those five urgent commands represent the formula for reviving a moribund church.

1. WAKE UP

To whom is the command to "wake up" addressed? At first glance it seems to be addressed to the entire church, since it is the church as a whole that has died. In this sense, it might be considered similar to Jesus's words to Lazarus as he lay in the tomb: "Lazarus, come out" (John 11:43). But if that is the case, then none of the five commands that Jesus issues to Sardis are efficacious—meaning that they do not necessarily accomplish the action they command. And even if they were efficacious, "Wake up!" would be the wrong com-mand in this context. That is an appropriate thing to say to someone who is sleeping—not to a corpse.

It is best to think of this, then, as a command addressed to those within the church who are genuine believers. In other words, it is addressed to those who are not dead but only asleep. This tells us a couple of things. First, it suggests that revival begins with a few individuals who wake up to the condition of those around them and begin to be concerned for them. Revivals begin with the faithful, fervent prayer of true Christians. It is generally acknowledged that the amazing revivals in Ulster in 1859 began with a small group of businessmen who met in a remote schoolhouse for early-morning prayer. The revivals that came to the United States at about the same time began with a small group who met for prayer in New York City. Second, this command suggests that Christians should not necessarily leave a dead church. Leaving an apostate church is one thing—no Christian should support or be a part of a church that denies either Christ or the gospel. But a dead church is not necessarily doing that. It may actually profess right doctrine. If it does, the right course for a believing member is to seek its renewal, not its burial.

2. STRENGTHEN WHAT REMAINS

This command involves action, for renewal is not merely a matter of prayer. It also involves careful work with those who are spiritually alive, though they may be mere babes in Christ or sleeping themselves. We would call this work teaching, training, or discipling. There are many commands for us to do this in Scripture—such as Isaiah 35:3–4, for example: "Strengthen the weak hands, and make firm the feeble knees. Say to those who have an anxious heart, 'Be strong; fear not!'" And later, speaking of the work of God's servant, Isaiah says that "a bruised reed he will not break, and a faintly burning wick he will not quench" (Isa. 42:3)—his work will be to restore and strengthen, not to destroy.

3. REMEMBER WHAT YOU RECEIVED AND HEARD

This third command is also directed to genuine believers, for it is a charge for them to recall God's blessing to them in the past. This blessing that they are to remember is a specific blessing. John Stott argues that what they have received is the Holy Spirit, on the grounds that "sound doctrine alone cannot reclaim a church from death."[5] But the next verb in the sentence is "heard," which clearly refers to sound or apostolic teaching; and the word "received" is often used as a technical term for the accurate receiving of God's Word. It is the term Paul used when he passed on the words that ministers use when they officiate at the Lord's Supper: "For I received from the Lord what I also delivered to you" (1 Cor. 11:23).

Moreover, it is precisely the Word of God, properly taught and blessed by God, that brings revival. Nothing else does it. Charles Finney, the father of modern revivalism, said that revival "is not a miracle . . . in any sense. It is a purely philosophical result of the right use of the constituted means"—meaning that it could be produced by such techniques as conversion stories, the anxious bench, altar calls, and "invitation" music.[6] But that is not true. It is the Holy Spirit operating through the preaching of the Bible that regenerates sinners.

Peter described genuine conversion as being "born again, not of perishable seed but of imperishable, through the living and abiding word of God" (1 Peter 1:23). Which is also why Paul gave Timothy the directions that he did for remaining true to Christ in the evil end times that were coming. I quoted these directions earlier:

> But as for you, continue in what you have learned and have firmly believed, knowing from whom you learned it and how from childhood you have been acquainted with the sacred writings, which are able to make you wise for salvation through faith in Christ Jesus. (2 Tim. 3:14–15)

This passage is saying that the Bible is entirely sufficient for evangelism and Christian growth.

---

5. John R. W. Stott, *What Christ Thinks of the Church: Insights from Revelation 2–3* (Grand Rapids: Wm. B. Eerdmans, 1958), 92; see also 93–96.

6. Charles G. Finney, *Lectures on Revivals of Religion* (New York, 1835), 12, quoted in Richard Hofstadter, *Anti-Intellectualism in American Life* (New York: Vintage Books, 1963), 109.

4. KEEP IT

The fourth step for reviving a dead church is obedience—for it is not sufficient to hear the Word of God only; we must also obey what we hear. Moreover, we must keep on obeying it—the verb that is translated "keep" in this verse is a present imperative that carries the idea "obey and keep on obeying." It is the same word that was used earlier, in the first beatitude of the book: "Blessed is the one who reads aloud the words of this prophecy, and blessed are those who hear, and who *keep* what is written" (Rev. 1:3). The greater our knowledge, the greater our responsibility and obligation. Do you know the Bible? Have you been taught sound doctrine? Then you, above all others, must show it by your obedience to Jesus Christ.

5. REPENT

The final word Jesus gives the church in Sardis is "repent"—a requirement that is also urged upon the churches at Ephesus, Pergamum, and later Laodicea. Repentance is necessary because the nominalism of a church like the one in Sardis is a sin, and sins require repentance. Repentance is a specific turning away from sin and to Jesus. But what if those in the church in Sardis do not repent? Then Jesus warns that he "will come like a thief" (Rev. 3:3), when they least expect his coming.

The image of Christ coming like a thief is borrowed from Matthew 24:42–44, where it refers to his sudden appearance as Judge at the end of time. But here it is probably a warning of a judgment to fall specifically on the church at Sardis if it refuses to repent—a judgment that would come earlier than the final judgment and would anticipate it. If so, this warning would parallel the one Jesus gives to the church in Ephesus: "I will come to you and remove your lampstand from its place, unless you repent" (Rev: 2:5). What a warning! Jesus is saying that he will not tolerate a nominal church forever. He calls the Sardinians to repentance and tells those who are genuine believers to get busy, to pray, and to work for renewal. And if that does not happen, the day will come when Jesus will remove the dead church entirely. We have seen this in many places. Once there was a strong church in North Africa, but it is almost nonexistent today.

The same thing has happened to the church in other areas of the world. Will that not be the case for many churches in the United States, if we do not repent? Will it not be the case for you, if you fail to turn from a faith that is merely a formality to a genuine trust in and obedience to Jesus Christ?

THE FAITHFUL FEW

The story of the church in Sardis has been a sad story, for there are few things sadder than the death of a church that was genuinely alive at one time. But there is something good even here. There was a remnant of faithful believers in Sardis—people who had "not soiled their garments" by lusting after the world and its pollution (Rev. 3:4; see also James 1:27; Jude 23).

God always keeps a remnant—even in a dead church. When he saw the wickedness of man before the deluge and concluded that "every intention of the thoughts of his heart was only evil continually" (Gen. 6:5), there was nevertheless one family—the family of Noah—that was upright. Noah was "a righteous man, blameless in his generation," and he "walked with God" (v. 9). Even in the wicked cities of Sodom and Gomorrah, there was righteous Lot—who, in spite of his sinful yearnings for the world, is nevertheless called "righteous" and was "greatly distressed by the sensual conduct of the wicked" (2 Peter 2:7). In Elijah's day there were yet "seven thousand in Israel, all the knees that have not bowed to Baal" (1 Kings 19:18). Even in the evil days preceding the birth of Jesus there were still those, such as Anna, "who were waiting for the redemption of Jerusalem" (Luke 2:38).

To this remnant in Sardis, who had "not soiled their garments," Jesus makes four great promises. (1) They will "walk with" Christ (Rev. 3:4)—which refers to their being in heaven. (2) They will be dressed "in white" (v. 5). White is a prominent color in Revelation; the book speaks of white robes, white horses, white clouds, white stones, and a white throne. White stands for purity in almost any culture, but in ancient times white robes were also worn on festive occasions and at victory celebrations. When a Roman military triumph was celebrated, the citizens all dressed in white, and the city was called an *urbs candida* (a "city in white"). (3) Jesus will never "blot [their names] out of the book of life" (v. 5). The Book of Life is mentioned again in Revelation (see 13:8; 17:8; 20:12, 15; 21:27), but it first appears in Exodus 32:32–33, where Moses expresses his willingness to be blotted out of God's book if it would secure the salvation of his people. (4) Jesus "will confess [their names] before [his] Father and before his angels" (Rev. 3:5; see also Matt. 10:32–33; Luke 12:8–9).

To be acknowledged by Jesus is the exact opposite of the experience of the people in the parables of Matthew 25, who are not acknowledged by Christ, whose names are not written in the Book of Life, and who are banished from his presence: "Depart from me, you cursed, into the eternal fire prepared for the devil and his angels" (v. 41).

Is your name written in the Lamb's Book of Life? You can be a member of a church like the one at Sardis and be as spiritually dead as your church is, or you can have your name entered on the rolls of a living church; you can hold a certificate of baptism with your name prominently displayed; you can be acknowledged as a Christian by those with whom you work . . . and yet not have your name written in the only book that really matters. Jesus told his disciples to rejoice—not that they were able to do miracles but that their names were "written in heaven" (Luke 10:20). Is your name written there? Can you rejoice in that knowledge today? Today, the city of Sardis is a ruin—the church is gone. But those in it who were faithful to Christ now walk with him in paradise and are confessed by him before his Father and the holy angels.

11

TO THE CHURCH IN
PHILADELPHIA

Revelation 3:7–13

How do you measure success as a Christian? The investment firm of Morgan Stanley Dean Witter measured success "one investor at a time." Meanwhile, their customers measured success by the return on their portfolios. Others measure success by the size of their houses, the amount that they pay for their cars, or the money in their bank accounts. But how should a Christian measure success?

One answer is found in Jesus's letter to the church in Philadelphia, which contains nothing in the way of condemnation. Christ had only praise for this church—because, as he said, "You have kept my word and have not denied my name" (Rev. 3:8). This is the only real measure of success in the Christian life. The church in Philadelphia was not famous. It was not large or rich or prominent. It had only a small amount of strength. But because it had kept his word and not denied his name, Christ's letter to the church was one of unqualified commendation.

THE CITY OF BROTHERLY LOVE

Philadelphia was not large. In fact, it was the smallest of the seven cities in Revelation. Nor was it old. It had been named for Attalus II, the king of Pergamum from 159–138 BC. Attalus was called *Philadelphos*, meaning "brother lover," because of his loyalty to his brother Eumenes, and the civic name Philadelphia came from this personal nickname.

The city did have a wonderful location. It was the easternmost of the seven cities, about thirty miles southeast of Sardis and a hundred miles east of Smyrna, and it was located on an important road in a valley, as well as being located at the borders of three provinces: Mysia, Lydia, and Phrygia. This made it an important gateway to the east. Xerxes, the Persian king, rested nearby on his way to make war against Europe. In a sense, Philadelphia was a link between two continents. It exists to this day, as the modern city of Alaşehir.

Philadelphia was founded as a Greek city, with the purpose of spreading the Greek language and culture into Lydia and Phrygia—which means that it was a missionary city from the beginning. And it was successful in this commission. The great scholar and traveler William Ramsay reports that Greek had become the language even of the countryside by AD 19—the Lydian tongue being almost entirely forgotten.[1] Philadelphia was so Greek-centered that it came to be called "a little Athens." Similarly, the church there was a small missionary enclave within a dominant surrounding culture of paganism.

One other thing is important about Philadelphia. The valley on the edge of which it sat was volcanic. The soil was rich and therefore well suited to growing grapes, but the area was troubled by earthquakes and tremors. After the earthquake of AD 17, which destroyed Sardis and Philadelphia as well as ten other Asian cities, tremors continued for years and the people never really felt safe in the city afterward. In fact, the majority left Philadelphia and erected their homes in the open spaces outside the city, where they would be safe from collapsing masonry. This is probably the context for Christ's promise to the one who is given entrance to God's city: "Never shall he go out of it" (v. 12).

---

1. See William M. Ramsay, *The Letters to the Seven Churches of Asia: And Their Place in the Plan of the Apocalypse* (London: Hodder and Stoughton, 1904), 391–92.

THE HOLDER OF THE KEY

In his opening words to the church, Jesus describes himself in two ways.

HE IS "THE HOLY ONE, THE TRUE ONE"

Throughout the Bible—and nowhere more than in the book of Revelation—holiness is the distinguishing attribute of God. When God appeared to Moses at the burning bush on Mount Sinai, he told Moses, "Do not come near; take your sandals off your feet, for the place on which you are standing is holy ground" (Ex. 3:5). In Leviticus he told Moses, Aaron, and the people, "Be holy, for I am holy" (Lev. 11:44, 45)—a verse that Peter picked up in his first letter (see 1 Peter 1:15–16). Isaiah heard the seraphim who surround the throne of God singing, "Holy, holy, holy is the LORD of hosts; the whole earth is full of his glory!" (Isa. 6:3). In the chapter of Revelation after this, the living creatures who surround God's throne are likewise constantly singing, "Holy, holy, holy, is the Lord God Almighty, who was and is and is to come" (Rev. 4:8). When Jesus calls himself "holy," he is clearly identifying himself with God, for God alone is holy.

"The true one" is a translation of *alethenos*, which means not true as opposed to false, but something that corresponds to reality as opposed to a mere appearance or show. This is how Jesus used the word in John's gospel when he referred to himself as "the true bread," "the true vine," and so on. He meant that he is the bread that satisfies and the vine that actually nourishes the grapes. However, in Hebrew thought, true also meant trustworthy or faithful—as in Psalm 146:6, which describes God as the one who "keeps faith forever." The word "true" recalls the promises that were made to Israel throughout the Old Testament and indicates that they have now come to faithful fulfillment in the Messiah, Jesus Christ. He is the true or genuine Messiah, as opposed to those who "say that they are Jews and are not, but lie" (Rev. 3:9).

HE "HAS THE KEY OF DAVID"

This phrase is not a direct reference to the vision of Jesus in Revelation 1, as is the case with most of the descriptive phrases in the letters to the other churches—though it does remind us of verse 18 of that chapter, in which Jesus says, "I have the keys of Death and Hades." The phrase is actually a quotation of Isaiah 22:22, in which "the key of the house of David" is assigned to a man named Eliakim, who became chief steward in the house of King Hezekiah. The full text of that verse says, "I will place on his shoulder the key of the house of David. He shall open, and none shall shut; and he shall shut, and none shall open."

In Isaiah, Eliakim replaced a man named Shebna, who was an unfaithful steward, and the fact that he was given the key to the house of David meant that he controlled access to the king. A similar position today might be the chief of staff who arranges the daily schedule for the White House and who thus controls access to the president. This idea of a key and a door establishes the theme of the letter to the church in Philadelphia, in which it appears in four forms: (1) Jesus has opened the door to God's kingdom for the faithful in Philadelphia, because they are saved people (see v. 7); (2) he has set an "open door" of opportunity before them (see v. 8); (3) he will make them pillars in the temple of God, which he has opened (see v. 12); and (4) they will never have to leave God's city (see v. 12). Jesus accomplishes all this because he is the only genuinely faithful steward—both "the holy one" and "the true one" (v. 7).

John Stott calls attention to the fact that, in this verse, the key is in the hand of Christ—not in the hand of Peter, as many Christians mistakenly believe.

> Jesus certainly said to Peter, "I will give you the keys of the kingdom of heaven" (Mt. 16:19). And Peter used them. By his proclamation of the gospel the first Jews were converted on the day of Pentecost. Through the laying on of his hands (with John) the Holy Spirit was given to the first Samaritan believers; and through his ministry the first Gentile, Cornelius the Roman centurion, was born again and baptized. By the use of the keys committed to him Peter opened the Kingdom of heaven to the first Jews, the first Samaritans, and the first Gentiles (Acts 2:14–41; 8:14–17; 10:44–48). But now the keys are back in the hands of Christ, and if men use them at all today it

is only in the secondary sense that they are privileged to preach the gospel through which sinners believe and are saved.[2]

THE OPEN DOOR

In verse 8 Jesus builds on his reference to the door from verse 7; having spoken as the one "who opens and no one will shut, who shuts and no one opens," he now adds, "Behold, I have set before you an open door, which no one is able to shut."

This could mean that he has given the believers in Philadelphia entrance into the kingdom of heaven—which, of course, he has. Quite a few commentators feel that the context demands this interpretation. But this verse might also refer to a special opportunity for preaching the gospel, particularly since the image of an open door is often found with this meaning elsewhere in the New Testament. Paul told the Corinthians that "a wide door for effective work has opened to me" (1 Cor. 16:9) and that when he went to Troas "a door was opened for me in the Lord" (2 Cor. 2:12). He reported to the church in Antioch that God "had opened a door of faith to the Gentiles" (Acts 14:27). Philadelphia was a missionary church in a missionary city. So the promise that Jesus gives is that its witness to him there will be successful.

Still, neither of those ideas exhausts the meaning of this sentence. For when we read that Jesus has opened a door that no one can shut and we realize that the verb is in the perfect tense—meaning that Christ opened the door once and for all and that it stands open today because of that past act—we also realize that it is by his death on the cross for sin that he has opened this door. Most people like open doors—open doors suggest opportunity—whereas closed doors are frustrating. But of all the doors that have ever been or ever will be opened, the greatest of all is the door of salvation that Jesus has opened for all who enter through faith in himself.

The Gospels are filled with invitations to enter by that door.

2. John R. W. Stott, *What Christ Thinks of the Church: Insights from Revelation 2–3* (Grand Rapids: Wm. B. Eerdmans, 1958), 108.

"Come to me, all who labor and are heavy laden, and I will give you rest" (Matt. 11:28). Revelation itself ends on this note: "The Spirit and the Bride say, 'Come.' And let the one who hears say, 'Come.' And let the one who is thirsty come; let the one who desires take the water of life without price" (Rev. 22:17). You may enter through the door that Christ has opened. But be warned: it will not be open forever. One day it will be shut. The day of opportunity will end, and those who have not entered by faith in Jesus Christ will be excluded forever. The women in Christ's parable cried, "Lord, lord, open to us." But Jesus answered, "Truly, I say to you, I do not know you" (Matt. 25:11–12).

Do you find that difficult to believe? That the same Christ who has opened the door of salvation will one day close and lock it? Listen to Jesus's words in Luke 13:24–28.

> Strive to enter through the narrow door. For many, I tell you, will seek to enter and will not be able. When once the master of the house has risen and shut the door, and you begin to stand outside and to knock at the door, saying, "Lord, open to us," then he will answer you, "I do not know where you come from." Then you will begin to say, "We ate and drank in your presence, and you taught in our streets." But he will say, "I tell you, I do not know where you come from. Depart from me, all you workers of evil!" In that place there will be weeping and gnashing of teeth, when you see Abraham and Isaac and Jacob and all the prophets in the kingdom of God but you yourselves cast out.

Jesus is warning that the day of opportunity will not last forever. Therefore, if you are going to believe in Jesus and be saved, you must believe in him now. The Bible says, "Behold, now is the favorable time; behold, now is the day of salvation" (2 Cor. 6:2).

THE FOURFOLD REWARD

It is the pattern of these letters to follow Jesus's identification of himself with words of both commendation and criticism. In the case of this church there is no condemnation. Thus, Jesus follows his praise of the congregation with a fourfold statement of the reward they will receive for being faithful.

THEY WILL PREVAIL OVER OPPOSITION FROM THOSE "WHO SAY THAT THEY ARE JEWS AND ARE NOT" (V. 9)

When Jesus calls the Jews in this city "those of the synagogue of Satan" and adds that they "say that they are Jews and are not, but lie," he may mean that the Jews of Philadelphia had so compromised with the customs of the Greek city that they no longer deserved to be called Jews. The Jewish Talmud itself says things like this. In one place it says that "the wines and the baths of Phrygia have separated the ten tribes from Israel,"[3] meaning that the Jews who had gone into Phrygia had adapted to its way of life so thoroughly that they were no longer truly Israelites.

On the other hand, Jesus may mean that the Jews of Philadelphia were doing Satan's work by persecuting the Christians. Since John, the author of Revelation, is the same person who wrote the gospel that bears his name, it is hard not to interpret what Jesus says in Revelation within the context of a conversation that occurs in John 8 between Jesus and the Jewish leaders—one that makes the very point that they were persecuting the righteous.

Jesus was rebuking the leaders because they were plotting to kill him. He said, "You seek to kill me because my word finds no place in you. I speak of what I have seen with my Father, and you do what you have heard from your father" (John 8:37–38).

Jesus was referring to the devil, of course; and they probably understood him, because they retorted, "Abraham is our father" (v. 39).

Jesus said, "If you were Abraham's children, you would be doing the works Abraham did, but now you seek to kill me, a man who has told you the truth that I heard from God. This is not what Abraham did. You are doing the works your father did" (vv. 39–41).

"We were not born of sexual immorality," they protested. "We have one Father—even God" (v. 41).

---

3. Rabbi Helbo, quoted in the Babylonian Talmud, *Shabbat*, chap. 22, folio 147b.

Jesus then spoke deliberately, saying, "You are of your father the devil, and your will is to do your father's desires. He was a murderer from the beginning" (v. 44). If John has this incident in mind here in Revelation, he is saying that the Jews in Philadelphia were doing the same things to the Christians that the Jews of Jerusalem had done to Jesus Christ. Their persecution of the church was Satan's work. But Jesus had prevailed. He had been raised from the dead, and he is now seated on the throne of heaven. Every knee will bow to Jesus as he sits on that throne. So those who are seated with him there will one day see these very persecutors bow and acknowledge that Jesus has indeed saved and loved his people. This is the promise of Revelation 3:9.

The Jews of John's day expected that the Gentiles would bow before the children of Israel (see Isaiah 45:14; 49:23; 60:14; Zech. 8:20–23). But this is a reversal. Here the promise is that Jews will bow to those Gentiles who have accepted Jesus as Savior, because such Gentiles have become the true Israel by believing in the true Messiah, while those who have rejected the Messiah have thereby repudiated their status as true Jews. As Paul told the Romans, "No one is a Jew who is merely one outwardly, nor is circumcision outward and physical. But a Jew is one inwardly, and circumcision is a matter of the heart, by the Spirit, not by the letter" (Rom. 2:28–29).

THEY WILL BE KEPT "FROM THE HOUR OF TRIAL THAT IS COMING ON THE WHOLE WORLD" (V. 10)

I said in the first study in this book that the troubles to come at the end of history are also seen throughout history, in line with what John says about the Antichrist in 1 John 2:18 ("You have heard that antichrist is coming, so now many antichrists have come"). The church in every age has had trials. But although that is true, this verse refers specifically to the time of especially bad tribulation that is to come in the last days. Indeed, one purpose of Revelation is to describe these trials and to prepare its readers for them. We know that this is the case for two reasons. First, the trials that are spoken of here are trials that are going to come upon "the whole world," not simply upon the church through persecution by unbelievers. Second, they will affect "those who dwell on the earth," and in Revelation this phrase always refers to unbelievers.

This is the first indication in Revelation of the harsh general judgment to come. These particularly harsh judgments have not come yet. Still, tribulations come in lesser ways throughout history, as I have indicated, and it is interesting to note that Jesus did preserve the church in Philadelphia through various trials for many centuries. The city withstood many invasions for more than a thousand years, and although it finally fell to the invading Muslims in the fourteenth century, it is reported that there is still a Christian community in Philadelphia that is presided over by a bishop.

THE ONE WHO CONQUERS WILL BE MADE "A PILLAR IN THE TEMPLE OF MY GOD" (V. 12)

This could be a general promise that the believers in Philadelphia will receive a sure and prepared place in Christ's kingdom. But it may also be a reference to the two pillars Solomon set up in the porch of the great temple that he built. He called the first pillar Jachin, which means "he established," and the second pillar Boaz, which means "in him is strength" (see 1 Kings 7:15–22). If this is what Jesus means, then this is a fitting reward for the faithful in this city. They have been described as having "little power." But they have stood firm in *Christ's* power and are to be made pillars of strength in his kingdom.

THE VICTOR WILL RECEIVE THE "NAME" OF GOD, OF THE CITY OF GOD, AND OF CHRIST (V. 12)

The citizens of Philadelphia knew something about receiving a new name. When their city was destroyed by the same earthquake that had destroyed Sardis and the other ten cities of Asia Minor, they were aided by Tiberius Caesar (who reigned AD 14–37), who had also contributed to the rebuilding of Sardis, and they renamed their city Neocaesarea (the "new city of Caesar") in gratitude to him. Later, when the emperor Vespasian (who reigned AD 69–79) also helped the city, they renamed it Flavia, which was Vespasian's family name. In time the name reverted to Philadelphia.

Believers being given the names of the Father and the Son, and even having them written on their foreheads, occurs again later in Revelation: "Then I looked, and behold, on Mount Zion stood the Lamb, and with him 144,000 who had his name and his Father's name written on their foreheads" (Revelation 14:1). In chapter 7, the name that is written on the foreheads of the 144,000 is referred to as a seal (see vv. 3–4). Similar imagery also occurs in Revelation 22:4, where those who bear the name of God on their foreheads are permitted to see him. Clearly, having the name of the Father written on one's forehead has to do with belonging to God and therefore being safe in him.

Having the name of God's city ("the new Jerusalem"), as well, must mean something similar. It refers to a person's citizenship in Zion. It indicates that, like Abraham, we have looked "to the city that has foundations, whose designer and builder is God" (Heb. 11:10) and that we now have a secure place in that eternal city of God.

What is Christ's "new name"? This is one of those many points on which the book of Revelation explains itself. Christ's new name is revealed in Revelation 19:16. There Jesus is presented as a rider on a white horse—clearly as a conqueror—and we are told that "on his robe and on his thigh he has a name written, King of kings and Lord of lords." If the believers in Philadelphia are to be given this new name, it is because they have conquered in life and are now to reign with Christ.

THE CHALLENGE

Finally, having acknowledged the faithfulness of this small church—that it had kept Christ's word and not denied his name (see Rev. 3:8)—and having spoken of four great rewards for the people because of their faithfulness, Jesus offers a challenge: "Hold fast what you have, so that no one may seize your crown" (v. 11).

And do you know something? They did. Edward Gibbon, the author of *The History of the Decline and Fall of the Roman Empire*, blamed Christianity for the collapse of Rome's great empire, which he loved. But in a remarkable passage toward the end of that great masterpiece, he wrote about the cities that are addressed in Revelation and noted this about them:

> In the loss of Ephesus, the Christians deplored the fall of the first angel, the extinction of the first candlestick of the Revelations; the desolation is complete; and the temple of Diana or the church of Mary will equally elude the search of the curious traveler. The circus and three stately theaters of Laodicea are now peopled with wolves and foxes; Sardis is reduced to a miserable village; the God of Mahomet, without a rival or a son, is invoked in the mosques of Thyatira and Pergamum; and the populousness of Smyrna is supported by the foreign trade of the Franks and Armenians. Philadelphia alone has been saved by prophecy, or courage. At a distance from the sea, forgotten by the emperors, encompassed on all sides by the Turks, her valiant citizens defended their religion and freedom above fourscore years, and at length capitulated with the proudest of the Ottomans. Among the Greek colonies and churches of Asia, Philadelphia is still erect, a column in a scene of ruins: a pleasing example that the paths of honor and safety may sometimes be the same.[4]

How does a Christian measure success? I gave one answer at the beginning of this study, which was based on verse 8: "you have kept my word and have not denied my name." But that is only one way of looking at the question. There is another answer, too: success means still standing when the battles of life are over, or when Jesus comes again.

I have always remembered a line from the first of the many popular *Rocky* movies. Because of a promotional fluke, Philadelphia's Rocky Balboa has been brought out of oblivion and given a chance to fight the heavyweight champion of the world, Apollo Creed. No one thinks that Rocky has a chance—and neither does he, really, although he loses the fight in the end only by a close decision. But

---

4. Edward Gibbon, *The History of the Decline and Fall of the Roman Empire* (Norwalk, CT: Easton Press, 1974), 6:2230.

Rocky takes the challenge seriously and goes into rigorous training. He gives it everything he has. Yet as the day of the fight draws near, in a reflective mood, he confides to his girlfriend, "I can't beat him. . . . All I want to do is go the distance."[5] Rocky means that he just wants to last all fifteen rounds of the fight without getting knocked out sooner.

That is not a bad approach for Christians. How do you measure success? One way is just to go the distance. Jesus Christ says, "Hold on! Don't give up! Don't let anyone take your crown! And remember, I am coming soon!" Can you remember that? Can you hang on? Jesus doesn't ask for heroics. He just wants those who are his to persevere. But to those who do persevere, who endure to the end, he promises his own new name—the name of a conqueror—and a crown of glory that will never tarnish or be snatched away.

5. "I Can't Beat Him," *Rocky*, directed by John G. Avildsen (1976; Beverly Hills, CA: Metro-Goldwyn-Mayer Studios, 2006), DVD.

12

TO THE CHURCH IN LAODICEA

Revelation 3:14–22

Doors have an interesting feature: they can be opened to let someone either in or out, or they can be shut to keep someone from getting either out or in. We see both these uses for doors in the last two letters of Jesus to the churches. In the case of Philadelphia, Jesus had set an open door before the church. It signified an entrance into Christ's kingdom and a door of missionary opportunity. It was a door that no one could shut (see Rev. 3:8). In the case of Laodicea, however, the church had closed the door of their fellowship to keep Christ out (see v. 20). It was a door that the church itself needed to throw open.

Christ's letter to the church in Philadelphia contained no criticism. That letter was a bright high point in this collection. Sadly, his letter to the church in Laodicea contains no praise. Laodicea was a church that was self-satisfied and complacent—and what was worse is that it was not even aware of its condition. The comic strip philosopher Pogo famously said, "We have met the enemy, and he is us."[1] That was true of the Laodicean church. They themselves were the enemy. No mention is made in this letter of persecution from the Roman authorities or the Jews, nor of the pernicious influence of false teachers. Everything seemed to be going along quite well in Laodicea. The problem with this church was its own spiritually complacent, sinful state. At least Pogo said that he had "met the enemy."

1. Walt Kelly, *Pogo*, April 22, 1971.

The believers in Laodicea had not met the enemy, because they did not know that they *were* the enemy.

Jesus called the church in Laodicea lukewarm. Is that not a fair assessment of many churches today? John Stott thought so. "Perhaps none of the seven letters is more appropriate to the twentieth-century church than this. It describes vividly the respectable, sentimental, nominal, skin-deep religiosity which is so widespread today. Our Christianity is flabby and anemic. We appear to have taken a lukewarm bath of religion."[2]

THE CITY OF LAODICEA

Laodicea was located about forty-five miles southeast of Philadelphia and about a hundred miles east and slightly south of Ephesus. It lay in the Lycus valley, along with Hierapolis and Colossae. It had been founded in about the middle of the third century BC by Antiochus II (who reigned 261–246 BC) to guard the way to Phrygia and had been settled with Syrians and Jews from Babylon. Antiochus had named the city after his wife, Laodice.

A number of features of the city color Jesus's words to this church. For one thing, Laodicea was located near an area of hot springs, though it did not have a good water supply itself. Water had to be brought into the city, from a town that today is called Denizli, through a six-mile-long aqueduct—which meant that the water was lukewarm by the time it got to Laodicea. A famous school of medicine was also located there—one that produced, among other things, a remedy for weak eyes. We call the substance *collyrium*; they called it "Phrygian powder." The Laodiceans also raised sheep that produced a soft, black wool. It was woven into highly prized black cloth and carpets.

Most of all, Laodicea was famous for its wealth. It lay at the meeting point of three great highways, and although it had a slow beginning, it had grown into a prosperous trading and financial

2. John R. W. Stott, *What Christ Thinks of the Church: Insights from Revelation 2–3* (Grand Rapids: Wm. B. Eerdmans, 1958), 116.

center under Roman rule. Laodicea was the home of bankers, traders, and millionaires. The citizens had received help from the government to rebuild their city after the earthquake of AD 17, which had also destroyed Sardis and Philadelphia. But four decades later, Laodicea had become so proud of its wealth that it declined government aid when it was destroyed by the earthquake of AD 61. Tacitus wrote, "One of the famous cities of Asia, Laodicea, was that same year overthrown by an earthquake, and, without any relief from us, recovered itself by its own resources."[3] When Cicero was on his way to govern an Asiatic province in 51 BC, he cashed large bank drafts in Laodicea, as he reports in two of his surviving letters.

The church in Laodicea, along with churches in Hierapolis and Colossae, must have been founded during Paul's two-year ministry in Ephesus (which is described in Acts 19:10), though not by Paul himself. The church was probably founded by his colleague Epaphras, who is commended in Colossians 4:12–13 for his hard work among the Christians of these cities. Paul considered Laodicea to be part of his mission field (see Col. 2:1) and asked the Colossians to convey greetings to the believers there, among whom were "Nympha and the church in her house" (Col. 4:15). He says that he wrote a letter to this church (see Col. 4:16), but it has been lost—unless it was a copy of the letter to the Ephesians, as some scholars hold.

By the time John wrote Revelation, the spiritual condition of the church in Laodicea had deteriorated badly. The church members had become just like the people around them. They had the same proud attitude. They thought that their wealth was proof of God's special favor toward them. Worst of all, they had no awareness of their sin. They did not think that they needed to repent—because, well, they were doing just fine. The church in Sardis was described as nearly dead, but at least it had a remnant of faithful believers. No remnant is mentioned in the church in Laodicea. What Jesus tells the Christians in Laodicea is that he is disgusted with them. They make him sick. He is ready to spit them out.

3. *The Annals of Tacitus*, trans. Alfred John Church and William Jackson Brodribb (London, 1876), bk. 14.27.

JESUS'S SELF-DESCRIPTION

What terrible language! Anyone who has read Dale Carnegie's best-selling self-improvement book, *How to Win Friends and Influence People*, knows that you do not get people to do what you want by criticizing them—least of all in language like this. But Jesus does criticize this church. What is more, he begins this letter by insisting that his evaluation of the church is right, because he is "the Amen, the faithful and true witness, the beginning of God's creation" (Rev. 3:14).

These descriptive phrases do not call back to the vision of the risen Christ that John reports in Revelation 1, but the words "faithful witness" are found in John's own introduction of Jesus in verse 5 of that chapter. Jesus is the one who told "the truth, the whole truth, and nothing but the truth" in his trial before Pilate and who continues to speak the truth today—however painful it may be. Here his witness is called both "faithful and true."

"Amen" is a common word that means "truly" or "so be it," and it is regularly used to express assent or agreement. It occurs many times throughout the Bible—ten times in the book of Revelation alone. Only twice is it used as a name, however—here and in Isaiah 65:16: "He who blesses himself in the land shall bless himself by the God of truth." The Hebrew text of that final phrase is literally "the God of the Amen." Therefore, when Jesus calls himself "the Amen, the faithful and true witness," he is not only stressing the total truthfulness and reliability of whatever he says but also joining himself to God the Father as the entirely faithful one. Paul incorporates a somewhat similar use of "amen" into 2 Corinthians 1:20: "For all the promises of God find their Yes in him. That is why it is through him that we utter our Amen to God for his glory."

"The beginning of God's creation" stresses Jesus's role as the source of and Lord over all created things—and above all, over the church, which is God's new creation. Paul uses the same word "beginning" in Colossians 1:18, where he says of Jesus: "He is the head of the body, the church. He is the beginning, the firstborn from the dead, that in everything he might be preeminent."

JESUS'S ASSESSMENT OF THE CHURCH

We need to look carefully at Jesus's evaluation of the church in Laodicea and ask, What is it that makes the Lord sick? Strikingly, it is not what we might expect. He was not disgusted with them because of some false doctrine—as dangerous as false doctrine is. He was not disgusted because they had fallen into idolatry or compromised with the morality of the pagan culture around them. He was not disgusted because they had left their first love. These things are bad, of course; he challenges the other churches in these areas. But that is not what made him sick. What made Jesus sick was that the people in the church were lukewarm, that they were sinfully self-satisfied, and that they were oblivious to their impoverished condition.

1. THEY WERE LUKEWARM

Jesus says,

> I know your works: you are neither cold nor hot. Would that you were either cold or hot! So, because you are lukewarm, and neither hot nor cold, I will spit you out of my mouth. (Rev. 3:15–16)

The nearby city of Hierapolis had well-known medicinal hot springs. The nearby city of Colossae had pure, cold, drinkable water. Laodicea had bad water, and when it tried to bring water in through the aqueduct from modern-day Denizli, all it could get was tepid water. This may be the background for these words. But we do not need that kind of archeological trivia in order to get Christ's point. The church in Smyrna was hot—flaming with zeal. The church in Sardis was cold, as a corpse is cold. Laodicea was neither hot nor cold. It was alive, but sadly apathetic. It was like the character in *Pilgrim's Progress* whom Bunyan called "Mr. Facing Both Ways." Christian? Yes, but not passionately. The church in Laodicea was perfectly able to get along with the world around it. It was what a man once called another dispassionate person: "as insipid as the white of an egg." Some students of Revelation have trouble understanding how Jesus can say that he would rather the church be cold than merely indifferent, as if that were better. But, of course, it is better. A dead church can always be resurrected. A cold church can be challenged. But what do you do with a church that is merely lukewarm? It is hard to do anything with such people. The only thing Jesus seems able to do is to spit them out and start again.

How could a body of believers who knew the greatest news that the world has ever heard become indifferent to that gospel or lukewarm in living it out? There can be only one explanation. They had drifted so far from Christ that they had lost the joy of their salvation. How unnecessary! How tragic! Yes—but how true of many churches and professing Christians in our day, as well. They may be Christians, but they have no zeal for Christ or for winning lost persons to the Savior.

2. THEY WERE SELF-SATISFIED

This goes along with their lukewarm condition, for the reason that they were lukewarm is that they were blissfully content as they were. They thought they had everything they could possibly want and had achieved everything that could reasonably be expected of them. Jesus describes their condition when he says, "For you say, I am rich, I have prospered, and I need nothing" (v. 17). Was their boast in material wealth or spiritual riches? No doubt it was in both. The Christians in Laodicea had prospered materially, and (as rich people often do) they supposed that their happy state was due to their own inherent superiority—in their case, spiritual superiority. "God must be pleased with us, because we are doing so well," was their thinking.

3. THEY WERE IGNORANT OF THEIR TRUE CONDITION

Jesus says that the Laodiceans did not realize that they were "wretched, pitiable, poor, blind, and naked" (v. 17). In all the Bible I do not think there is a more comprehensive, devastating denunciation of an alleged people of God than this short sentence. These people thought they were exceedingly blessed—they were rich and prospering. But they were actually wretched. They thought they were so well off that they should be envied—that the whole world should strive to be like them. But Jesus says they were actually to be pitied. They thought they were rich—spiritually as well as materially. They were like Israel in the Old Testament days, about whom Hosea wrote, "Ephraim has said, 'Ah, but I am rich; I have found wealth for myself; in all my labors they cannot find in me iniquity or sin'" (Hos. 12:8). But the believers in Laodicea were actually poor in the things of God. They also thought they were spiritually perceptive—"a guide to the blind, a light to those who are in darkness, an instructor of the foolish, a teacher of children" (Rom. 2:19–20). But they were blind even to their own debased condition. They thought they were clothed in righteousness and good deeds. But they were spiritually stripped before God.

JESUS'S COUNSEL TO THE CHURCH

What is Jesus going to say to people like this? He is disgusted with them. He is about to spit them out of his mouth (see Rev. 3:16). But surprisingly, after he has explained their state and how he sees them, instead of speaking harshly he stoops to offer counsel. And the reason he offers them counsel is, as he explains in verse 19, because he loves them. For all their failures, this is nevertheless a church composed of his people, whom he loves and wants to bring to repentance.

His words are remarkably gentle. These self-satisfied materialists disgust him, but he still speaks tenderly to them, advising them to buy "gold refined by fire" so that they can become truly rich, "white garments" to cover their shameful nakedness, and "salve" to put on their eyes so that they can see (v. 18).

Refined gold is a biblical image for a life that has been purified from sin or a faith that has been strengthened through suffering. Job 23:10 says, "But he knows the way that I take; when he has tried me, I shall come out as gold." Malachi uses the image to describe God's work of judgment. He asks, in words that are well known to us through Handel's *Messiah*, "But who can endure the day of his coming, and who can stand when he appears? For he is like a refiner's fire and like fullers' soap. He will sit as a refiner and purifier of silver, and he will purify the sons of Levi and refine them like gold

145

and silver" (Mal. 3:2–3). Peter also speaks of the faith of believers being purified in this manner.

> In this you rejoice, though now for a little while, if necessary, you have been grieved by various trials, so that the tested genuineness of your faith—more precious than gold that perishes though it is tested by fire—may be found to result in praise and glory and honor at the revelation of Jesus Christ. (1 Peter 1:6–7)

"White garments" convey the same idea. White stands for purity and the reward of living for Christ. A white garment was promised to the faithful in Sardis, because they had not "soiled their garments" (Rev. 3:4). Later in Revelation we find this counsel, which is obviously from Jesus himself: "Behold, I am coming like a thief! Blessed is the one who stays awake, keeping his garments on, that he may not go about naked and be seen exposed" (16:15).

Finally, "salve to anoint your eyes, so that you may see" is a picture of the healing we need so that our natural spiritual blindness can be cured. The words remind us of the blind man of John 9, who received sight when his eyes were anointed by Jesus (see vv. 1–7). He was only a poor, blind beggar. He had no claim on Jesus at all. But when Jesus restored his sight, the man began to grow in spiritual vision, calling Jesus first "the man" (v. 11), then "a prophet" (v. 17), thirdly a man "from God" (v. 33), and finally "Lord"—at which point "he worshiped him" (v. 38). That is the healing we need, as well, if we are to have the spiritual sight that enables us to repent of our sin and come to Christ. John Newton, the former slave trader turned preacher, was as spiritually blind as anyone could be. But after he was converted, he wrote of his experience,

> Amazing grace! How sweet the sound
> That saved a wretch like me!
> I once was lost, but now am found,
> Was blind, but now I see.[4]

4. John Newton, "Amazing Grace," 1779.

146

JESUS'S TENDER APPEAL

What would get this church of self-satisfied, blind materialists to come to Jesus for the gold of upright character, the white garments of personal righteousness, and the salve that would enable them to see? Not Christ's counsel alone. People receive good counsel every day and yet pay no attention to it. If anything would draw them to Christ, it would be apprehending what Jesus says next: "Those whom I love, I reprove and discipline" (Rev. 3:19). What draws us is Christ's love. But notice that this is a love expressed not in indifference—which was the sin of the Laodicean church—but rather in honest rebuke and discipline. This verse is a close quotation of Proverbs 3:12, which says that "the LORD reproves him whom he loves." It is because Jesus loves us that he prods us to repent.

And to be zealous! The New International Version translates this part of Revelation 3:19 as "be earnest," which is right, but it obscures the unique sense of the word in this letter. The Greek word is *zeleue*, from which we get our words "zeal," "zealous," and "zealot." The literal meaning is to be "hot" or "boiling"—the exact thing that these lukewarm believers were not. They needed to be heated up if they were to please Christ. They needed to be zealous in serving him.

There is a story about a village atheist in a small Tennessee town who was never known to go to church. His name was Uncle George. While the Christians were in church on Sunday or for a midweek meeting, he would sit in front of the village store and whittle small wood figures and ridicule the church. One day, the church caught fire. There was no fire department in the village, so the people formed a bucket brigade and Uncle George pitched in. He was actually at the head of the line throwing water on the flames. The pastor said, "This is the first time I ever saw you at church, George."

"Yes," George said, "but this is the first time I ever saw a church on fire."[5]

---

5. J. Ralph Grant, *Letters to the Seven Churches and Other Sermons* (Grand Rapids: Baker Book House, 1962), 72–73.

When we get on fire for Jesus Christ, the world will begin to listen to us and some people will be saved.

OUTSIDE THE FAST-CLOSED DOOR

Revelation 3:20 is often used wrongly as an evangelistic text. It is used to picture Jesus standing helplessly at the door of the sinner's heart and begging to come in. Conversion is not like that; Jesus accomplishes conversion by using the preaching of his Word to bring the dead sinner to life and draw the antagonistic rebel to himself. But here Jesus is standing outside the door and is knocking. He is knocking at the closed hearts of those who are his but who have turned their backs on him and shut him out of their complacent, self-satisfied, worldly Christian lives. This is an image not of calling unbelievers to give their hearts to him but of calling drifting, worldly believers to sincere repentance and renewal. Steve Gregg rightly says, "Familiar as an evangelistic text for sinners, this verse, in context, actually expresses Christ's feeling of being an outsider from his own church, desiring to be invited back in."[6]

I have been in many churches from which Christ has been locked out. The people inside have found him to be too honest, too disturbing, too commanding, too holy for their worldly, compromising state. Are you like that? Are you a Christian who has shut the door on Jesus Christ because you do not want him to intrude? Because you are satisfied with your insipid, sinful, worldly life and do not want to change it?

Perhaps you have seen a copy of the painting by Holman Hunt that hangs in St. Paul's Cathedral in London. In this painting, Jesus stands by a closed door. Its hinges are rusty. There is no handle on the outside of the door. Vines cover its side posts and lintel. Jesus's hand is poised in the air, uplifted and ready to knock. Many stories have been told about this picture, but here is one that is to the point. A little girl stood with her father, looking at the picture

6. Steve Gregg, ed., *Revelation: Four Views; A Parallel Commentary* (Nashville: Thomas Nelson, 1997), 80.

very seriously. She was deeply moved. Finally she asked, "Daddy, did he ever get in?"[7] It was a very good question. Apparently Jesus did not get into the church in Laodicea, for it soon ceased to be. If you are shutting Jesus out, will he ever get in to eat and fellowship with you?

In the letter to the church in Thyatira, Christ's appeal was to a remnant (see Rev. 2:24). In Sardis there were still "a few" who were faithful (see Rev. 3:4). Here the appeal is to "anyone" (see Rev. 3:20). It is to the individual believer. It is to you.

THE PROMISE

In John's vision in Revelation 1, Jesus is seen standing in the midst of the lampstands that represent the seven churches (see v. 13). In the vision that is to come in chapters 4 and 5, he is pictured as a Lamb standing before the Father's throne (see 5:6). Here he is seen as one who is seated with the Father on his throne and who offers the right to sit with him to all who heed his words and overcome. The important fact is that he is already enthroned. The promise is that those who overcome in this life will reign with him in his kingdom.

The final exhortation, as in the other churches' letters, is to hear what the Spirit is saying. Will you hear it? Will you alter your life as a result?

Bishop Francis J. McConnell once painted a word picture of the Boxer Rebellion in China, in which hundreds of Chinese Christians were martyred. He pictured them kneeling with their heads on the execution blocks and the executioners standing with drawn swords in their hands. All the Christians needed to do in order to escape death was to grunt a mere word, indicating that they were willing to recant their Christianity. "What would I have done under those circumstances?" the bishop asked himself. Then he answered, "I speak not only personally but in a representative capacity, for I think the rest of you are very much like myself. With my head on the block I

7. Grant, *Letters to the Seven Churches*, 75.

think I should have said, 'Hold on! I think I can make a statement that will be satisfactory to both sides.'"[8]

Christians have probably taken that approach in every age. But that is exactly what makes Christ sick. Don't let it be true of you. Don't live a lukewarm Christian life. Get on fire for Christ now. Love him. Invite him in. And serve him while you can.

8. Grant, 66.

13

How Worship
Should Be Done

Revelation 4:1–8

I want to describe an extraordinary worship service for you. It took place on a day that had been set apart as a festival for worshiping God. There had been a miracle, which was the occasion for this special worship time, and the leader of the congregation had planned everything carefully. The people rose early, offered sacrifices, and then enjoyed what we might call a fellowship meal. Everyone took part. They were so involved in their worship that they began to dance before God. It was a very special time. Does that sound like anything you have ever heard of or witnessed? There is a lot of worship like that today.

The only problem is that the worship I have just been describing was the worship of the golden calf by Israel while Moses was on the mountain receiving the law from God, and this worship provoked God's anger. God told Moses, "Let me alone, that my wrath may burn hot against them and I may consume them" (Ex. 32:10).

Clearly not everything that is called worship pleases God! Many sincere churchgoing contemporary people suppose that we can do whatever occurs to us as long as it is fervent enough, appeals to the masses, or is sufficiently inventive. But if we take the story of the golden calf seriously—as we must—we must also understand that not only do some kinds of worship fail to please God, but some even provoke him to wrath.

This is a view of the throne in heaven - not the entire creation

Where do we learn to worship? Where do we learn what kind of worship pleases God? We can learn this from many Bible passages, of course—among them, and high on the list, is that magnificent collection of praise songs that we know as the Psalms. But surely there is no passage of the Bible that better shows us how worship should be done than the fourth and fifth chapters of Revelation, which open a door into heaven and give us a glimpse of the entire creation joining in praise of the triune God. In the first part of chapter 4, which we are looking at in this study, four living creatures praise God day and night, saying, "Holy, holy, holy, is the Lord God Almighty, who was and is and is to come" (v. 8)..

But you mock this setting on pg 154 ...

A DOOR STANDING OPEN IN HEAVEN

Revelation 4 begins with a picture of "a door standing open in heaven" and with a voice calling to John, saying, "Come up here, and I will show you what must take place after this" (v. 1). This is the third door mentioned so far in Revelation. The first was the door that Jesus said he had opened for the believers in Philadelphia—"an open door, which no one is able to shut" (3:8). It was a door of opportunity. The second was the door that the believers in Laodicea seem to have closed against Christ. Jesus pictured himself standing before the door and knocking (see 3:20). Now there is a door that is opened into heaven, and John is invited to "come up" and be shown the first of the visions that form the heart of this book. This third door is the door of revelation. It is God's revelation to John, and it is John's purpose to take us through that door to see life and the troubling episodes of history from the divine perspective.

This is the point at which the various interpretations of Revelation begin to diverge—and understandably so, since there are many questions that any thoughtful commentator must raise from this point forward. For example, what does the imagery of the visions signify? When are these things supposed to occur? How does John use the passages that he seems to have drawn from the Old Testament? Does he use them in their original Old Testament sense, or does he reinterpret them? What is symbolic? What is literal? One helpful hint

What has happened is 152 repeated. There are types which must be fulfilled.

about how we should proceed is found in Hebrews 9:23, which says that the parts of the earthly tabernacle were "copies of the heavenly things." This phrase suggests that we can apply some of what we are told about Israel's earthly worship to what we are shown of the heavenly worship in Revelation.

There is one interpretation of these verses that we ought to handle right away, and that is the view of dispensationalists, who see John's being taken up into heaven as a picture of the supposed rapture of the church before the tribulation. J. A. Seiss is quite dogmatic at this point, though not all dispensationalists are as certain as he is.[1] John Walvoord admits that the rapture is not explicitly taught in this passage, though he finds it represented as a type.[2] Why should dispensationalists see John's being taken up into heaven in this light?

The obvious reason is that dispensationalists are committed to the idea of a rapture for other reasons, even before they get to Revelation, and this is the best place for them to insert it. They interpret the letters of chapters 2 and 3 as a preview of the history of the church and the judgments of chapters 6 through 16 as that final period of intense tribulation from which most of them believe the church will be delivered. They argue that "after this" means "after the church age."

But there is no reason to interpret any of these words in that way. John's experience of being caught up to heaven is not the rapture of the saints—even assuming that there is such a thing as a rapture. This experience is his alone, meaning that he alone is given the revelation that he is now communicating to us. Again, "after this" does not carry such a heavy weight of chronology. The phrase occurs again and again in Revelation (see Rev. 7:9; 15:5; 18:1; 19:1; 20:3) and most often refers merely to a sequence of disclosures. In chapter 4, all that it indicates is that after John received the letters to the seven churches, he heard a voice summoning him to the vision of chapters

---

1. See J. A. Seiss, *The Apocalypse: Lectures on the Book of Revelation* (1900; repr., Grand Rapids: Zondervan, 1970), 87, 95–101. "That door opened in heaven is the door of the ascension of the saints" (p. 96).

2. See John F. Walvoord, *The Revelation of Jesus Christ* (Chicago: Moody Press, 1966), 103.

4 and 5. That is, this is a sequence of John's experiences, not of his-torical events.[3] *But John's experiences are historical events*

We have to remember the purpose of Revelation: to show us everything from God's point of view. The throne-room vision of chapters 4 and 5 is to remind believers at all times and in all places that the holy, omnipotent, and omniscient God is in control of his-tory. Moreover, since this is also a worship scene, it tells us that because God is in control of all things, we and all the creation must make it our primary activity and duty to worship him.

No. It is to make known

A THRONE AND THRONES IN HEAVEN

What John sees, when he is "in the Spirit" and is caught up to pass through the door that has been opened into heaven, is the throne of God Almighty. The word *throne* occurs more than a dozen times in these two chapters and about forty times in Revelation over-all. God's throne is mentioned in every chapter of the book except chapters 2, 8, and 9. What a magnificent scene! What an amazing revelation! It seems to have inspired George Frederick Handel to write his great musical masterpiece, the *Messiah*—for when the great composer was asked how he had come to write the oratorio, he sup-posedly answered, "I saw heaven opened and God upon his great white throne."

God is Spirit

We need to be careful about assuming that this is a literal description, however. For one thing, what John is sharing with us is a vision—something like a dream—and dreams are not usually to be interpreted literally. If this were not a dream, then it would be necessary to imagine a literal, material throne in heaven, with a physical Deity seated upon it, surrounded by twenty-four other literal thrones, as well as to imagine that Jesus, who is introduced as part of the scene in the next chapter, actually looks like a lamb with seven horns and seven eyes. That is absurd, of course, and we realize

Why burden the text w/ an overlay of philoso assumptions that are not biblical. This is demeaning to the word of God. The Word is always worthy of honor, especially from those in

3. For a sound critique of the dispensationalists' interpretation of Revelation 4:1, see Craig S. Keener, *Revelation*, The NIV Application Commentary (Grand Rapids: Zonder-van, 2000), 177–79.

his house.

it as soon as we state the problem this way. What these chapters are actually doing is describing the universe from the aspect of heaven. William Hendriksen says, "The purpose of this vision is to show us, in beautiful symbolism, that all things are governed by the Lord on the throne."[4]

Remember the flow of the book. We have witnessed the condition of the church on earth, where weak and very human believers are struggling for Christ amid temptations from the world, the flesh, and the devil. What is their future? Will they triumph? Or will they be defeated? To show us the outcome, John is now lifted to heaven, where we see the almighty God upon his throne. The recipients of his letter who are threatened by the shadow of Caesar's throne are to know that there is a greater throne than Caesar's and that the path of history is determined by him who turns even the hearts of kings to do his will (see Prov. 21:1). *The one who sits on the throne is your LORD and your God.*

THE THRONE OF GOD (VV. 2–3, 5–6)

John does not describe God, because God cannot be described (see Ex. 20:4). All he says is that he saw someone "seated on the throne" (Rev. 4:2). This is God himself, of course, and all John can say about him is that he "had the appearance of jasper and carnelian" (v. 3). Jasper is an unknown stone (though we have a stone called jasper today), but since it is later said to be as clear as crystal (see Rev. 21:11), it is likely to be identified as a diamond. Carnelian is a deep red–colored jewel. There is no point in trying to find special significance in these colors. John is simply using the image of valuable stones to suggest God's radiance or glory.

There are several more descriptive features of God's throne. First, it is surrounded by "a rainbow that had the appearance of an emerald" (Rev. 4:3). An emerald is green, which is not the color one that would normally attribute to a rainbow. A rainbow is usually thought of as having many colors. Nor does green have any special significance here. And the only biblical significance of the rainbow is that

---

4. William Hendriksen, *More Than Conquerors: An Interpretation of the Book of Revelation* (Grand Rapids: Baker Book House, 1940), 84.

it was the sign of the covenant that God made with Noah following the great flood of Genesis 6–9. It signifies a covenant of grace (see Gen. 9:12–17), and its reappearance in Revelation—coming at the very end of the Bible, as it did at the beginning—indicates that God is eternally the same. He is and always has been a covenant-making, covenant-keeping God.

"Flashes of lightning, and rumblings and peals of thunder" (Rev. 4:5) move us from the first book of the Bible to the second, as they recall the appearance of God on Mount Sinai in the days of Moses (see Ex. 19:16). These words appear again, almost unchanged, in Revelation 8:5; 11:19; and 16:18—in each case at the conclusion of a series of judgments. This is meant to be awe-inspiring and frightening. It is a reminder that God is holy and that evil and those who practice it will be judged.

The sea of glass (see Rev. 4:6) is the heavenly model for the laver in Solomon's temple (2 Chron. 4:2–6), though even before the temple, the elders in Moses's day saw something like this as well (see Ex. 24:10–11). It is mentioned again in Revelation 15:2. Some modern commentators view the sea in terms of the Babylonian creation myth, in which it represents evil and the source of evil—but in spite of the fact that the beast emerges out of the sea later in Revelation, there is no reason to think of any pagan myth here. John is not drawing from the world of ancient myth at all. He is drawing on images from the Old Testament, and in the Old Testament the laver was used for purification by the priests who served in the temple. The reason the sea is described as being like "a sea of glass, like crystal" is probably because there will be no need for purification in heaven, since all who enter heaven will have been saved from and cleansed of all sin. Later, John will write of the heavenly city, "Nothing unclean will ever enter it, nor anyone who does what is detestable or false, but only those who are written in the Lamb's book of life" (Rev. 21:27).

TWENTY-FOUR THRONES AND TWENTY-FOUR ELDERS (V. 4)

Who are the elders? There are countless theories about who they might be, which range from identifying them as angels to saying that they represent the twenty-four priestly rotations under the Old Testament temple system. The most obvious view is that they represent the entire people of God, under both the old and new dispensations, with the number twenty-four coming from a combination of the twelve patriarchs of Israel and the twelve apostles—much as the patriatchs and apostles are represented by the twelve foundations and twelve gates of the heavenly Jerusalem that are described in Revelation 21:12–14.

The way that the elders are pictured makes them a natural link with and follow-up to the promise that was given to the churches in the previous two chapters—that the one who conquers will reign with Jesus on his throne. White garments signify the elders' holiness, for they are now in glory. Crowns symbolize their victory over sin. Similarly, Jesus told the church in Sardis, "The one who conquers will be clothed thus in white garments" (Rev. 3:5) and told the believers in Laodicea, "The one who conquers, I will grant him to sit with me on my throne, as I also conquered and sat down with my Father on his throne" (v. 21).

There is an expanding picture of the heavenly worshipers throughout Revelation 4 and 5: first, the twenty-four elders and four living creatures; second, innumerable angels; and finally, "every creature in heaven and on earth and under the earth and in the sea, and all that is in them" (5:13). But the elders, who represent the church, are mentioned first (see 4:4) and last (see 5:14), since they alone are able to testify to the grace that God showed in their redemption.

THE FOUR LIVING CREATURES

One of the most striking pictures in Revelation is the description of the "four living creatures." We read, "Around the throne, on each side of the throne, are four living creatures, full of eyes in front and behind: the first living creature like a lion, the second living creature like an ox, the third living creature with the face of a man, and the fourth living creature like an eagle in flight. And the four living creatures, each of them with six wings, are full of eyes all around and within" (Rev. 4:6–8). There are variations within the details, but these must be the same creatures that Isaiah observed during his vision of heaven that is recorded in Isaiah 6, in which the prophet calls them *seraphim*, and that appear in Ezekiel 1:4–25 and 10:1–22, where they are called *cherubim*.

William Hendriksen notes the following parallels between the creatures in Revelation and the creatures, or cherubim, in Ezekiel:

- There are four of them (Ezek. 1:5; Rev. 4:6).
- They are called "living creatures" (Ezek. 1:5; Rev. 4:6).
- They are compared to a man, a lion, an ox, and an eagle (Ezek. 1:10; Rev. 4:7).[5]
- They are connected with the throne (Ezek. 1:26; Rev. 4:6).
- Fire moves to and fro among them (Ezek. 1:13; Rev. 4:5).
- They are covered with eyes (Ezek. 1:18; 10:12; Rev. 4:8).
- A rainbow circles the throne (Ezek. 1:28; Rev. 4:3).[6]

Lucifer was one of these exalted cherubim before he fell and became Satan.

THE WORSHIP OF THE FOUR LIVING CREATURES

The first of the five worship hymns in these two chapters (which are found in Rev. 4:8, 11; 5:9–10, 12, 13)[7] is the song of the four living creatures that is recorded in verse 8. As we saw with the worshipers themselves, who expand from the elders and the four living

5. The church fathers linked these creatures to the four gospel writers in various ways but without exegetical support. Athanasius had Matthew as the man (representing Christ in his humanity), Mark as the ox (picturing Christ as a servant), Luke as the lion (emphasizing Christ as King), and John as the eagle (portraying Christ as God). Victorinus had Matthew as the man, Mark as the lion, Luke as the ox, and John as the eagle. Augustine suggested Matthew as the lion, Mark as the man, Luke as the ox, and John as the eagle. Augustine's system corresponds most closely to the actual emphases of the Gospels, so his view gradually prevailed.

6. See Hendriksen, *More Than Conquerors*, 86–87.

7. It is the first not only of these five hymns but also of many more throughout the book—see Revelation 7:10, 12, 15–17; 11:15, 17–18; 12:10–12; 15:3–4; 16:5–7; 18:2–8; 19:1–8.

creatures to the angels and eventually to "every creature in heaven and on earth" (5:13), there is also a progression within these hymns. The first two are addressed to God the Father, first as the holy and eternal God, then as the Creator. The next two hymns are addressed to Jesus Christ, the Lamb, first as the Redeemer of mankind, then as the one who is supremely worthy to receive all "power and wealth and wisdom and might and honor and glory and blessing" (v. 12). The last hymn is addressed to both the Father and the Son—"To him who sits on the throne and to the Lamb" (v. 13).

The first hymn, the song of the four living creatures, is a clear and obvious echo of what Isaiah heard in the similar vision that is recorded in Isaiah 6: "Holy, holy, holy is the LORD of hosts; the whole earth is full of his glory!" (v. 3).

What is the point of these hymns? I have already said that they show how worship should be done by focusing on the worship of those created beings who are in heaven. But they also show the meaning of this vision of God being seated on the heavenly throne. They show that he is the utterly exalted one, that he is the focal point and ultimate object of the entire creation—of all he has made—and that he alone is to be praised by every intelligent creature in the universe. In other words, to refer to the celebrated first question of the Westminster Shorter Catechism, "What is the chief end of man [and of every other intelligent creature in the universe]?" The answer: "Man's chief end is to glorify God and to enjoy him forever." That is the ultimate meaning of these visions.

HOW WE SHOULD WORSHIP

So how should we worship? In both of these chapters, the song of the cherubim is echoed by the praise of the elders, who represent the entire church. They add to the praise of God the Father at the end of chapter 4, and in chapter 5 they join with the four living creatures (see vv. 8–10) and in the final praise chorus (v. 13). They are the last persons mentioned in this section: "and the elders fell down and worshiped" (v. 14). So the elders are our pattern for worship, and the question for us is this: Do we worship as they do? Can each of us echo the song of the four living creatures and the other mighty angels?

We are going to be exploring the characteristics of the worship of God in heaven as we move on, but we can notice a number of its most important features here.

TRUE WORSHIP IS THE WORSHIP OF GOD ALONE

Is anything in Revelation 4 and 5 more obvious than this? Here, in the act of worship, the entire creation is focused utterly on God. And so must we be, if we are really worshiping. We must have our attention fixed on God himself and no other. In a sense, this is merely our obedience to the first and second of the Ten Commandments.

> You shall have no other gods before me.
>   You shall not make for yourself a carved image, or any likeness of anything that is in heaven above, or that is in the earth beneath, or that is in the water under the earth. You shall not bow down to them or serve them. (Ex. 20:3–5)

It is also our obedience to what Jesus called the first and greatest commandment, which he drew from Deuteronomy 6:5: "You shall love the LORD your God with all your heart and with all your soul and with all your might" (cf. Matt. 22:37). If we are concentrating on something else, however good it may be in itself, we are not worshiping God.

TRUE WORSHIP HONORS GOD FOR HIS GODLIKE ATTRIBUTES

Worship assigns to God his true worth. We will never do this exhaustively, of course, for we are finite beings and God is the Infinite One. We will never probe his attributes to their depth or be able to exhaust our awestruck worship of God throughout the infinite duration of eternity. But the fact that we cannot praise God exhaustively does not mean that we cannot praise him rightly or that our praise is without eternal value.

In the case of this first hymn, God is praised for three great attributes—one in each of its three phrases: holiness ("Holy, holy, holy"), sovereignty ("is the Lord God Almighty"), and eternity ("who was and is and is to come!"). That last phrase has already occurred twice in Revelation—in verses 4 and 8 of chapter 1.

THE BEST WORSHIP IS CEASELESS WORSHIP

The best worship is continuous, for it is rendered to God day and night (see v. 8). We cannot do this ourselves, of course, except in the sense that our entire lives should be ordered to God's glory. But we can literally worship ceaselessly alongside others. And we are. It is happening right now around the world, in every land and by countless Christian congregations, as praises are given to God continuously by his redeemed and grateful people.

THE FULLEST WORSHIP IS WITH OTHERS

Should we worship God individually, when we are by ourselves in our own times of prayer and Bible study? Of course. But we must not forsake worshiping him with others, either, for there is something in the corporate worship of God by the assembled people of God that is right and beneficial. Especially beneficial! For worshiping with others keeps us on track and reminds us that God is God, that he is in control of history, that we are his people, and that our chief end is to glorify and enjoy him.

Here are two wise and wonderful paragraphs by Craig S. Keener written to remind us of precisely that:

> As late first-century Christians gained courage to declare that the emperor had no clothes, we must declare the same for the idols of our generation. Caesar did not create (4:11) and is not eternal (4:8), nor did he redeem us by his blood (5:9); he had no control over ultimate hope. In view of present knowledge about the narrow parameters essential for the formation of life in the universe, we can see God's loving design in creation today in greater detail than our forebears. Only in the depths of worship, as we stand in awe of God's majestic glory, do all other competing claims for affection and attention recede into their rightful place. God alone is God, and

he alone merits first place—beyond every other love, every other anxiety, every other fear that consumes us.

If God's grandeur dwarfs the emperor's majesty, it also challenges in a different way the numbing triteness of modern Western culture. God's greatness summons our attention: Who are we to be overwhelmed by the mortal emperor or our present trials? That God is Lord of history and has everything under control helps us view everything else in life the way we should. Praise puts persecution, poverty, and plagues into perspective; God is sovereignly bringing about his purposes, and this world's pains are merely the birth pangs of a new world (Rev. 21–22).[8]

That is why worship matters. If you do not join with other believers in faithful, true, and beneficial worship of almighty God, you will be cowed by the apparent powers of this antagonistic world and engulfed by the trivialities of our evil culture. You need reminding—constantly. But if you truly worship, you will be able to stand firm.

8. Keener, *Revelation*, 182.

14

THE WORSHIP OF THE ELDERS

Revelation 4:8–11

We are studying the worship of God as it is pictured in Revelation 4 and 5, in order to improve our worship, and we have seen that true worship is (1) the worship of God alone, (2) acknowledgment of God's attributes, (3) ceaseless (in heaven, at least), and (4) best when it is also done with others. But there is one additional and obvious aspect of worship that I did not even mention in the previous study—namely, that worship is best expressed in song! These two chapters of Revelation are filled with hymns—five in all—and there are many more hymns later in the book. Isn't it interesting that heaven's worship is expressed in words that can be set to music—in words to be sung?

This is more than interesting, of course; it is important—for music is a gift from God that allows us to express the deepest responses of our hearts to him, and to his truth, in meaningful and memorable ways. It is a case of our hearts joining with our minds to say, "Yes! Yes! Yes!" to the truths we are embracing.

From time to time I have reflected on the absence of singing in our contemporary Western culture, because it suggests to me that most people are unable to feel or respond to anything at a very deep level. We have music, of course. Oh, do we have music! We can't escape it. We have it piped in everywhere. "Popular" songs blast us from radios, televisions, and countless loudspeakers. Yet people do not sing. They used to sing. They sang together around pianos in the 1920s and in the music halls to keep their spirits up during the two world wars. They sang patriotic ballads and love songs, ethnic music, and old favorites from the past. But not today. We live in a frantic but joyless culture, and while people sometimes understand the words of the popular songs they hear, they do not join in singing them. One of the saddest things about today's youth culture is that the youth do not sing. They are world-weary. They have no joy.

About the only place left in Western culture where singing still happens is in church, where it is done by Christian people. The reason is obvious: we have something to sing about! Like the saints in heaven, we want to praise our God "with heart and soul and voice,"[1] and singing the revelations of God together is how we do it best— and always have! See if you do not echo the sentiments of this poem by the medieval theologian John Scotus (AD 810–877):

> Homer once sang of his Hellenes and Trojans
> And Vergil composed verse about the descendants of Romulus;
> Let us sing about the kindly deeds of the king of Heaven
> whom the world never ceases joyously to praise.
> Homer and Vergil took pleasure in speaking about the flames that brought
> sudden destruction to Troy and about the struggles of their heroes,
> but our delight is to sing of Christ
> drenched in blood after vanquishing the prince of this world.
> They were both learned in how to compose falsehoods
> with an appearance of truth and how to deceive [in] Arcadian verse;
> we prefer to sing hymns of fine praise
> to the power of the Father and His true wisdom.
> Let us therefore hold the supreme victories of Christ
> as brilliant stars in our minds.
> Behold the four corners of the world are clasped by the wooden cross.[2]

"To sing of Christ" is what Christians have always done—though not always as well as they might have or should have. It is what the

---

1. Heinrich Suso, "Good Christian Men, Rejoice," ca. 1328; trans. John M. Neale, 1853.
2. Quoted in Douglas Jones and Douglas Wilson, *Angels in the Architecture: A Protestant Vision for Middle Earth* (Moscow, ID: Canon Press, 1998), 15.

four living creatures, the elders, the angels, and the entire creation are doing today in heaven. We join that great heavenly choir rightly, wisely, and joyously when we sing the praises of our great God.

THE SONG OF THE ELDERS AND THE LIVING CREATURES

Whenever any of the created beings praise God, the elders soon join them. In Revelation 4:9, we see them adding their praise of God as Creator to the living creatures' worship of God for being holy, sovereign, and eternal. The elders' hymn begins with the words "Worthy are you" (v. 11)—which is worship in its most literal sense, since worship is the act of ascribing all true worth to God. This is what the four living creatures did in their hymn (see v. 8) and what the elders' song also does—they give honor to God. Since the elders join in the praise that is offered by the living creatures, we can assume that they too acknowledged God's holiness, sovereignty, and eternity. Taken together, the worship in these two hymns begins with who God is and continues with what he has done.

GOD IS HOLY

Holiness is the only attribute of God that the Bible repeats three times in a row, as in Revelation 4: "Holy, holy, holy, is the Lord God Almighty." This attribute is what sets God apart from everything else and is the first characteristic that human beings are aware of when they are brought into his presence. It is also what makes God terrifying. When he appeared on Mount Sinai with the same "flashes of lightning, and rumblings and peals of thunder" that John saw coming from the throne (v. 5), even Moses said, "I tremble with fear" (Heb. 12:21).

There is not much recognition of God's holiness today, even among the most serious Christian people, which more than anything else explains why our worship services are so often trivial. An awareness of the holy has been crowded out by our grossly material, self-centered, entertainment-oriented, ticky-tacky culture. Douglas Jones and Douglas Wilson recognize the problem.

165

We who are now alive do not remember how to apprehend [the] beauty and holiness of our God; we are so unlettered by modernity that we no longer ache to think of it. Our inability to comprehend such things pervades everything we do. Some hope that postmodernism will show the way out, but a postmodernist is nothing more than a modernist who has admitted his cultural illiteracy . . . which is not the same thing as reading. Christians by and large do not stand against this folly with a clear understanding of antithesis. Coming to worship the Lord in "the beauty of holiness" somehow gets translated into the "warmth of niceness." Almost entirely gone is the experience of being run through, pierced by the numinous. We acknowledge that some things are "pretty" or "nice," and desire to be dabbed by them. We say we call for the gods of glory and beauty but summon up the imbecilic and grinning demons of kitsch.[3]

The elders did not fall for this. Rather, they joined the cherubim in singing, "Holy, holy, holy, is the Lord God Almighty, who was and is and is to come!" (Rev. 4:8).

GOD IS SOVEREIGN

Holiness may be the characteristic of God that human beings first recognize and are most terrified by, but the attribute that is most emphasized in Revelation is his sovereignty. That is because John's readers needed to know that God is ruling history. Nothing ever takes place that is contrary to his overriding will, and no circumstance of life can ever ultimately defeat or harm the Christian.

This is what the four living creatures are praising when they call God "the Lord God Almighty" (v. 8). That is the name *Jehovah Sabaoth*, which means "God, the Sovereign One." This is also what the elders are acknowledging when they use the words "our Lord and God" (v. 11). "Lord and God" were the words that the emperor Domitian insisted upon as his titles, to be used whenever anyone addressed him. People had to say *Dominus et Deus* (or, in Greek, *kyrios kai theos*): "Lord and God." But Domitian was not Lord

3. Jones and Wilson, 46.

and God. He was only a man—a very evil man who persecuted Christians. There is one who is Lord and God, and this true Lord and God brought even the powerful Domitian to judgment in time. Those to whom John wrote needed to know this, for it was only knowledge of the truly sovereign God that would enable them to stand firm when the times of persecution came.

In the Greek text, each of the nouns in the second line of verse 11—"glory," "honor," and "power"—is preceded by the definite article, which indicates totality. It is not that God should be glorified, honored, or ascribed power along with Caesar or any other ruler. It is rather that he alone is to receive all the honor, all the glory, and all the power. For all things are from him and are sustained by him, as Paul wrote: "From him and through him and to him are all things. To him be glory forever. Amen" (Rom. 11:36).

GOD IS ETERNAL

When we acknowledge that God is eternal, we mean that he transcends time. He had no beginning, and he will have no end. Moreover, we confess that he is always the same in his eternal being. That is what the words "who was and is and is to come" mean (Rev. 4:8). God is past ("was"), present ("is"), and future ("is to come"). But there is more to that last phrase, since it is not merely the future form of the verb "to be." The future of "be" is "will be." By saying "is to come" instead of "will be," this hymn indicates that the eternally existing God is yet to come in *judgment*. That is, he is the one before whom all hearts are open and all desires are known, as well as the one with whom we must deal.

This is emphasized in the repeated phrase that is used to introduce the actual song of the elders. For we are told that when the four living creatures give honor and thanks to him "who lives forever and ever" (v. 9), the elders fall down and also worship him "who lives forever and ever" (v. 10). This phrase seems to be borrowed from Daniel 4:34 and 12:7, where it is contrasted with the limited duration of the reigns of all earthly kings.

In the first passage, the phrase occurs within the final testimony of the chastened King Nebuchadnezzar, who expected that his own kingdom would endure forever but instead was judged for his arrogance and ended by confessing boldly, "I blessed the Most High, and praised and honored him who lives forever, for his dominion is an everlasting dominion, and his kingdom endures from generation to generation" (Dan. 4:34).

In the second passage, Daniel hears an angelic figure swear the truth of his words "by him who lives forever" (12:7)—that is, by God. It is a passage in which the overthrow of the wicked is prophesied, the salvation of the righteous is assured, and God is declared to be in complete control—not only of the ultimate end but even of the chronological progression of world history. When the twenty-four elders join in the song of the four living creatures, they are adding their names to this important doxological confession.

GOD AS THE CREATOR

After the four living creatures praise God in respect to his essential nature—holiness, sovereignty, and everlastingness are essential and unique qualities of God—the elders praise him for the glory of his created works. They cry, "Worthy are you, our Lord and God, to receive glory and honor and power, for you created all things, and by your will they existed and were created" (Rev. 4:11).

There are three emphases in this hymn. First, all that exists has been made by God—nothing exists other than what he has created. Second, the creation is the result of God's free will to create and nothing else—no external force or power acted upon God to cause him to do what he did. Third, God not only has created the universe but also continues to sustain its existence by his sovereign will and power.

1. EVERYTHING THAT EXISTS HAS BEEN CREATED BY GOD

The elders who are before God's throne must know more of the wonder of God's creation than we do in our current earth-bound state, but we know enough about the creation to be overwhelmed by God's creative majesty and power and to praise him in awestruck wonder.

How vast the heavens are! When we look up into the sky on a clear night, we see perhaps ten thousand points of light. A few of these are the planets of our solar system shining back reflected light. Thousands belong to the special grouping of stars that is known as the Milky Way—to which our sun belongs. Other thousands are entire galaxies, which shine as one point because they are so distant. We say ten thousand points because that is what we can see with unaided eyes. But these ten thousand are only the tiniest fraction of the existing stars. A typical galaxy contains billions of individual stars, and our galaxy alone contains two hundred billion. The Milky Way's form is of a giant spiral that rotates majestically in space, its glowing arms trailing behind it like the distended points of a pinwheel. Our sun is in one arm of the spiral, which makes a complete rotation in 250 million years. These figures are staggering. And this is only our galaxy. There are thousands of others that are visible to the naked eye—and billions more within range of earth-based telescopes. The Hubble telescope, which is located in space above the earth, is detecting and photographing even more.

The galaxies of stars display a seemingly unending array of beauty. Some are spirals, like ours. Others are nearly spherical clusters. Others are flattened out like pancakes. Still others are irregular. All the stars in the heavens are clustered together in these intricate and beautiful groupings.

The galaxies are scattered about in an irregular pattern, and between them are vast expanses of space. The distance from one edge of an average galaxy to the other edge is approximately six hundred thousand trillion miles. The average distance from one galaxy to another is twenty million trillion miles. If these numbers were written out in zeros, they would fill up several lines of type. To avoid such large numbers, astronomers generally use a unit of distance called a "light-year." A light-year is the distance that light travels in one year, at the speed of 186,000 miles per second—which is approximately 6 trillion miles. Translated into this unit of measurement, the size of an average galaxy is approximately a hundred thousand light-years.

The Andromeda Galaxy is the galaxy closest to our own Milky

Way. It is separated from us by two and a half million light-years. This means that the light that is coming to us now from Andromeda has taken more than two million years to get here. Put in other terms, this means that when we look at Andromeda, what we see is the galaxy as it existed not a moment ago but two million years in the past.

The galaxies are not fixed in space but rather moving away from one another at tremendous speeds. Vesto Melvin Slipher, who was the first to discover this fact, found that the galaxies he could observe were moving away from the earth at several million miles per hour. His scientific followers, particularly Milton Humason and Edwin Hubble, showed that the most distant galaxies were retreating from us at the rate of a hundred million miles per hour. Moreover, everything is retreating from everything else. Nothing is coming toward us, nor is anything coming toward any other galaxy. This means that the universe is expanding. By working backward from the present position of the galaxies and their known speed of retreat, astronomers have placed the origin of the universe approximately fifteen billion years in the past.

When we turn to the stars themselves, we find equal evidence of variety, design, and mystery. Not all stars are alike, though they seem to follow a similar cycle: they are born, burn, grow old, and eventually die. At any given moment, millions of stars are being born in space. Each one is born as a cloud of interstellar gas contracts under the force of gravity between the atoms that compose it. As the cloud contracts, its temperature rises. Finally, the hydrogen within the ball of condensed gas ignites in a reaction similar to that which occurs in the explosion of a hydrogen bomb. This energy halts any further condensing of the gas, and the star continues to burn for billions of years. Our sun is at this stage.

The wonders of the macrocosm (the world of large things) are mirrored in the microcosm (the world of small things). There are electrons, protons, neutrons, and a seemingly endless variety of particles that are barely understood. The distances between these particles are, proportionately to their size, comparable to some of the distances that are involved in the solar system. If we were to take the simplest of atoms, the hydrogen atom, and blow it up billions upon billions of times, to the point at which the proton at its center would now be the size of a ten-inch soccer ball, the electron that circles its nucleus would now be the size of a golf ball and would be circling the proton at a distance of five miles. There would be nothing else within the circle.[4]

The saints in heaven praise God for the wonders of his creation. Shouldn't we, who are part of that creation, do so in our worship as well?

2. GOD ACTED WITH PERFECT FREEDOM IN CREATING

This is the second point of the elders' worship hymn—they do not merely say "You created all things" but also add "and by your will they . . . were created" (v. 11). This means that creation was the result of God's utterly free will and nothing else. No external force or power acted upon God to cause him to do what he did, for there were no other beings, entities, forces, or powers in that distant, eternal time before creation. Nor was God under obligation to create because of anything within himself. God did not need the atoms or the stars or the galaxies. He did not need the quarks and the quasars. He did not need us. That he created us was due solely to his own good pleasure.

This should be profoundly humbling to anyone who thinks about it. It was humbling to Arthur Pink, who wrote,

> God was under no constraint, no obligation, no necessity to create. That he chose to do so was purely a sovereign act on his part, caused by nothing outside himself, determined by nothing but his own mere good pleasure; for he "worketh all things after the counsel of his own will" (Eph. 1:11). That he did create was simply for his manifestative glory. . . . God is no gainer even from our worship. He was in no need of that external glory of his grace which arises

---

4. I have borrowed the description of the wonders of God's heavenly and earthly creation from James Montgomery Boice, *Genesis: An Expositional Commentary*, vol. 1, *Creation and Fall (Genesis 1–11)* (1982; repr., Grand Rapids: Baker Books, 2006), 38–40.

from his redeemed, for he is glorious enough in himself without that. What was it that moved him to predestinate his elect to the praise of the glory of his grace? It was, as Ephesians 1:5 tells us, "according to the good pleasure of his will."

. . . The force of this is [that] it is impossible to bring the Almighty under obligations to the creature; God gains nothing from us.[5]

Human beings always want to make God somehow dependent on us. But that will not work. Our believing in God adds nothing to his perfections; our doubting him takes nothing away.

3. GOD CONTINUOUSLY SUSTAINS THE UNIVERSE BY HIS WILL AND POWER

The line of the elders' hymn that reads "by your will they existed" (v. 11) means that the universe exists from moment to moment only because God continues to keep it in existence.

There is a change of tenses between the verbs that the English Standard Version renders as "existed" (*esan*) and "were created" (*ektisthesan*). The first is an imperfect and means, more literally, "they continue to have their being." The second is an aorist, which indicates a past, completed act: "they have been created." Because the imperfect precedes the aorist, this verse has been interpreted to mean that all things existed first and eternally in the mind of God (they always "were there") but then were brought into actual being by God's creative act. That is possible. But it is better to take this as the New International Version renders it in its translation: "they were created and have their being." The verse is saying that God not only brought all things into being but also now freely sustains all things in their existence by his will. If God should cease to sustain them, they would instantly be gone or disappear.

You exist only because of God's continuing good pleasure.

5. Arthur W. Pink, *The Attributes of God: A Solemn and Blessed Contemplation of Some of the Wondrous and Lovely Perfections of the Divine Character* (Grand Rapids: Baker Book House, n.d.), 2–3.

WHAT THE ELDERS DO

Is this humbling? It should be; it is meant to be. It was humbling to the elders, who showed the state of their hearts through two forms of what we call nonverbal communication.

First, they fell on their faces before God. In some languages, the word for *worship* literally means "to prostrate oneself before another," which is what the elders do. But the point of their prostration is to not so much to show worship itself but more so to show that their own honor—for they are dressed in white and wear crowns—is nothing in comparison with God's honor, since he alone is altogether worthy. Satan may have led millions to suppose that he is the prince of this world and the god of this age, but now mighty beings—the four living creatures—show the way of true worship; and the redeemed saints, who have learned the truth about God and themselves, are glad not only to prostrate themselves before him but also to "cast their crowns before the throne" (Rev. 4:10).

And that is the second part of the elders' nonverbal communication. Reginald Heber wrote in his famous hymn on the holiness of God,

> Holy, holy, holy!
> All the saints adore thee,
> Casting down their golden crowns
> Around the glassy sea.[6]

By placing their crowns at God's feet, the elders confess that the victories they have achieved were won only by God's power and by his grace. They persevered, but it was only because God persevered with them.

One day you will stand before almighty God. If you are not a Christian—have not been saved by the redeeming blood of Jesus Christ alone—it will be to hear God's dreadful condemnation of your sin. If you are a believer in Christ, it will be to hear God's welcome

---

6. Reginald Heber, "Holy, Holy, Holy," 1826.

173

and to join with every creature in heaven and on earth in praising him. But let me ask: When you stand before God in order to begin the worship that will last forever and ever, will you have a crown to lay down? Will you have done anything of which you can say, "This was accomplished by God's power and grace alone"? Will you be able to say, "To God be the glory"?

15

THE LION WHO IS THE LAMB

Revelation 5:1–8

There is a story about a small boy who was very absorbed in drawing and coloring an elaborate picture. His mother asked him what he was doing. "I'm drawing a picture of God," he told her.

"That's nice," she said. "But, you know, nobody knows what God looks like."

"They will now!" he answered triumphantly.

Nobody does know what God looks like, of course. This is why even the prophet John has not attempted to describe him in Revelation 4. He does not even call him "God," in fact. He refers to him only as "one seated on the throne" (v. 2), "he who sat there" (v. 3), and "him who is seated on the throne" (v. 10). But there is a way that we do see God: we see him in Jesus Christ, the second person of the Trinity. Jesus told Philip, "Whoever has seen me has seen the Father" (John 14:9), and John himself wrote in the fourth gospel, "No one has ever seen God; the only God, who is at the Father's side, he has made him known" (John 1:18).

In Revelation 5 we see God on the throne with Jesus standing nearby. Chapter 4 introduced God as the Creator of all things, though without describing him. In this chapter we have a vision of God the Redeemer—which means a vision of Jesus, the second person of the Trinity—and he *is* described. Chapter 4 ended with the worship of the Creator alone. This chapter will end with the worship of the Creator and Redeemer together, as every creature in heaven and on earth and under the earth and in the sea joins in singing. "To him who sits on the throne and to the Lamb be blessing and honor and glory and might forever and ever!" (Rev. 5:13).

These two chapters are important for understanding Revelation. They show us the relationship of the Father to the Son, of course. But mostly they show Jesus and unveil his role in carrying forward the eternal plan of God in history. Chapter 5 begins with a vision of a scroll that is sealed with seven seals. No one is worthy to open the scroll, reveal its contents, and put the flow of history into motion. But Jesus is worthy. He has won the victory and is therefore worthy to do all that is desired or required. He will break the seals, and God's purpose will be worked out. We do not need Jesus to show us that life is filled with troubles, but we do need him to guarantee that the suffering of God's people has meaning and is part of God's good plan.

THE SEVEN-SEALED SCROLL

By now we should know that nearly every symbol in Revelation has been given a multiplicity of interpretations by commentators. So we should suspect—rightly—that this has also been true of the scroll with which chapter 5 begins. What is this scroll? And what is in it? There have been five major ideas about what it is or what it contains.

First, in the Roman world, it was customary for a person's last will to be sealed with seven seals, which is why some adopt the view that the scroll in this chapter is *the last will and testament of Christ.* Its contents would then be a description of the kingdom of God, which the people of God are to inherit—what Peter speaks of as "an inheritance that is imperishable, undefiled, and unfading, kept in heaven for you" (1 Peter 1:4). The problem with this view is that the breaking of the seals does not reveal the nature or launch the arrival of the kingdom, but rather describes the outpouring of God's judgments on the earth.

A second view is that this is *the book of the redeemed.* The strength of this view lies in the frequent mentions of the Lamb's "book of life" throughout Revelation (see 3:5; 13:8; 17:8; 20:12, 15;

21:27). Its weakness is similar to that of the previous interpretation: the breaking of the seals does not disclose the names of the redeemed but rather the nature and outpouring of God's just judgments.

Third, the scroll may be *the Old Testament*. The idea here is that only Jesus Christ can fully explain the meaning of the Old Testament, as he did in his conversation with the disciples on the road to Emmaus following his resurrection: "And beginning with Moses and all the Prophets, he interpreted to them in all the Scriptures the things concerning himself" (Luke 24:27). This view has in its favor the fact that the book of Revelation is in one sense a sustained reflection upon the Old Testament from a Christian point of view. But aside from that, the idea is completely arbitrary. There is nothing in the chapter to suggest in any way that the scroll is to be seen as the Old Testament.

Fourth, the scroll may be *a list of the judgments of Revelation 6–16*. This is much closer to the context of Revelation as a whole. Besides, this scroll in Revelation 5 probably refers to the scroll that is mentioned in Ezekiel 2:9–10, which likewise was written "on the front and on the back" and contained "words of lamentation and mourning and woe." After he had eaten this scroll, Ezekiel was able to prophesy to Israel. This is a good interpretation and probably what John has in mind. But it is only half the total picture, since the message of these next chapters is not merely the outpouring of God's judgments on the world but also the preservation of the elect and the culmination of earth's history—which leads to interpretation number five.

Finally, the scroll may contain *God's total plan of judgment and redemption*. George Eldon Ladd states this view well.

The easiest identification of John's scroll is that it contains the prophecy of the end events, including both the salvation of God's people and the judgment of the wicked. It is God's redemptive plan for the denouement of human history, the overthrow of evil, and the gathering of a redeemed people to enjoy the blessings of God's rule. Although John, surprisingly, does not describe the actual opening of the scroll, the breaking of the sixth seal brings us to the end of the world—the last day; and in view of the fact that the opening of the seventh seal is accompanied by no specific event like the first six, we may conclude that the contents of the scroll consist of the material in Revelation 7:1–22:21. The events accompanying the breaking of the seals are not the end itself, but the events leading up to the end, while the contents of the scroll are that complex of events, both redemptive and judicial, which will accompany the end of this world and the introduction of the world to come.[1]

In other words, the scroll represents God's eternal, all-comprehensive decree—his purpose with respect to the entire universe. Its being sealed indicates that God's plan is both unrevealed and unexecuted. Opening the scroll by breaking its seals means revealing and carrying out God's plan—which is why Jesus must do it! A sealed scroll reminds the reader of Daniel 12, where the prophet was told to "shut up the words and seal the book, until the time of the end" (v. 4). Now the events of the end have come, and Jesus will reveal them.

THE ENIGMA OF HISTORY

No sooner had John seen the scroll in God's hand than he saw an angel as well, who asked in a loud voice, "Who is worthy to open the scroll and break its seals?" (Rev. 5:2). When no one was found worthy to either open the scroll or look inside, John wept. Why? There are two obvious reasons.

First, apart from the person and redeeming work of Jesus Christ, history is an unfathomable enigma—which is why people who have rejected the Bible's message are so pessimistic about life today. Rudolf Bultmann was a New Testament scholar who did not think that the Bible gives us any sure revelation about Jesus—or about anything else, for that matter. He wrote about history, "We cannot claim to know the end and the goal of history. Therefore the question

---

1. George Eldon Ladd, *A Commentary on the Revelation of John* (Grand Rapids: William B. Eerdmans, 1972), 81.

of meaning in history has become meaningless."[2] George Eldon Ladd, who quotes Bultmann's negative judgment, explains that since "Christ, and Christ alone, has the key to the meaning of human history," it is "not surprising that modern thinkers are pessimistic; apart from the victorious return of Christ, history is going nowhere."[3]

But it was not only the fear that the ultimate meaning of history might never be revealed that caused John to weep; he was troubled not merely because of his ignorance. He was also troubled because, until the scroll was opened, God's purposes in history would remain unaccomplished as well as unknown. Hendriksen explains,

> You will understand the meaning of these tears if you constantly bear in mind that in this beautiful vision the opening of the scroll by breaking the seals indicates the execution of God's plan. When the scroll is opened and the seals are broken, then the universe is governed in the interests of the church. Then, God's glorious, redemptive purpose is being realized; his plan is being carried out and the contents of the scroll come to pass in the history of the universe. But if the scroll is not opened it means that there will be no protection for God's children in the hours of bitter trial; no judgments upon a persecuting world; no ultimate triumph for believers, no new heaven and earth, no future inheritance.[4]

We can put it this way: If the cross of Christ is the decisive event that stands at the very center of history and explains everything—the event that is what history is about—then the resurrection and thus the decisive victory of Christ is the assurance that the plan of God, which is centered in the cross, will indeed be carried out. Nothing will defeat the Almighty. But none of the judgments that fill the following pages can be poured out until the slaughtered but risen Lamb breaks the scroll's seals.

---

2. Rudolf Bultmann, *History and Eschatology: The Gifford Lectures 1955* (repr., Edinburgh: University Press, 1957), 120.

3. Ladd, *Commentary on the Revelation of John*, 82.

4. William Hendriksen, *More Than Conquerors: An Interpretation of the Book of Revelation* (Grand Rapids: Baker Book House, 1940), 89.

HE IS WORTHY

"Who is worthy to open the scroll and break its seals?" asked the mighty angel. No creature, either in heaven or on earth, was able to step forward. But when John wept because "no one was found worthy to open the scroll or to look into it" (v. 4), an elder was able to arrest his tears by pointing to Jesus. "Weep no more; behold, the Lion of the tribe of Judah, the Root of David, has conquered, so that he can open the scroll and its seven seals" (v. 5). In the previous chapter, God alone was called "worthy" (4:11). But now we find that the conquering Christ is worthy also.

He is given two new names.

THE LION OF THE TRIBE OF JUDAH

This is the only place in the entire Bible where this exact phrase occurs. However, it harks back to Genesis 49:9, where Jacob, delivering his dying blessing to his sons, calls Judah "a lion's cub" (see also Ezek. 19:2–3, 5–6). The tribe of Judah was the tribe that produced David and the other great kings in his line. Jesus was a descendant of this line through Joseph, his adopted father, and also (I believe) through Mary, his mother. As a lion, he is the greatest of this strong line.

THE ROOT OF DAVID

This exact phrase is not found in the Old Testament either, though it is based on Isaiah 11, where the prophet speaks of "a shoot from the stump of Jesse" (v. 1) and "the root of Jesse" (v. 10). Jesse was David's father, and the verses that speak of his "shoot" or "root" are prophecies concerning the promised messianic king. This is a surprising but wonderful combination of words. "Shoot" means that the Messiah was to be Jesse's descendant, but "root" means that he is that from which Jesse himself comes. This is the exact point that Jesus made when he demanded of his enemies whose son the Christ was to be.

> They said to him, "The son of David." He said to them, "How is it then that David, in the Spirit, calls him Lord, saying,

180

" 'The Lord said to my Lord,
"Sit at my right hand,
until I put your enemies under your feet" ' "?

If then David calls him Lord, how is he his son?" (Matt. 22:41–45)

The only possible answer is that the Messiah would be God's Son as well as David's—a divine Messiah, who Paul would later write "was descended from David according to the flesh and was declared to be the Son of God in power according to the Spirit of holiness by his resurrection from the dead, Jesus Christ our Lord" (Rom. 1:3–4).

The elder says something else about the Lion of Judah and the Root of David. He tells John that this great figure "has conquered" (Rev. 5:5), which Jesus clearly has done by his incarnation, death, and resurrection. His enemies (just as ours are) are Satan, sin, and death. Jesus has triumphed over each enemy. He has triumphed over Satan and his hosts (see Heb. 2:14–15; see also Matt. 12:29; Luke 10:18; John 12:31; 16:11; Col. 2:15) and has "abolished death and brought life and immortality to light through the gospel" (2 Tim. 1:10).

WORTHY IS THE LAMB

What follows is one of the great dramatic scenes in a book that is known for its great dramatic scenes. John has been told that "the Lion of the tribe of Judah" is able to open the scroll and its seven seals (Rev. 5:5). But when he turns around to look in the direction that is indicated by the elder, he sees not a lion but a lamb—indeed, "a Lamb standing, as though it had been slain" (v. 6). The lion is the fiercest and strongest of the beasts—a fit image for a powerful, conquering Messiah. By contrast, a lamb is the weakest and most helpless of the animals. It is a strange juxtaposition. But Jesus is indeed both. In fact, it is by his becoming a lamb—a slaughtered one, at that—that he has conquered.

Christ is called a lamb twenty-eight times in Revelation. It is John's favorite name for Jesus—and it also occurs, not surprisingly, in John's gospel. In fact, his gospel contains perhaps the most important reference to Jesus as a lamb, for it is there that John the Baptist points him out as "the Lamb of God, who takes away the sin of the world!" (John 1:29).

John the Baptist's words are the culmination of the Old Testament's teaching about the way of salvation through sacrifice—which is the gospel. The first indication of this gospel is in Genesis 3, where God promised a Savior who would destroy the works of the devil and bring the people of God to paradise, and he illustrated how that would happen by killing animals and clothing Adam and Eve with their skins. The sacrifice of the animals taught the principle of vicarious atonement—the innocent dying for the guilty—while the use of their skins to clothe Adam and Eve taught the principle of imputed righteousness. I think our first parents understood those doctrines and believed them, trusting God's word about the Savior who would come, which is why they responded as they did. Adam called his wife "Eve," which means "life-giver" or "mother," because he thought she would give birth to the Messiah and was looking to him as the Savior, while Eve called her firstborn "Cain," which means "here he is" or "acquired." Our first parents made a mistake about when the Savior would come, thinking that Eve's firstborn was the deliverer. But they had the right idea: they were looking for the Lamb who would take away their sin and bring salvation.

We find the sacrifice of animals all through the Old Testament, and it always points forward to the perfect sacrifice to be made by Jesus Christ. The killing of the lambs at the time of the Passover showed how those who were covered by the blood would escape spiritual death. The sacrifices that were made on the Day of Atonement showed how God's wrath against sin could be turned aside and how the sin of the people could be borne away so that it might not rise up against them ever again. These were powerful pictures. But all who had understanding in such matters knew that "it is impossible for the blood of bulls and goats to take away sins" (Heb. 10:4). They were looking for a Savior to come. And he has come! That Savior is Jesus.

This is what Jesus explained to the disciples on the Emmaus road in the conversation I referred to earlier. The two disciples were returning home after the weekend in which Jesus had been crucified, and they were in a despondent mood. Jesus asked why they were downcast, and they replied—not recognizing the risen Savior—that it was because of what had happened to Jesus of Nazareth. They explained how he was "a prophet mighty in deed and word before God and all the people" and how their "chief priests and rulers delivered him up to be condemned to death, and crucified him" (Luke 24:19–20). "But we had hoped," they said, "that he was the one to redeem Israel" (v. 21). The disciples knew that Jesus was powerful. He had done many miracles, after all. But he had been killed—which meant, as they saw it, that he had not been powerful enough. His enemies had proved stronger than he was; and death was clearly stronger, too. Jesus had been defeated, and the expectation that he might have been able to redeem Israel was dispelled forever.

Jesus reproved them, saying, "O foolish ones, and slow of heart to believe all that the prophets have spoken! Was it not necessary that the Christ should suffer these things and enter into his glory?" (vv. 25–26). Then, "beginning with Moses and all the Prophets, he interpreted to them in all the Scriptures the things concerning himself" (v. 27). That is a sermon I wish I had heard, for it is one in which Jesus showed, by using the whole of the Old Testament, that the Savior was to triumph through suffering. It was by becoming the true sacrificial Lamb that he was eventually to reign as the Lion of the tribe of Judah.

TRIUMPH THROUGH SUFFERING

This was the most practical message that the churches to which John was writing could hear. And it is practical for us, too—particularly for those of us who are interested in power, prestige, and worldly influence. Christ has conquered, just as we will. We are going to be triumphant. But he did not conquer by calling forth the mighty armies of heaven or by confounding his enemies by a sudden burst of glory. He conquered by suffering, just as we are called to suffer. This was a great mystery to the Old Testament saints—how the suffering of the Servant of God was related to the conquering Messiah. But Jesus insisted that this was taught throughout the Old

Testament (see Luke 24:27), and the New Testament teaches that we are to follow his example in this: "For to this you have been called, because Christ also suffered for you, leaving you an example, so that you might follow in his steps" (1 Peter 2:21).

G. K. Beale makes this point well.

> In their struggle against the world, believers should remember that Christ also suffered at the hands of the world but triumphed over it. His destiny is to be theirs, if they persevere. This is why the saints are described as "those who follow the Lamb wherever he goes" and in 14:4–5 are even likened to the lamb of Isa. 53:7–9. . . . For the same reason they are said to have "washed their robes . . . in the blood of the Lamb" (7:14) and to have overcome the devil "because of the blood of the Lamb" (12:11).
>
> . . . While he was suffering the defeat of death, he was also overcoming by creating a kingdom of redeemed subjects over whom he would reign and over whom the devil would no longer have power.[5]

Jesus was defeated physically, but in the very moment of his death—and by means of it—he was spiritually victorious. It is by suffering for truth and righteousness, as Jesus did, that we win battles. Paul wrote of his suffering,

> So we do not lose heart. Though our outer self is wasting away, our inner self is being renewed day by day. For this light momentary affliction is preparing for us an eternal weight of glory beyond all comparison. (2 Cor. 4:16–17)

TWO MORE CHARACTERISTICS

When John turned and saw the "Lamb standing, as though it had been slain," he noticed two more of the Lamb's characteristics.

---

5. G. K. Beale, *The Book of Revelation: A Commentary on the Greek Text* (Grand Rapids: William B. Eerdmans, 1999), 353.

It had "seven horns" and "seven eyes, which are the seven spirits of God sent out into all the earth" (Rev. 5:6). Once again, we have to remind ourselves that this is a dreamlike vision. We are not to think that Jesus is literally in heaven in the form of a lamb with seven horns and seven eyes. The very thought is ludicrous. This is symbolized revelation, and it is clearly meant to teach two things about Jesus.

JESUS IS OMNIPOTENT

Throughout the Bible, a horn is a symbol of power—appearing as such first in Deuteronomy 33:17 and then later in 1 Samuel 2:1 and 10; Psalm 18:2 and 112:9, and elsewhere. The image arose among a people who raised animals and noticed that the strongest animals had strong horns. Here the Lamb has seven horns because seven is a number that indicates the fullness of a thing. It is a way of saying that Jesus is omnipotent. He exercises the rule and power of the Father. As he told the disciples,

> All authority in heaven and on earth has been given to me. Go therefore and make disciples of all nations, baptizing them in the name of the Father and of the Son and of the Holy Spirit, teaching them to observe all that I have commanded you. And behold, I am with you always, to the end of the age. (Matt. 28:18–20)

JESUS IS OMNISCIENT

In a parallel way, the Lamb who represents Jesus also has seven eyes, which indicates that he is able to see and know everything. He is omniscient. The background for this concept is Zechariah 4:10, which speaks of the seven lamps of the menorah as "the eyes of the LORD, which range through the whole earth."

Here in Revelation 5, John identifies the seven eyes with "the seven spirits of God sent out into all the earth" (v. 6). These seven spirits are first introduced in chapter 1, verse 4, where they seem to be a way of describing the Holy Spirit as being multifaceted or omnipresent. While this interpretation is a bit uncertain, it would mean that Jesus is filled with the Spirit—and if this is so, it would mean that the entire Trinity appears together in these verses from

Revelation 5: the Father on the throne, the Son before the throne, and the Spirit emanating from both the Father and the Son throughout the earth.

The climax of this section comes in verse 7 when the Lamb approaches the throne and takes the scroll from the hand of God Almighty. At this point, the four living creatures and the twenty-four elders from chapter 4 respond by falling down before the Lamb, just as they had previously done before the throne of the Father, and by worshiping him in prayer and singing the hymns that we will examine in our next study.

Daniel 7:13–14 is the only Old Testament passage in which a divine individual is described as approaching the throne of God to receive authority. The text says, "Behold, with the clouds of heaven there came one like a son of man, and he came to the Ancient of Days and was presented before him. And to him was given dominion and glory and a kingdom, that all peoples, nations, and languages should serve him; his dominion is an everlasting dominion, which shall not pass away, and his kingdom one that shall not be destroyed." That son of man was Jesus, of course; and what Daniel saw was the same thing John was allowed to see from Patmos. John's Lamb is the Lord of glory. Why not bow before him as he unrolls the scroll that reveals the outworking of the perfect purposes of God in human history?

16

"Worthy Is the Lamb"

Revelation 5:9—14

Worship is a serious mental activity. It consists of praising God for who he is; and in order to do that, we need to understand who he is, at least in part. God reveals who he is in the Bible. So in order to worship rightly we have to study the Bible and think clearly. Still, worship is no mere recognition of facts—even biblical or theological facts. It is done with the heart as well as with the head, which means that the facts of Scripture—especially those that concern the character and works of God—call for a passionate response.

By what vehicle should we respond? By words, certainly. The Bible is filled with words for us to read, learn, and sometimes memorize—but also to sing. Singing provides a unique joining of biblical content and emotional assent. Music alone does not do this joining and is not itself worship, though it can prepare us for worship by quieting our minds and freeing our hearts to hear the voice of God in Scripture. And words alone, while we can and do respond to them personally and joyfully, do not accomplish all that words and music together can. Praise words become far more joyful, and also a part of us, when we sing them—which is why Paul told the Colossians, "Let the word of Christ dwell in you richly, teaching and admonishing one another in all wisdom, singing psalms and hymns and spiritual songs, with thankfulness in your hearts to God" (Col. 3:16).

When we sing, we confess that the words we have heard are true, we rejoice in those truths, and we stand together with others who make the same confession.

A NEW SONG

And there is another thing. As we learn more about God and experience more and more examples of his grace, we want to sing new songs that express this new knowledge or experience we have gained. And that brings us to Revelation 5:9. In Revelation 4 we were introduced to two of heaven's praise songs: the first by the four living creatures ("Holy, holy, holy, is the Lord God Almighty, who was and is and is to come!"—v. 8) and the second by the twenty-four elders ("Worthy are you, our Lord and God, to receive glory and honor and power, for you created all things, and by your will they existed and were created"—v. 11). These songs are as old as creation itself and are presumably what God was referring to when he described to Job the picture of how "the morning stars sang together and all the sons of God shouted for joy" (Job 38:7).

But those songs are different from the one we come to in this part of Revelation. When the Lamb, who had been slain and has conquered, comes and takes the scroll from the hand of him who sits upon the throne, the four living creatures and the twenty-four elders, who had been worshiping God as the Creator, immediately sing "a new song" of praise to the Lamb (Rev. 5:9), who is also our Redeemer.

Some commentators put this event in the future, at the start of that time of God's final judgments on the earth and its people. But it is far more natural to think of this as having taken place in heaven when Jesus ascended there following his death and resurrection. And this song of praise continues to be sung! Jesus's death and resurrection was a truly new event in history, and it called for "a new song," which is what we see in Revelation 5:9 and what the saints in glory continue to sing.

Actually, there are three new songs in this chapter of Revelation. We have seen two songs of praise to the Father. Now we see two songs of praise to Jesus followed by a final hymn of praise to the Father and Son together. The first song highlights Jesus's work as Redeemer, the second highlights the praise that is due to him for his redeeming work, and the third highlights the praise that is due to the first two persons of the Godhead together.

Singing "a new song" is not in itself a new idea, however. These words are common in the Old Testament—especially in the Psalms, where they usually mark the response of God's people to some new act of deliverance (see, for example, Pss. 33:3; 40:3; 96:1; 98:1; 144:9; 149:1; see also Isa. 42:10). These new songs seem to happen again and again, for the people of God are always experiencing new blessings from his hand. As late as Psalm 149, the psalmist is calling for a new praise song: "Sing to the LORD a new song, his praise in the assembly of the godly" (v. 1). The same is true in Revelation. We have one new song in chapter 5. But we have another new song as late as chapter 14: "The voice I heard was like the sound of harpists playing on their harps, and they were singing a new song before the throne and before the four living creatures and before the elders" (vv. 2–3).

Why do the four living creatures and the twenty-four elders sing a new song in chapter 5? William Hendriksen writes, "They sing a new song . . . because never before had such a great and glorious deliverance been accomplished and never before had the Lamb received this great honor."[1] I can say the same thing another way: the reason a new song is sung to Jesus now is because, having redeemed his people, he has taken the scroll that will determine the flow of future history, and that means that he is controlling history in the interests of those whom he has redeemed. Jesus is the sovereign God—and, as Paul wrote, "He must reign until he has put all his enemies under his feet. The last enemy to be destroyed is death" (1 Cor. 15:25–26).

THE SONG OF THE REDEEMED

So we turn now to these three hymns—especially to the first, which praises the Lord Jesus Christ as the Redeemer of his people. It is the longest and most complete of the three new songs, because the work of which it speaks is the most important of all the saving

1. William Hendriksen, *More Than Conquerors: An Interpretation of the Book of Revelation* (Grand Rapids: Baker Book House, 1940), 91.

189

works that God has done. The hymn has these words: "Worthy are you to take the scroll and to open its seals, for you were slain, and by your blood you ransomed people for God from every tribe and language and people and nation, and you have made them a kingdom and priests to our God, and they shall reign on the earth" (Rev. 5:9–10).

This is an amazingly comprehensive declaration. It begins by ascribing worth to Jesus—the same thing that was ascribed in the previous hymn to God. So it has the effect of linking Jesus to God, affirming his deity, and also anticipating the last of the five hymns, which ascribes praise, honor, glory, and power "to him who sits on the throne and to the Lamb" explicitly (v. 13). Jesus is honored as God because he is God.

This final hymn's explanation of why Jesus is worthy is comprehensive, too, though it is done in few words.

JESUS WAS "SLAIN"

That Jesus was crucified is a fact of history—and an amazing fact, at that, when we consider who Jesus Christ is. It is amazing that God, the immortal God, could become man in order to accomplish our salvation by his death. How can the immortal die? Or even become a man, for that matter? The Greeks considered it the height of foolishness even to think that God could appear in human flesh, not to mention die on a cross. But that is exactly what Jesus has done, and it is what he is praised for in this hymn. It is what he will be praised for eternally.

JESUS "RANSOMED PEOPLE FOR GOD"

An interpretation of the historical fact of Jesus's death—one that explains what the crucifixion was about—is that it was a means of ransoming God's people. Jesus's death was no mere fluke of history, and even less so a meaningless tragedy. On the contrary, it was the very essence of the work God was doing in Christ for our salvation. Jesus was purchasing men and women for God at the cost of his own precious blood. In a word, he was *redeeming* us from the power and penalty of sin.

I find it interesting that the elders are praising Jesus as Redeemer rather than as Lord or Savior or Son of God, or as one of the countless other titles or functions for which he could be praised. Later in Revelation Jesus will be hailed as "King of kings and Lord of lords" (19:16), but he is not being praised as "King of kings" by the elders here—though he is praised for making us "a kingdom" (5:10). Jesus is our high priest, too, but he is not praised for being a priest in this chorus, either. Instead, it is because he has made *us* "priests" (v. 10).

Why is Jesus praised as Redeemer, here, rather than being honored with one of his many other noble titles? I think Benjamin B. Warfield had the answer years ago when, in 1915, he addressed the incoming students of Princeton Theological Seminary on the subject of *Redeemer* and *redemption*, showing how wonderful those words are.[2] He argued that there is no title of Christ that is more precious to the true people of God than *Redeemer* is, because this title "gives expression not merely to our sense that we have received salvation from [Jesus], but also to our appreciation of what it cost Him to procure this salvation for us. It is the name specifically of the Christ of the cross. Whenever we pronounce it, the cross is placarded before our eyes and our hearts are filled with loving remembrance not only that Christ has given us salvation, but that He paid a mighty price for it."[3]

In proof of his claim that no title of Christ is more precious to the people of God than *Redeemer*, Warfield appealed not to great works of theology that deal with the cross—though there are many of them—but to the church's hymnody. Many of the hymns in the hymnbook that was used in those days at Princeton celebrated the Lord as our Redeemer, and Warfield listed them.

> Let our whole soul an offering be
> To our *Redeemer's* Name

---

2. See Benjamin Breckinridge Warfield, "'Redeemer' and 'Redemption'" (opening address, Princeton Theological Seminary, Princeton, NJ, September 17, 1915), quoted in *The Person and Work of Christ*, ed. Samuel G. Craig (Philadelphia: Presbyterian and Reformed, 1950), 325–48.
3. Warfield, 325.

While we pray for pardoning grace,
    Through our *Redeemer's* Name

Almighty Son, Incarnate Word,
    Our Prophet, Priest, *Redeemer*, Lord

O for a thousand tongues to sing
    My dear *Redeemer's* praise

All hail, *Redeemer*, hail,
    For Thou hast died for me

All glory, laud and honor
    To Thee *Redeemer*, King[4]

These are only six of the hymns that Warfield listed; he cited twenty-eight in all. But then, in case the students had missed his point, he did the same thing all over again with the words *ransom* and *ransomed*, which are very close synonyms of *redeem*. He found twenty-five examples of hymns that use those words. Isn't that why the elders, who represent the people of God from both the Old and New Testament periods, praise Jesus as the one who "ransomed," or purchased, them for God with his blood? Isn't it because they are remembering that Jesus died to redeem them personally, and remembering as well the greatness of the cost?

I said above that this hymn is an amazingly comprehensive statement of both why Jesus is worthy of praise and, in support of that, what he accomplished for us by redeeming us. Notice further what the hymn of the four living creatures and the twenty-four elders teaches us about this redemption.

First, it is a *particular* redemption. This means it is a redemption that actually accomplished its purpose of purchasing and setting free a particular people for God from the penalty and power of sin. The verse does not say that Jesus purchased salvation for every individual

---

4. Warfield, 326.

but only that he has purchased salvation for some people—namely, those whom he has also made kings and priests in order to serve God. His death may have benefited others in a general way—as an inspiring example, for instance. But it actually redeemed only the elect.

This is a point on which theological traditions have disagreed, for many want to stress the universal nature of Christ's atonement to the exclusion of its particularity. "Christ must have died for all people," they say. "How else can we offer the gospel to all people. Don't we have to be able to say, 'Christ died for you'?" The real question, of course, is not whether the death of Jesus Christ has sufficient value to atone for the sins of the entire world, or whether it benefits all people in some limited sense, or whether it can be proclaimed to all people. The real question concerns the *design* of the atonement—that is, what God the Father actually intended to do, and did do, by sending his Son to die for us. We can express the matter in such questions as these: Did Jesus's death actually redeem anyone? Did his sacrifice of himself make a true propitiation for our sins? Did it reconcile any specific individual to God? Was his death an actual atonement? If the answer to these questions is yes, then for whom did he do these things? When the question is asked in this way, we can see that there are only three possible answers.

1. Jesus's death was not an actual atonement, but only something that made atonement possible. The atonement becomes actual when the sinner repents of his or her sin and believes on Jesus.[5]
2. Jesus's death was an actual atonement for the sins of God's elect people, with the result that these—and only these—are delivered from sin's penalty.
3. Jesus's death was an actual atonement for the sin of all people, with the result that all people are saved.

5. This is what Lewis Sperry Chafer taught. He wrote, "Christ's death does not save either actually or potentially; rather it makes all men saveable." "For Whom Did Christ Die?" reprinted in *Bibliotheca Sacra* 137, no. 548 (October–December 1980): 325, quoted in Michael Horton, *Putting Amazing Back into Grace: Embracing the Heart of the Gospel*, rev. and updated ed. (Grand Rapids: Baker Books, 2005), 107.

We can dismiss the third possibility immediately, for all orthodox Christians agree that not all persons will be saved. On the contrary, the Bible teaches clearly that some will not be saved and that in some cases specific individuals are lost. Pharaoh is an example. So is Judas—Jesus said that "it would have been better for that man if he had not been born" (Matt. 26:24). If we eliminate the third possibility, which is actually universalism, then we are left with only options one and two: (1) Jesus's death was not an actual atonement but merely made atonement possible, or (2) Jesus's death was an actual atonement for the sins of those elect persons whom the Father had previously determined to give to him.

This leads us to study the terms that the Bible actually uses to talk about Christ's death.

Redemption is one of the most important. Does the Bible say that Jesus redeemed his people by his death or only that his death made their redemption possible? Clearly it teaches that Jesus's death was an actual redemption—that it actually freed certain people to serve God. Peter wrote, "You were ransomed from the futile ways inherited from your forefathers, not with perishable things such as silver or gold, but with the precious blood of Christ, like that of a lamb without blemish or spot" (1 Peter 1:18–19). What kind of redemption would this be if the death of Jesus only made redemption possible—and if, as a result, some of those for whom he died were still in bondage? In order for there to be a real redemption, the person who has been redeemed must be liberated. Therefore, when the Bible says that Jesus redeemed us by his death on the cross, that redemption must be an effective redemption, and those who have been redeemed must be actual beneficiaries of it.

The same thing is true in the case of whatever term we consider. Was Christ's work of turning aside God's wrath a real *propitiation*, or did it only make propitiation possible? What kind of a propitiation would this be if Jesus turned the wrath of God aside through his death but God nevertheless poured it out on the sinner? If Jesus made propitiation for sin through his death, then either that propitiation must be for all the sins of all the people of the world, as a result of which all people are or will be saved (the view of universalists), or else it must be a propitiation for the sins of his elect people, who are saved, and for no one else.

Or consider *reconciliation*. Reconciliation means "to make one" or "to establish peace," as between warring parties. What kind of reconciliation would be accomplished if the parties who have been reconciled are still fighting? Reconciliation like that would not be reconciliation at all. Yet reconciliation is what the Bible says Jesus accomplished through his death on Calvary.

Or consider *atonement*. Did Jesus's death actually atone for the sins of his people, or did it merely make atonement possible?

The answers to all these biblical questions are obvious, and the elders recognize the true meaning of what they are saying when they praise Jesus as the one who "ransomed people for God from every tribe and language and people and nation" (Rev. 5:9). He did it for those people only—but he really did do it. His death saved his people.

Second, although this is a particular redemption, it is nevertheless universal in its scope—for those who are purchased for God are, we are told, "from every tribe and language and people and nation" (v. 9). This is a common phrase in Revelation. In chapter 7 John sees "a great multitude that no one could number, from every nation, from all tribes and peoples and languages" (v. 9), and in chapter 14 he says, "I saw another angel flying directly overhead, with an eternal gospel to proclaim to those who dwell on earth, to every nation and tribe and language and people" (v. 6). Similar words occur—though not necessarily to describe the redeemed people—in Revelation 10:11; 11:9; 13:7; and 17:15.

JESUS MADE THOSE WHOM HE RANSOMED "A KINGDOM AND PRIESTS"

As the end result of the fact that Jesus died for his people's salvation, they became "a kingdom and priests." This is a repeated theme in Revelation. We studied the meaning of these words when we came to them in Revelation 1:6, and they occur again in Revelation 20:6: "They will be priests of God and of Christ, and they will reign with him for a thousand years."

This is not the place to discuss the nature of the millennium.

The place for that is chapter 20, which is the only place in the Bible where the concept occurs. But it is hard to escape the thought that when the four living creatures and the twenty-four elders say here that the saints "shall reign on the earth" (5:10), what they are pointing to surely looks like a future, earthly, thousand-year reign with Christ. Those who interpret the millennium to mean the church age argue that believers are reigning with Jesus in the church now. But although there is a sense in which we rule now, it is hard to believe that our present rule exhausts the meaning of this promise. We may also be said to rule with Christ in heaven when we get there, and that is certainly true. But Revelation 5:10 says "on the earth"—not in heaven. I would argue that a literal, future, earthly reign is the only reasonable meaning of these words and that such a reign is also suggested elsewhere in the Bible, as in 1 Corinthians 6:2: "Or do you not know that the saints will judge the world?"

THE SONG OF THE ANGELS

After hearing a new song from the living creatures and the elders, John looks out beyond the immediate vicinity of the throne and sees "many angels, numbering myriads of myriads and thousands of thousands" (Rev. 5:11). These numbers are not to be taken literally, of course. The largest number in the Greek language is ten thousand, so multiplying thousands upon thousands merely means innumerable. What is being said here is that the innumerable hosts of heaven join the four living creatures and the twenty-four elders in singing these last songs. Having noted what Jesus accomplished by his death, the heavenly armies now ascribe to God the glory that is his just due—first to Jesus alone, then to Jesus together with the Father.

Seven things are ascribed to Jesus in the first hymn, and four of them are repeated in the final song. All of them are ascribed to Jesus elsewhere in the New Testament as well:

- power (see 1 Cor. 1:24)
- wealth (see 2 Cor. 8:9; Eph. 3:8)
- wisdom (see 1 Cor. 1:24)

- might (see Eph. 6:10; 2 Thess. 1:9)
- honor (see Heb. 2:9)
- glory (see John 1:14; Heb. 2:9)
- blessing (see Eph. 1:3–6)

Again, this list is comprehensive, meaning that all honor and praise belong to Jesus and none of it to us, for salvation has been accomplished by the work of Christ alone. And also by the Father, who planned it. This is why Paul ends his great doxology in Romans 11 in much the same way, saying, "For from him and through him and to him are all things. To him be glory forever. Amen" (v. 36).

Nature joins the redeemed in singing the final song of Revelation 5, because God and the Lamb are responsible for both creation and redemption and because nature can certainly give God honor—especially for creation. First we hear the song of angels and elders and living creatures: "Worthy is the Lamb who was slain, to receive power and wealth and wisdom and might and honor and glory and blessing!" (v. 12). Then every creature on earth and in heaven and under the earth joins the chorus: "To him who sits on the throne and to the Lamb be blessing and honor and glory and might forever and ever!" (v. 13).

What is left after that? Nothing—except to do what the four living creatures and the twenty-four elders do: "The four living creatures said, 'Amen!' and the elders fell down and worshiped" (v. 14).

17

THE FOUR HORSEMEN
OF THE APOCALYPSE

Revelation 6:1–8

One of the most disturbing movies I have ever seen is Francis Ford Coppola's classic reflection on the Vietnam War, *Apocalypse Now*. The film tracks an American officer who is sent upriver into the heart of the war-torn countryside in order to find and eventually assassinate a renegade commander who has holed up in an inaccessible region. Forging deep into the battle zone, the officer arrives at a remote river outpost in the middle of a shattering firestorm. Shells are exploding everywhere. Men are being blown to bits. Those who are fighting have the wide-eyed, desperate look of men who are virtually insane, and the whole scene is bathed in the red-orange color of the exploding bombs and automated fire. It's a scene out of Dante's *Inferno*. It is hell.

"Who's in charge here?" the officer asks.

Nobody answers his question.[1]

Many observers of the world scene would recognize that this is a portrait of our times: no one is in charge, and we are all headed for eventual destruction. But silence is not the answer that the author of the Bible's great apocalypse gives to the question "Who's in charge?"

---

1. Author's recollection of "Do Lung Bridge," *Apocalypse Now*, directed by Francis Ford Coppola (1979; Hollywood, CA: Paramount, 1999), DVD.

John answers that God is in charge and that world events—even those that are most terrifying—are controlled by Jesus Christ, who is the Lord of history. He states this boldly when he describes how the Lamb who is before the throne takes the scroll from the hands of God the Father and begins to break its seals.

THE BREAKING OF THE SEALS

The breaking of the seals in Revelation 6–8 continues the vision of heaven that is described in chapters 4 and 5, but with a change along the lines that I mentioned in an earlier study in this book. This change concerns the flow of Revelation, which takes the form of a constant shifting between a scene in heaven and what is happening on earth. Chapters 4 and 5 were set in the throne room of heaven. Now we look to earth to see what is happening here, and what we see are the calamities of world history being released by the One who alone is worthy to break the scroll's seals. As Jesus breaks the seals, the events that they portend unfold, as symbolized in the case of the first four seals by four variously colored horses and their riders, who go out from God's presence in order to bring suffering to the earth. They are the famous "four horsemen of the apocalypse."

There is an echo here of two visions that are described by Zechariah. One is of a rider on a red horse, behind whom are red, brown, and white horses (see Zech. 1:8–11). These riders are sent out to survey the earth, and they return in time to report that the whole earth is at rest and in peace (see v. 11). The second vision is in Zechariah 6:1–8. It is of four chariots that are pulled in turn by four red, black, white, and dappled horses. These chariots are described as the spirits of heaven going to the ends of the earth, though Zechariah does not say what they are doing.

John would have been aware of these visions and may have been thinking of them, but the scene that he describes is quite different. In Revelation 6, the world is not at peace—it is at war. And what is most significant, God is not sending his messengers into the world to discover whether the world is at peace or at war but in order to *bring* war and its terrible aftermath to those who have not heeded his call to repentance—and who must now experience his just judgments. It is Jesus who breaks the seals and thus brings judgment. In case we miss the significance of this, even the call that summons the four riders to "Come!" is spoken by the four living creatures who surround the throne of the Almighty and who speak for God.

"Come!" is the Greek imperative *erchou*. It can mean either "come" or "go." Here it means "Be going!" or "Come out and get going!"

THE RIDER ON THE WHITE HORSE

When the Lord Jesus Christ breaks the first of the seven seals that bind God's scroll, the first living creature cries, "Come!" and a white horse appears in heaven. John writes, "I looked, and behold, a white horse! And its rider had a bow, and a crown was given to him, and he came out conquering, and to conquer" (Rev. 6:2).

Who is this rider? No one who is acquainted with the voluminous literature on the book of Revelation will be surprised to learn that there is more than one view of the answer. Some identify the rider with Jesus Christ. Others see him as the Antichrist, or at least as representing the kind of false christs or deceptive religious teachers that are common in the world. Still others see the rider as representing mere military figures or tyrants—in other words, as the spirit of conquest.

VIEW ONE: THE RIDER IS CHRIST

Quite a few commentators identify the rider on the white horse as Jesus Christ, or as the gospel of Christ that is being preached and winning converts throughout the earth. Examples would be George Eldon Ladd, who says, "The rider is not Christ himself but symbolizes the proclamation of the gospel of Christ in all the world,"[2] and William Hendriksen, who argues that the rider actually is Jesus Christ. Hendriksen supports this view with seven arguments.

---

2. George Eldon Ladd, *A Commentary on the Revelation of John* (Grand Rapids: William B. Eerdmans, 1972), 99.

1. "This view is in harmony with the context." Revelation 2 and 3 portrayed Jesus standing in the midst of his churches—and whenever Jesus is present, the devil gets busy. Concerning the Lamb, we are told, "Behold, the Lion of the tribe of Judah, the Root of David, has conquered" (Rev. 5:5)

2. "This view is in harmony with a careful word study." The horse is white, and white is associated with heaven and with purity. Therefore, according to Hendriksen, the rider cannot be the devil or the Antichrist. The rider also receives a crown, as does Christ in Revelation 14:14. Finally, in Revelation, "to conquer" refers to Christ or to believers (see Rev. 3:21; 5:5), with only a few exceptions.

3. "This interpretation is demanded by the parallel passage in the book of Revelation itself." In Revelation 19:11, the rider on the white horse is explicitly identified as Christ.

4. "The idea that the Conqueror upon the white horse is the Christ is in harmony with the very genius and purpose of the book of Revelation." The theme of the book is the victory of Christ and his church. Revelation 17:14 says that "the Lamb will conquer them, for he is Lord of lords and King of kings, and those with him are called and chosen and faithful."

5. "The view that the rider on the white horse in 6:2 is the Christ is in harmony with what is found in Matthew 10:34, where Jesus says he has come to bring a sword to the earth."

6. "This interpretation is strongly supported by its parallel in Psalm 45:3–5, which describes a victorious, conquering King." That psalm clearly refers to Christ.

7. Zechariah 1:8–11 is another parallel passage that may be cited in support of this view.[3]

Hendriksen concludes, "Our Lord Jesus Christ is conquering now; that is, throughout this present dispensation his cause is going forward, for he is exercising both his spiritual and his universal

3. William Hendriksen, *More Than Conquerors: An Interpretation of the Book of Revelation* (Grand Rapids: Baker Book House, 1940), 93–96.

Kingship. By means of the Word (gospel: Matt. 24:14) and the Spirit, the testimonies and the tears of his disciples, his own intercession and their prayers, the angels of heaven and armies on earth, the trumpets of judgment and the bowls of wrath, our Lord is riding forth victoriously, conquering and to conquer. That, in all probability, is the meaning of the rider on the white horse."[4]

VIEW TWO: THE RIDER IS THE ANTICHRIST OR FALSE RELIGIOUS TEACHING

The points that have just been summarized are impressive, but none of them are totally convincing when examined carefully, and not all commentators are convinced by them. A second class of commentators see the rider on the white horse as the Antichrist or as representing deceptive religious teaching. Most dispensationalists hold to this view. So does J. Ramsey Michaels, who writes, "The concern over false prophets in chapters 2–3 suggests false prophecy as the most likely interpretation. . . . And to the degree that the antichrist figure in the book of Revelation is associated with false prophecy . . . the first rider is 'antichrist' as well."[5] Billy Graham takes this view as well, devoting three chapters of *Approaching Hoofbeats: The Four Horsemen of the Apocalypse* to a study of the false or deceptive religion that is represented by this rider.[6]

Here are some arguments in favor of this view:

1. The language of conquering is not used as exclusively of Christ as Hendriksen suggests. It is used elsewhere to describe the beast oppressing the saints (see Rev. 11:7; 13:7).
2. The four horses in this passage, as well as in the Old Testament background passages of Zechariah 1:8–11 and 6:1–8, are in the same category. That is, in each individual passage all four horses have the same nature and do the same things. So, in

4. Hendriksen, 96.

5. J. Ramsey Michaels, *Revelation*, The IVP New Testament Commentary Series (Downers Grove, IL: InterVarsity Press, 1997), 101.

6. See Billy Graham, *Approaching Hoofbeats: The Four Horsemen of the Apocalypse* (Waco: Word Books, 1983), 73–119.

Revelation, all four horses are evil agents or instruments of judgment.

3. If the white color suggests Christ, it might also suggest an imitator of Christ, who would be the Antichrist. If this is the case, and if the rider also stands for false religious teaching, then the pattern of the horses and their riders fits the description, in a general way, of woes that are found in Matthew 24:4–14. There Jesus warns of false prophets, wars and rumors of wars, famines, earthquakes, persecutions, and apostasy.

VIEW THREE: THE RIDER IS MERELY A MILITARY FIGURE—THE SPIRIT OF CONQUEST

I am not satisfied with either of these first two views and therefore turn to the third—namely, that the rider on the white horse merely represents the spirit of conquest or militarism that leads to the evils that are symbolized by the riders that follow him. As G. K. Beale puts it, "Conquest (the first rider), together with civil unrest (especially for persecuted Christians—the second rider), leads to famine (the third rider) and death (the fourth rider)."[7]

I think it is too early in the book of Revelation to apply to the vision of the rider on the white horse what is said of the Antichrist, who does not appear until much later; and the similarities between the description of this rider and the vision of Christ riding a horse in Revelation 19 are all weak. The Christ of chapter 19 carries a sword, which is identified as the Word of God. This rider carries a bow. The Christ of chapter 19 has been crowned with "many crowns." This rider has only one crown. The words for *crown* are not even the same—in chapter 19 the word for *crown* is *diadema*, which is the royal diadem of authority; while the word in chapter 6 is *stephanos*, which is the wreath of victory at athletic games. In addition, Christ *has* conquered. This rider is merely "conquering, and to conquer."

A few historical details also point in the direction of this horse and rider representing conquest. The rider of Revelation 6 has a bow, and

---

7. G. K. Beale, *The Book of Revelation: A Commentary on the Greek Text* (Grand Rapids: William B. Eerdmans, 1999), 371.

the bow was the characteristic weapon of the Parthian cavalry, for whom white was also a sacred color. The Parthians were a threat to the eastern flank of the Roman Empire at this time, having defeated a Roman army in AD 62—not many years before John wrote his apocalypse. What John may be suggesting, then, under divine inspiration, is a successful Parthian invasion that would disrupt the Roman peace, which would mean world war. Incidentally, a historical memory of the fear with which the Romans regarded the Parthian army survives in our English expression "a parting shot"—meaning a final retort. Originally the expression was "a Parthian shot," and it referred to the accurate, devastating arrows of the Parthian archers who were able to strike and kill enemies while they were galloping on their horses.

Revelation 6:2 may also be merely a picture of any conquering general. When a Roman general celebrated a triumph, he either rode through Rome on a white horse or entered the city riding a chariot that was pulled by white horses. Noting this and other arguments, Leon Morris says (rightly, in my opinion), "The four horsemen must surely be taken together, and they all indicate destruction, horror, terror. This one surely stands for war."[8] Similarly, Robert Mounce summarizes this image by saying, "John has in mind military conquest in general."[9]

THE RIDER ON THE RED HORSE

If we identify the first of the four horsemen as representing military conquest—and even if we cannot—the identification of the second, third, and fourth riders is not difficult. Clearly they stand for war's destructive swath, particularly in terms of bloodshed; for poverty and famine, which often follow conquest; and for death, which is war's ultimate legacy. Bloodshed is symbolized by a red horse and poverty and famine by a black horse, while the fourth and final horse is the color of a corpse.

8. Leon Morris, *The Book of Revelation: An Introduction and Commentary*, rev. ed. (Grand Rapids: Wm. B. Eerdmans, 1988), 101–2.
9. Robert H. Mounce, *The Book of Revelation* (Grand Rapids: Wm. B. Eerdmans, 1977), 154.

But maybe I am moving too quickly. I have identified the second horseman as the destructive swath of war, and particularly as bloodshed—which is suggested by the fact that the horse is red, the color of blood, and that the rider has been given a sword. Most writers would agree, in broad terms. But William Hendriksen wants to narrow this interpretation a bit. He believes that this horse and rider refer specifically to the persecution of Christians rather than to war and its results in general. This fits the pattern that he sees in Revelation: first the advance of the gospel, which then results in the persecution of believers, and finally judgment on the wicked and the salvation of God's people. He argues the following:

1. "This explanation is in striking accord with the immediate context." Whenever Christ and his gospel appear, persecution immediately follows.
2. "This view is confirmed by the parallel passage, Matthew 10:34"—in which Jesus says he has come to bring not peace but a sword.
3. "Slay," or "slaughter," is the normal word not for killing in warfare but for killing believers. Hendriksen cites 1 John 3:12 and Revelation 5:6, 9, 12; 6:9; 13:8; and 18:24 as proof.
4. "When the fifth seal is opened John sees 'the souls of those who have been slaughtered for the Word of God'."
5. The sword (*machaira*) signifies the sacrificial knife.[10]

This last point is questionable, though it is supported by Beale, who agrees that "slay" or "slaughter" is used by John only for the killing of Christ or his followers.[11] Moreover, it seems significant that the breaking of the fifth seal, in Revelation 6:9, discloses those who had been killed for their testimony. Still, verse 4 does not seem to be speaking about persecutions. It says that the rider of the red horse was "permitted to take peace from the earth, so that people should slay one another." This is describing worldwide slaughter, not

---

10. Hendriksen, *More Than Conquerors*, 99–101.
11. See Beale, *The Book of Revelation*, 379.

the persecution of believers specifically. As far as the word *machaira* is concerned, the English Standard Version uses the wording "a great sword," because of the many who are killed—which is a very different idea from a sacrificial knife.

The people to whom John was writing would have been well aware of the slaughter that accompanies war. From 67 to 37 BC, the thirty years before the reign of Herod the Great, no fewer than 100,000 men in Palestine alone had perished in abortive revolutions. The civil wars that were launched by the assassination of Julius Caesar had been settled by the triumph and ascension of Octavius Augustus (63 BC–AD 14), but thousands had lost their lives in those wars, and they had caused untold suffering. In faraway Britain, in AD 61, Queen Boadicea had rebelled against Rome and been crushed by Rome's armies. She committed suicide, and 150,000 men perished in that conflict. War always brings widespread suffering and death—as it is doing in many areas of the world today.

THE RIDER ON THE BLACK HORSE

Hendriksen relates the symbolism of the rider on the black horse to the poverty that would have befallen many of the Christians who refused to worship Caesar or the tutelary deities that were worshiped in the various manufacturing guilds of Rome. But if the red horse does not refer to the persecution of Christians specifically, there is no reason to restrict the poverty that is symbolized by the rider on the black horse to Christians, either. The black horse simply represents the deprivations that normally accompany war, when the regular avenues of supply are interrupted and the fruit of that year's harvest is destroyed.

Verse 6 says, "A quart of wheat for a denarius." A quart of wheat was enough for one person for one day, and a denarius was a working man's wages for a day. Normally, a denarius bought from eight to sixteen quarts of wheat or barley.[12] But in the times of scarcity that are described here, a person who received a day's wage

---

12. See the second speech of Cicero, *In Verrem*, bk. 3, sec. 188.

would have to spend it all just to buy enough to stay alive. If he had a family, he could buy barley, which was cheaper ("three quarts of barley for a denarius"), but he would not have enough left over for the other necessities of life. This would be a bare subsistence economy. What about the words "do not harm the oil and the wine"? They indicate that the luxuries of the rich are being protected at the same time that the necessities of the poor are growing scarce.

An example of this situation comes from the very time in which John may have been writing. During the reign of the emperor Domitian, the Roman Empire experienced a serious shortage of grain and an abundance of wine. Domitian decreed that no more vineyards should be planted and indeed that half the vineyards in the provinces should be cut down. This caused riots in Asia Minor, where John was writing, because one of the principle sources of income for that area was the production and sale of wine. Responding to that fierce reaction, Domitian relented and enacted a contrary edict to the effect that those who allowed their vineyards to go out of production should be prosecuted. The result was an exact picture of what John seems to be describing in Revelation: a case in which grain was scarce but was still forbidden from interfering with the supply of wine and oil.[13]

THE RIDER ON THE PALE HORSE

The fourth horse is of a livid, or pale, greenish color, which symbolizes disease and death. The word that is translated "pale" is *chloros*, from which we get the words "chlorophyll" (the substance that makes plants green) and "chlorine" (a pale or greenish gas). Behind this pale horse comes Hades—the abode of the dead. Death and Hades are given power over "a fourth of the earth, to kill with sword and with famine and with pestilence and by wild beasts of the earth." This is a natural progression—the sword is the sword of war; war is followed by scarcity, which leads to famine; those who are starving are susceptible to plague, which kills many; and at last, when the

13. See William Barclay, *The Revelation of John*, vol. 2, *Chapters 6 to 22*, rev. ed. (Philadelphia: The Westminster Press, 1976), 8.

restraining force of civilization is dissolving, the beasts move in from the forest to prey upon the weak. God warned the Jews of these very judgments in Ezekiel 14:21 (see also Lev. 26:21–26).

But notice: even these terrible judgments are controlled by God, since the power to kill that Death and Hades possess is authority that has been "given" to them (Rev. 6:8). By whom? By God, of course, and by the Lord Jesus Christ, who breaks the scroll's seals. God remains sovereign even over the worst of the horrors of war.

CHRIST IS IN CONTROL

Some writers on Revelation have trouble believing that Jesus is actually controlling war, bloodshed, famine, plague, and death—that he sends the woes that are portrayed by these horsemen. They do not want to make him the immediate cause of these judgments, arguing instead that he only permits or tolerates what unfolds here. But that is not the message of this book. The message of Revelation is that Jesus Christ is totally sovereign over all things, including the forces of evil in this world, and that he uses these things for God's purposes, as he always has. As far as the wicked are concerned, Revelation teaches that it is Jesus himself who is the judge and the executor of the judgments that are every person's due.

Moreover, the judgments that are depicted here will get worse, which is what the unfolding series of seals, trumpets, and bowls of God's wrath that follow the four horsemen and their judgments portend. For, after all, this is just war. The four horsemen of the apocalypse release only what human beings unleash against one another every day. Bruce Metzger says, "There are few chapters in Revelation that speak more directly to our time than this part of chapter 6. In books, in newspapers, in magazine articles, and in radio broadcasts, we read and hear about the Four Horsemen of the Apocalypse, who are riding across the earth today. We hear the cry for justice; we sense that there must be a judgment in which the guilty will not be able to escape."[14]

14. Bruce M. Metzger, *Breaking the Code: Understanding the Book of Revelation*

Very true. But what about the days that are still to come, when God will exercise his just judgments by breaking up nature and its destructive forces and by unleashing the Antichrist, the beast, and the false prophet, who will strike the world with their Satanic evil? In the days of Abraham, when God foretold the history of the Jewish people, he said that "the iniquity of the Amorites is not yet complete" (Gen. 15:16). These ancient enemies were to be spared for four hundred years. But the four hundred years did pass—their sin did reach its fullness—and then they were destroyed by the Jewish invasion of Canaan under the command of Joshua.

The pictures John paints in this last book of the Bible are not for our amusement; nor are they puzzles merely to exercise our minds. They are warnings of how seriously God takes sin and of how he is going to judge it fully in time.

Let me make this personal. The evil that is portrayed by the four horsemen is not merely something that is out there somewhere in the world and being practiced by other people. It is in ourselves—because the seeds of all this destruction are in ourselves. Billy Graham had it exactly right when he wrote, "The four horsemen are God's picture to warn us of our own sinfulness. They do not cause evil. They are a picture of a very human process."[15] What the four horsemen do, we do—or at least are very capable of doing. And the meaning of this is that we need to repent of our sin and turn to Jesus Christ, in whom alone salvation can be found. Do not blame others for evil. Blame yourself!

Liturgical prayers of confession sometimes contain the language "By my fault, by my own fault, by my own most grievous fault." That is it exactly. With our own fault is where we must start, because it is only when we turn from our own self-righteousness that we can find God's mercy in Jesus Christ.

(Nashville: Abingdon Press, 1993), 59.
   15. Graham, *Approaching Hoofbeats*, 113.

18

THE FIFTH SEAL

Revelation 6:9—11

Here is a question: in the sixteenth and seventeenth centuries, what was the most popular and widely read book among Christians in the English-speaking world, besides the Bible? The answer is John Foxe's *Book of Martyrs*, which contained the stories of Christians who had been killed for their testimonies throughout the centuries of Christian history.

John Foxe was born in 1516—one year before Luther posted his "Ninety-Five Theses" on the door of the Castle Church in Wittenberg. Foxe studied at Oxford, fled England when Queen Mary took the throne, and, while abroad, began his great study, which was originally called the *Actes and Monuments of These Latter and Perilous Days*. The massive *Book of Martyrs* was published in 1563. It was an immediate success. It went through four editions in Foxe's lifetime, and its impact continued for generations, strengthening the faith of countless English Christians and forming a view of the competing religions of the day that helped to ensure the triumph of Protestantism in Britain.

The stories of those who have embraced death rather than renounce their faith in Jesus Christ are always powerful! And it is not only in Foxe's work that we find references to them. We also find such references in the eleventh chapter of Hebrews. In the latter half of that chapter, the author reminds his readers of the martyrs of the Old Testament period.

Some were tortured, refusing to accept release, so that they might rise again to a better life. Others suffered mocking and flogging, and even chains and imprisonment. They were stoned, they were sawn in two, they were killed with the sword. They went about in skins of sheep and goats, destitute, afflicted, mistreated—of whom the world was not worthy. (vv. 35–38)

Indeed, the world was not worthy!

In the sixth chapter of Revelation, we see these martyrs beneath the throne of God in heaven, and they are crying out to God, "O Sovereign Lord, holy and true, how long before you will judge and avenge our blood on those who dwell on the earth?" (Rev. 6:10).

GOD'S MARTYRS

The martyrs are revealed to John when the fifth of the seven seals is opened. The seals, like the seven trumpets that follow them, are broken into groups of four, two, and one, respectively—with a pause between the sixth and seventh of both the seals and trumpets. As far as the seals are concerned, the first four have described the conditions that will prevail on earth until the coming of the Lord at the final judgment. But now the focus changes, and what we observe are those who have died and who will die for Christ during the same period.

Does this change in focus surprise us? It should not—and for two reasons.

First, we have been prepared to think about the martyrs by the first three chapters of Revelation. Jesus told the church in Smyrna, "Behold, the devil is about to throw some of you into prison, that you may be tested, and for ten days you will have tribulation. Be faithful unto death, and I will give you the crown of life" (Rev. 2:10). And in the letter to the church at Pergamum, he referred to "Antipas my faithful witness, who was killed among you" (Rev. 2:13). Martyrs are mentioned again in Revelation 13:15, 18:24, and 20:4.

The second reason that the disclosure of martyrs in chapter 6 should not surprise us is that Jesus made clear in his teaching that those who followed him would experience persecutions and suffering. He did so in his sermon on the Mount of Olives, which we have already looked at several times as an outline of what we find being discussed at greater length in Revelation. For example, in Matthew 24, after Jesus has spoken of the conditions that will prevail before he comes again—"wars and rumors of wars," as well as "famines and earthquakes," which he calls "the beginning of the birth pains" (vv. 6–8)—he continues, "Then they will deliver you up to tribulation and put you to death, and you will be hated by all nations for my name's sake" (v. 9).

At the same place in Mark's parallel chapter, Jesus is quoted as saying,

> Be on your guard. For they will deliver you over to councils, and you will be beaten in synagogues, and you will stand before governors and kings for my sake, to bear witness before them. And the gospel must first be proclaimed to all nations. And when they bring you to trial and deliver you over, do not be anxious beforehand what you are to say, but say whatever is given you in that hour, for it is not you who speak, but the Holy Spirit. And brother will deliver brother over to death, and the father his child, and children will rise against parents and have them put to death. And you will be hated by all for my name's sake. But the one who endures to the end will be saved. (Mark 13:9–13)

Luke adds, "They will lay their hands on you and persecute you, delivering you up to the synagogues and prisons, and you will be brought before kings and governors for my name's sake" (Luke 21:12). The gospel of John does not contain a record of Christ's teaching on the Mount of Olives, but in the context of the Lord's final discourses to his disciples, John records him as saying, "They will put you out of the synagogues. Indeed, the hour is coming when whoever kills you will think he is offering service to God" (John 16:2).

In light of Jesus's teaching, what is surprising is not that Christians have been persecuted and killed all throughout the long annals of human history (which they certainly have been—the *Book of Martyrs* documents it) but that so many Christians have not been persecuted. It is surprising that you and I have not been persecuted.

It is worth noting, however, that by the end of the first Christian century, when John wrote Revelation, there had not yet been many martyrs. There had been a few. I mentioned Antipas, who had been killed in Pergamum. Stephen had been stoned in Jerusalem. James had been beheaded by Herod in the same city. Paul had been killed, and possibly Peter too. But there had not yet been any widespread arrests or executions of believers. This happened on a wide scale first under the emperor Domitian, who ruled from AD 81 to 96.

Since the years before then were relatively safe for Christians, we should probably conclude that here John is not describing the martyrs whom he had known or heard about but rather the vast host of believers who will have died for their faith throughout all ages of the church and in all places, before Jesus returns.

Why had they been persecuted? It was not because of their revolutionary activities or because they had been unruly or obnoxious. John reports that it was because of "the word of God and for the witness they had borne" (Rev. 6:9). A Latin expression says, "It is not death, but the cause of death, that constitutes a martyr." That is true! And what has made these individuals martyrs is that they died for Jesus Christ and the gospel. "The word of God" is the same thing as the truth of God, which is the gospel; whereas "the witness they had borne" is most likely the testimony that has been given to believers by Christ. It is all about him. We may recall that John used nearly these exact words to describe the cause for which he had been imprisoned on the island of Patmos. It was, he says, "on account of the word of God and the testimony of Jesus" (1:9).

When John says that he saw those who had been killed, for the word of God and for the testimony they had maintained, "under the altar," he does not want us to think of the souls of the martyrs somehow peeping out from underneath a literal stone or bronze altar, as if they were being squashed by it. This is symbolized revelation, and the meaning has to do with the associations that the altar has elsewhere in Scripture. There are several such associations.

1. The altar in the courtyard of the Jewish temple was the place

where the blood of sacrifices was poured out and the sacrifices them-selves were consumed. Therefore, the first thing that the altar is asso-ciated with is *the blood of Christ, which has atoned for sin*. The fact that the martyrs are "under the altar" suggests that their sins have been atoned for and that they have themselves been covered, in the sight of God, by Christ's righteousness. Donald Grey Barnhouse says rightly, "It is a figure that speaks of justification."[1] We are reminded that no one will be in heaven, whether they are martyrs or not, if their sin has not been atoned for by Christ's death.

2. Being "under the altar" also suggests that *the martyrs had sacrificed themselves for Christ's sake*. Jesus had taught his disciples, "If anyone would come after me, let him deny himself and take up his cross and follow me" (Matt. 16:24). The martyrs had done this, and their death was the result. They had followed closely in Christ's steps. This connection is made clear by the fact that the word that is translated "slain" in the phrase "those who had been slain for the word of God and for the witness they had borne" is the same word that was used earlier of Jesus, the Lamb: "Worthy are you to take the scroll and to open its seals, for you were slain, and by your blood you ransomed people for God from every tribe and language and people and nation" (Rev. 5:9)—and again, similarly: "Worthy is the Lamb who was slain, to receive power and wealth and wisdom and might and honor and glory and blessing!" (Rev. 5:12).

Robert Mounce states, "That the souls of the martyrs were under-neath the altar is a way of saying that their untimely deaths on earth are from God's perspective a sacrifice on the altar of heaven."[2] Paul was thinking of his own coming death in these terms when he told Timothy, "I am already being poured out as a drink offering, and the time of my departure has come" (2 Tim. 4:6), and when he wrote to the Philippians, "I am to be poured out as a drink offering upon the sacrificial offering of your faith" (Phil. 2:17).

3. The third thing that is associated with the altar is *the prayers*

---

1. Donald Grey Barnhouse, *Revelation: An Expositional Commentary* (Grand Rapids: Zondervan, 1985), 133.

2. Robert H. Mounce, *The Book of Revelation* (Grand Rapids: Wm. B. Eerdmans, 1977), 157.

that were offered up at the time of the sacrifices. Thus far we have been thinking of the great bronze altar that stood in the temple court because of the image of the sacrificial blood that was poured at its base. But there was also a golden altar of incense that stood in front of the curtain that was before the Most Holy Place in the temple (see Ex. 30:1–10). The blood that was shed on the Day of Atonement was poured on this altar once a year, but incense was burned on it every day—incense that symbolized the prayers of God's people (see Rev. 5:8). This altar is referred to explicitly in Revelation 8:3–4, where it is linked to these prayers of the saints.

> And another angel came and stood at the altar with a golden censer, and he was given much incense to offer with the prayers of all the saints on the golden altar before the throne, and the smoke of the incense, with the prayers of the saints, rose before God from the hand of the angel.

THE CRY OF THE MARTYRS

This last association of the altar has special relevance to Revelation 6, for what follows the disclosure of the martyrs beneath the altar is a description of their prayers. They are calling to God in a loud voice, "O Sovereign Lord, holy and true, how long before you will judge and avenge our blood on those who dwell on the earth?" (v. 10). This is a prayer for justice, obviously. But how can we reconcile a prayer like this with Jesus's prayer for God to forgive his enemies (see Luke 23:34) or with Stephen's prayer that seems to have echoed Jesus's petition: "Lord, do not hold this sin against them" (Acts 7:60)?

Let's begin by admitting that Christians have sometimes offered vengeful prayers and been anything but forgiving. We have often failed to show the spirit of our Master. But let's remember, too, that the prayers we are dealing with here are being offered not by sinful human beings but by those who have been cleansed from sin and who are now in a sinless condition. Or, to put it another way, these are righteous prayers. They are the kinds of prayers that Jesus himself might be making. Moreover, the only question that the martyrs are actually asking is "How long?" They are not disputing that justice will be done, nor are they pleading for it. Justice will be done, because God is a just and sovereign God. The Judge of all the earth must act rightly (see Gen. 18:25). The martyrs are only asking how long the conditions in which the people of God are slaughtered for their faith will continue.

Most importantly, it is not for their own wounded honor that they are praying, but for God's honor and God's glory. Hendriksen says that "these martyrs do not invoke retribution for their own sake but for God's sake. . . . Does not God affirm that the blood of his saints cries for wrath? (Gen. 4:10; cf. Heb. 11:4)?"[3] Actually, the martyrs are doing what Paul said to do in Romans 12:19: "Beloved, never avenge yourselves, but leave it to the wrath of God, for it is written, 'Vengeance is mine, I will repay, says the Lord.'"

This has been the prayer of God's people throughout history. "O LORD, how long shall the wicked, how long shall the wicked exult?" cried the psalmist (Ps. 94:3). "O LORD, how long shall I cry for help, and you will not hear?" asked Habakkuk (Hab. 1:2).

I mentioned that the prayer in Revelation 6:10 is made by the glorified saints and is thus a right and proper prayer. But let me add that we do not have to wait until we get to heaven in order to pray it. We do not have to be sinless in order to pray rightly. Is it not right to pray that God will be honored, that the righteousness of God will be vindicated, and that the wicked will be judged? What else would we pray—that evil might be allowed to work forever? That God would be eternally dishonored and disgraced?

Whether or not we pray for the vindication of the righteous and the judgment of the wicked ourselves, this is the prayer of the martyrs—and their prayers are answered. For, just two chapters later—in the very passage that speaks of the golden altar, the incense, and the prayers of the saints that went up to God from the angel's hand—we read, "Then the angel took the censer and filled it with fire from

---

3. William Hendriksen, *More Than Conquerors: An Interpretation of the Book of Revelation* (Grand Rapids: Baker Book House, 1940), 106.

the altar and threw it on the earth, and there were peals of thunder, rumblings, flashes of lightning, and an earthquake" (Rev. 8:5). This signifies God's just and final judgment, which follows the opening of the seventh seal.

THE MARTYRS' REWARD AND GOD'S ANSWER

This account of the opening of the fifth seal closes with two details. First, the martyrs are each given a white robe that signifies righteousness and victory. Some have understood these robes to be the saints' glorified bodies, but this is not the way white robes are used in Revelation. They signify *righteousness*, rather than symbolizing glory, in Revelation 7:9–11, where John sees a vast multitude praising God before the throne. Afterward, one of the elders tells him that "these are the ones coming out of the great tribulation. They have washed their robes and made them white in the blood of the Lamb" (v. 14). In other words, these are the justified saints.

Earlier, in Jesus's letter to the church at Sardis, white robes signify *victory*. He says to these believers, "You have still a few names in Sardis, people who have not soiled their garments, and they will walk with me in white, for they are worthy. The one who conquers will be clothed thus in white garments" (Rev. 3:4–5). White robes have this significance as well: they enable us to identify these martyrs when we see them again in Revelation 7:9, 13–14.

The second detail that closes the account of the opening of the fifth seal is God's answer to the martyrs' question, "O Sovereign Lord, holy and true, how long before you will judge and avenge our blood on those who dwell on the earth?" (Rev. 6:10). They are told to wait "a little longer, until the number of their fellow servants and their brothers should be complete, who were to be killed as they themselves had been" (v. 11). The number of the martyrs is not yet complete. The day of judgment is not yet here. But it will come. The martyrs, like us, must wait patiently. But they can wait in the knowledge that the day of retribution and final vindication *will* arrive.

This answer is the same as Peter's answer to those who were

impatient for the return of the Lord and for his judgment in Peter's day. He told them,

> Scoffers will come in the last days with scoffing, following their own sinful desires. They will say, "Where is the promise of his coming? For ever since the fathers fell asleep, all things are continuing as they were from the beginning of creation." For they deliberately overlook this fact, that the heavens existed long ago, and the earth was formed out of water and through water by the word of God, and that by means of these the world that then existed was deluged with water and perished. But by the same word the heavens and earth that now exist are stored up for fire, being kept until the day of judgment and destruction of the ungodly.
>
> But do not overlook this one fact, beloved, that with the Lord one day is as a thousand years, and a thousand years as one day. The Lord is not slow to fulfill his promise as some count slowness, but is patient toward you, not wishing that any should perish, but that all should reach repentance. (2 Peter 3:3–9)

Peter means that God is holding back his judgment until the full number of the elect is brought in. This is also what the *Book of Common Prayer* is saying when it asks, in its Order for the Burial of the Dead, "that it may please thee . . . shortly to accomplish the number of thine elect, and to hasten thy kingdom."

FINAL POINTS OF CONCLUSION

Our study of John's description of the opening of the fifth seal has enabled us to think about the martyrs, their position in heaven, their question for God, and God's reply to their question. But there is more to be learned from these verses. They teach us at least five things.

When we die, we go directly to heaven. This is obvious, isn't it? The resurrection of the bodies of those who have died does not occur until Revelation 20. Yet here in chapter 6, we already see the souls

219

of those who have died with God in heaven. And they are speaking to him and receiving answers. Over the years, there have been Christians who have posited a doctrine called "soul sleep," which says that we remain unconscious between the moment of our deaths and the day of the resurrection. But this passage refutes this spurious doctrine—as do other Bible verses. Jesus taught that the patriarchs were living in heaven, on the grounds that God "is not God of the dead, but of the living, for all live to him" (Luke 20:38). He told the believing thief who was crucified with him, "Today you will be with me in paradise" (Luke 23:43). Likewise, Paul wrote that to be "away from the body" is to be "at home with the Lord" (2 Cor. 5:8). This truth should be a deep comfort for dying Christians. They can know that as they die to life here, they will awake to life with God in heaven—and what is to come is surely better than what is past.

Although God's judgments are delayed, they will come. This should be a comfort to Christians who are suffering for their faith, but it should also be a warning and cause of terror for those who have been resisting the gospel.

Jesus spoke to the comfort Christians can take from this when he told the parable of a widow who was ignored by the judge who had charge of her case. She had nothing to bribe him with, so he kept putting her off. But she was not to be put off. She kept pleading for justice, and in the end he gave in and gave her the justice that she demanded. Jesus said, "Hear what the unrighteous judge says. And will not God give justice to his elect, who cry to him day and night? Will he delay long over them? I tell you, he will give justice to them speedily" (Luke 18:6–8).

If you are suffering for the cause of Christ, hear this and be encouraged. God will settle his accounts in time. But if you are the *cause* of oppression—if you have harmed one who bears the name of Christ or caused a little one to stumble—then tremble. Because judgment will come, and the Judge of all the earth will act rightly.

God's verdict will overturn man's verdict against the saints on earth. The martyrs have been condemned by earthly courts, which have judged them to be heretics, atheists, disturbers of the peace, haters of their fellow men, and not fit to live. Yet God has judged them to be saints and has honored them. He will also overturn those who speak against you.

But let me ask: Have you been true enough to God's Word to be rejected by any who are unbelievers? Most of us want to be accepted by the world. Have you chosen that path? Or have you entered the narrow path of discipleship that leads, from time to time—if not always—to the kinds of abuse that Jesus suffered? In his book on the four horsemen, Billy Graham ponders at one place whether he has "made the Christian faith look too easy" in his evangelistic campaigns. He asks himself, "In my eagerness to give away God's great gift, have I been honest about the price He paid in His war with evil? And have I adequately explained the price we must pay in our own war against the evil at work in and around our lives?"[4] There is a price, and we must ask whether we are willing to pay it.

The number of the righteous has been predetermined by God, and all whom he has given to Christ will surely be brought to him. This should encourage us to witness for Christ, since we can know that our witness will be effective. It should also encourage us to persevere in following after Christ, since we know that God will certainly persevere with us. He will bring us to heaven.

While we wait for the fulfillment of God's wise plan and promises, we can rest in God and trust his purposes for us, whatever the circumstances. This is what the martyrs did. Rowland E. Prothero tells the story of Louis Rang, a Huguenot pastor who was captured and condemned to die in Grenoble in 1745.[5] Rang was offered life if he would renounce his faith, but he rejected the offer and was led to the scaffold singing a French versification of Psalm 118:24, which might be roughly translated,

4. Billy Graham, *Approaching Hoofbeats: The Four Horsemen of the Apocalypse* (Waco: Word Books, 1983), 26.

5. See Rowland E. Prothero, *The Psalms in Human Life* (New York: E. P. Dutton, 1904), 225.

Here now is the happy day
For which we have been waiting.
Sing praise to God who gives us joy
And pleasures unabating.

A few weeks after the martyrdom of Rang, another Huguenot pastor, Jacque Roger, likewise strengthened himself with this verse. He was seventy years old and had escaped his enemies for nearly forty years—often by only a hair's breadth. When the soldiers finally tracked him down and asked who he was, Roger replied, "I am he whom you have sought for thirty-nine years; it was time that you should find me."[6] Roger spent his last days in prison encouraging other Protestant prisoners to remain true to the faith, and when the officers came to escort him to his place of execution, he quoted the same verse that Louis Rang had sung just weeks before.

The last of the Huguenot martyrs in France was Francois Rochette, who died in 1762. He was seized during a time of civil turmoil in Toulouse. As were the others, Rochette too was offered life if he would renounce his Protestant faith. He also refused. As he was led through the crowded streets, which were thronged with spectators, he encouraged the faithful to the very end and mounted the scaffold chanting, "Here now is the happy day for which we have been waiting."[7]

These martyrs were all able to rest in God, because they knew him.

6. Quoted in Prothero, 226.
7. See Prothero, 226–28.

19

THE SIXTH SEAL

Revelation 6:12–17

Martin Luther knew what it was to tremble before God and yet face the final judgment with confidence that God would accept him on that day. It was fear of God and of his righteousness that drove him into the monastery of the Augustinians at Erfurt when he was a young man. Luther entered the monastery, as he said, with one purpose only—to save his soul. But it was the discovery of the righteousness of God, imparted to him through Jesus Christ—the saving truth that he discovered while in the monastery—that enabled him to cease trembling and brought him back out of the monastery into the world as the leader of the Protestant Reformation.

A hymn of preparation for judgment that is known as "Luther's Hymn" captures the spirit of Luther's theology, though it was written many years later by an unknown theologian.

> Great God, what do I see and hear!
> The end of things created!
> The Judge of mankind doth appear
> On clouds of glory seated!
> The trumpet sounds; the graves restore
> The dead which they contained before:
> Prepare, my soul, to meet him.

This is the theme of the verses to which we have now come in our study of the book of Revelation. They describe what happens

223

when the sixth seal is opened and serve as a powerful warning of the judgment to come. They urge us to prepare to meet our Judge.

THE DAY OF THE LORD

In biblical language, the day of God's final judgment is referred to most frequently as the "day of the Lord." Literally, it is the "day of Jehovah," and it refers to the time when God will draw history to a close by punishing the wicked and vindicating the righteous. This day of the Lord is a frequent theme in the prophets. For example,

Wail, for the day of the LORD is near;
>   as destruction from the Almighty it will come!
Therefore all hands will be feeble,
>   and every human heart will melt.
They will be dismayed:
>   pangs and agony will seize them;
>   they will be in anguish like a woman in labor.
They will look aghast at one another;
>   their faces will be aflame.

Behold, the day of the LORD comes,
>   cruel, with wrath and fierce anger,
to make the land a desolation
>   and to destroy its sinners from it.
For the stars of the heavens and their constellations
>   will not give their light;
the sun will be dark at its rising,
>   and the moon will not shed its light.
I will punish the world for its evil,
>   and the wicked for their iniquity. (Isa. 13:6–11)

Let all the inhabitants of the land tremble,
>   for the day of the LORD is coming; it is near,
a day of darkness and gloom,
>   a day of clouds and thick darkness!

. . . .

"And I will show wonders in the heavens and on the earth, blood and fire and columns of smoke. The sun will be turned to darkness, and the moon to blood, before the great and awesome day of the LORD comes." (Joel 2:1–2, 30–31)

Peter was drawing on this imagery when he wrote, "But the day of the Lord will come like a thief, and then the heavens will pass away with a roar, and the heavenly bodies will be burned up and dissolved, and the earth and the works that are done on it will be exposed" (2 Peter 3:10).

Of even greater importance is the fact that Jesus himself used this imagery in his preview of the end times in Matthew 24. Quoting Isaiah 13:10 and 34:4, he said,

> Immediately after the tribulation of those days the sun will be darkened, and the moon will not give its light, and the stars will fall from heaven, and the powers of the heavens will be shaken. Then will appear in heaven the sign of the Son of Man, and then all the tribes of the earth will mourn, and they will see the Son of Man coming on the clouds of heaven with power and great glory. And he will send out his angels with a loud trumpet call, and they will gather his elect from the four winds, from one end of heaven to the other. (Matt. 24:29–31)

THE OPENING OF THE SIXTH SEAL

In the sixth chapter of Revelation, we have already been given a description of what human history will be like until the time of the end. It will be a time of military conquerors and tyrants, war, bloodshed, famine, and death. We have seen those who will be martyred for their faith during that entire period. They are gathered in heaven, waiting for God to be glorified by his judgment of the wicked and vindication of the righteous. That is our history at a glance. Therefore, there is nothing to stop us from moving forward rapidly to the end, as Jesus stretches out his hand and breaks the sixth seal. The text says,

When he opened the sixth seal, I looked, and behold, there was a great earthquake, and the sun became black as sackcloth, the full moon became like blood, and the stars of the sky fell to the earth as the fig tree sheds its winter fruit when shaken by a gale. The sky vanished like a scroll that is being rolled up, and every mountain and island was removed from its place. Then the kings of the earth and the great ones and the generals and the rich and the powerful, and everyone, slave and free, hid themselves in the caves and among the rocks of the mountains, calling to the mountains and rocks, "Fall on us and hide us from the face of him who is seated on the throne, and from the wrath of the Lamb, for the great day of their wrath has come, and who can stand?" (Rev. 6:12–17)

These verses fall into two distinct sections: the disruption of creation (vv. 12–14), and the terror of the human race (vv. 15–17). But in both cases, the imagery we see here is drawn from Old Testament descriptions of the final judgment: a great earthquake, the darkening of the sky, the changing of the moon's color to look like blood, the falling of the stars, the receding of the sky, the shaking of the mountains and the islands of the sea, the universality of the terror that ensues, and the attempt of the wicked to hide from God's wrath.[1]

Interestingly, both of the two sections mention seven objects being affected. The section about creation mentions the earth, the sun, the moon, the stars, the sky, and the mountains and islands of the earth, while the verses about the human race refer to kings, princes, generals, the rich, the mighty, slaves, and free men.

It is noteworthy that all this happens because of the opening of the sixth seal, when we might have expected it to coincide with the opening of the seventh seal. But the seventh seal introduces a pause.

---

1. Beale writes, "The judgment of the world is depicted with stock-in-trade OT imagery for the dissolution of the cosmos. This portrayal is based on a mosaic of OT passages that are brought together because of the cosmic metaphors of judgment that they have in common. The quarry of texts from which the description has been drawn is composed primarily of Isa. 13:10–13; 24:1–6, 19–23; 34:4; Ezek. 32:6–8; Joel 2:10, 30–31; 3:15–16; and Hab. 3:6–11 (cf. secondarily Amos 8:8–9; Jer. 4:23–28; and Ps. 68:7–8)." G. K. Beale, *The Book of Revelation: A Commentary on the Greek Text* (Grand Rapids: William B. Eerdmans, 1999), 396.

It is as if we come up to the very brink of destruction, but at this point do not quite go over. Instead, we have the blowing of the seven trumpets and the pouring out of the seven bowls of wrath. Even in judgment we see the patience and amazing mercy of God.

ARE THESE LITERAL EVENTS?

There is a question that we need to ask at this point, and it is not easy to answer: Are these catastrophic events—the earthquake, the darkening of the sky, the changing of the moon's color to look like blood, the falling of the stars, the receding of the sky, and the shaking of the mountains and the islands of the sea—to be taken literally? Or is this another example of what I have been calling symbolic revelation?

SYMBOLIC REVELATION

At first glance, it is most natural to interpret these descriptions of the end of time as symbols. For one thing, most of the descriptions we have seen thus far in Revelation have been symbols. The four horsemen are examples. We are not to think of them as four literal horses and riders that are sent from the throne room of heaven to bring turmoil to the earth. They stand for conquest, war, famine, and death, which men obviously bring on themselves. Symbolism is especially evident in the cases of Death, who is said to ride the fourth, pale horse, and of Hades, who is said to follow him. Death cannot be a literal person, and neither can Hades, which is the abode of the dead.

We can also observe that most of the Old Testament texts from which this imagery is taken refer to God's judgments on Israel, or on one of the surrounding nations, by using another nation to destroy it. These images would mean only that the world as the people of those nations knew it was ending. It would be as if we were to say in the midst of some great personal calamity, "The sky is falling" or "This is the end!"

A third argument for these descriptions being symbolic is that it is almost impossible to take some of them literally. How can the stars actually fall to earth? How can the sky roll up? How can every mountain and island be moved?

A LITERAL DESCRIPTION

Yet the matter might not be as simple as that. For one thing, we are not dealing with everyday events in this passage. This is the final judgment of mankind and the end of the world. It is not only natural but almost imperative to think of it as unfolding in extraordinary ways. And, although most of the Old Testament texts that employ this language are using the destruction to describe the natural outcome of war, not all of them do. When Isaiah 24 uses apocalyptic language, it seems to be referring to a literal future devastation of the earth that will affect all people—not merely those of a single, conquered nation. We find another example in Joel—a book that spans everything from the natural destruction it describes in chapter 1, which is brought by an invasion of locusts, to the judgments of the end time it describes in chapter 2. In that chapter, Joel is calling for repentance in view of the greater and final judgment. The reference to the end is even more marked in chapter 3.

> Multitudes, multitudes,
>> in the valley of decision!
> For the day of the LORD is near
>> in the valley of decision.
> The sun and the moon are darkened,
>> and the stars withdraw their shining.
>
> The LORD roars from Zion,
>> and utters his voice from Jerusalem,
>> and the heavens and the earth quake.
> But the LORD is a refuge to his people,
>> a stronghold to the people of Israel. (Joel 3:14–16)

Two New Testament texts also point us in the direction of a literal interpretation. One is Revelation 21:1, which speaks of "a new heaven and a new earth" to come, after "the first heaven and first earth had passed away." The other is 2 Peter 3:11–13, where Peter is arguing for a literal future destruction of the world on the basis of the literal destruction that already occurred, by water, at the time of the flood. Building on verse 10, which I quoted a few pages ago, he writes,

> Since all these things are thus to be dissolved, what sort of people ought you to be in lives of holiness and godliness, waiting for and hastening the coming of the day of God, because of which the heavens will be set on fire and dissolved, and the heavenly bodies will melt as they burn! But according to his promise we are waiting for new heavens and a new earth in which righteousness dwells. (vv. 11–13)

If we are thinking literally, it is not hard to imagine how events of this magnitude could happen. A single earthquake is terrifying enough. But what if there were earthquakes all along the great tectonic plates that line the Pacific Rim and pass through the middle of the Atlantic Ocean, through Europe, and through countless other places? Devastation like that would be beyond description. It would release volcanic activity, and the pulverized rock and ash that would spew into the upper atmosphere would darken the sky and alter the apparent color of the moon and sun. The stars would not fall to earth—in fact, a star could not even approach the earth without destroying it completely. But meteors would do damage of biblical proportions, and they would have been described as stars by people whose language did not have words for meteors or asteroids. Even today, magazines carry articles about the possibility of the earth being struck by a large meteor and about the destruction that this would cause. Movies such as *Armageddon* have been based on these same possibilities.

Are these descriptions to be understood literally? I tend to think so, but I really do not know. What I do know is that if they are not literal, it is because the reality will be even more terrifying than these symbols are.

THE TERROR OF THE HUMAN RACE

And human beings will be terrified. That is the point of the second section of these verses.

> Then the kings of the earth and the great ones and the generals and the rich and the powerful, and everyone, slave and free, hid themselves in the caves and among the rocks of the mountains, calling to the mountains and rocks, "Fall on us and hide us from the face of him who is seated on the throne, and from the wrath of the Lamb, for the great day of their wrath has come, and who can stand?" (Rev. 6:15–17)

Several things in these verses are worth noting.

A UNIVERSAL TERROR

This terror will devour everyone. Usually, when some great disaster strikes a country, there are people who have foreseen it and have made plans that enable them to escape. Dictators will have deposited fortunes in Swiss bank accounts. Generals will have planes waiting to whisk them to a safe haven in South America. Even common people will have ways of avoiding a disaster. But this won't be the case when God comes to execute his judgments. In that day, the rulers of the world's nations, those who serve under them, the directors of the military forces, the rich, the influential, and also the lower orders of society—the slaves as well as the free but poor men—will all cower before God and seek shelter in the caves and among the rocks of the mountains. Unlike previous, smaller judgments throughout history, this judgment will be a universal judgment, and the terror that accompanies it will be universal also.

J. A. Seiss suggests how terrifying this collapse of the creation would be: "Self-possession, unshaken courage, dignified composure, philosophic thinking, hopefulness, assurance, and the last remains of the stern intrepidity and statue-like imperturbability which characterize some men now, will then have vanished from humanity."[2]

2. J. A. Seiss, *The Apocalypse: Lectures on the Book of Revelation* (1900; repr., Grand

TERROR OF GOD

If the universe is being broken up, the sky darkened, the mountains shaken, and the islands moved, then we can well understand the terror of the surviving portion of humanity. But the terror that is spoken of here is not of death. On the contrary, by contrast with what is actually terrifying the people on this day, death would actually seem welcome. The people would gladly accept death if the mountains and rocks would fall upon them and wipe them out. No—the terror that is spoken of here is not of death but of God. He is what is terrifying the wicked. The wicked would rather die than appear before him.

But appear before him they must. In their lifetimes, as they went about their worldly concerns, they may never have given a single serious thought to God. They may even have claimed to be atheists. But on the brink of the final judgment, they all suddenly do believe in God and take him seriously—though what they try to do is hide from him. "Fall on us and hide us from the face of him who is seated on the throne, and from the wrath of the Lamb," they cry. It is what Isaiah described in his prophecy—a day when mankind will "enter the caverns of the rocks and the clefts of the cliffs, from before the terror of the LORD, and from the splendor of his majesty, when he rises to terrify the earth" (Isa. 2:21).

But the mountains will not move to cover them. The mountains answer to God and do as he commands. Nor will the rocks answer the people's frantic prayers. There is only one Rock who could have sheltered them from the judgment that is due them for their manifold sins—the Rock of Ages—and they have scorned that Rock. Now they are to be crushed by the One who was crushed by them and judged by the One whom they unjustly judged. What a mercy that there is still a Rock to which we can flee and a cross in which we can seek shelter!

CONCLUSION

Earlier in this study, I quoted Jesus's words from the sermon on the Mount of Olives in which he refers to these catastrophic

---

Rapids: Zondervan, 1970), 157.

judgments. All the signs are there, for Jesus has given us an outline of these and other end-times events in Matthew 24. We might even think of that chapter from the gospel as an outline of the whole of Revelation 6. But have you noticed that there is one thing missing in Revelation 6 that Jesus mentions in Matthew? What is it?

Obviously, it is the coming of the Son of Man in the heavens. His coming is described in Matthew 24:30–31; Mark 13:26–27; and Luke 21:27. The earthquakes, the darkening of the sky, and the moving of the mountains are all in Revelation 6. But not the second coming!

What does this mean? It means that even now, with the signs of God's judgment in the heavens, the ultimate judgment is withheld—so reluctant is God to unleash his fury on the human race. The sixth seal brings us to the very brink of judgment. But even when the seventh seal is broken—even then there is a pause while the seven trumpets are blown and the seven bowls of wrath are poured out. It is only at very the end of these warnings that the final, ultimate, and irrevocable judgment comes.

J. Ramsey Michaels puts it like this: "The prophecy given in 1:7 ('Look, he is coming with the clouds') is almost, but not quite, fulfilled."[3] And George Eldon Ladd says, "The breaking of each of the seals does not witness the opening of part of the book, chapter by chapter as it were; all of the seals are preliminary to opening the book. The sixth seal brings us to the threshold of the opening of the book and the great events of the end. The breaking of the seventh seal makes it possible for the book to be opened and its contents disclosed."[4] In other words, even at this point God's wrath is withheld, and whoever will flee *to* the Lamb of God, rather than *from* him, will be saved.

Five miles north of Mount Saint Helens, in the state of Oregon, there is a place called Spirit Lake. There used to be a recreation lodge on Spirit Lake, and the caretaker of that lodge was a man named Harry Truman, who bore the same name as the former president

3. J. Ramsey Michaels, *Revelation*, The IVP New Testament Commentary Series (Downers Grove, IL: InterVarsity Press, 1997), 110.
4. George Eldon Ladd, *A Commentary on the Revelation of John* (Grand Rapids: William B. Eerdmans, 1972), 109.

of the United States. In the early months of 1980, geologists began to pick up warning signs indicating that the mountain would soon explode in a terrible eruption. Radio and television stations broadcast the warning. The police patrolled the growing area of danger, herding people to safety. The region was emptying rapidly as thousands of vacationers abandoned tourist camps and hiking trails to flee for their lives.

Harry Truman refused to budge. Rangers warned him, and other residents begged him to join their exodus. His own sister called in order to try to talk some sense into him. But Harry ignored the warnings. From that beautiful lodge beside the lake, overlooking the snowy top of Mount Saint Helens, Harry stood his ground. He even appeared on national television, laughing and saying, "Nobody knows more about this mountain than Harry, and it don't dare blow up on him!"

But it did. At 8:31 on the morning of May 18, the mountain erupted, shooting tons of disintegrated rock into a towering cloud that reached more than ten miles into the sky. Concussive waves raced down the mountain, faster than the speed of sound—flattening Harry and everything else for miles.

Today Harry Truman is considered an Oregon legend. His face can be found on T-shirts, beer mugs, and posters. It is the image of a foolish man who would not listen to the warnings—a man who perished in the blast.[5]

The Bible offers this warning to anyone who is wise enough to listen: "Kiss the Son, lest he be angry, and you perish in the way, for his wrath is quickly kindled. Blessed are all who take refuge in him" (Ps. 2:12).

5. The story is told in Billy Graham, *Approaching Hoofbeats: The Four Horsemen of the Apocalypse* (Waco: Word Books, 1983), 13–14

AFTERWORD

Here ends the manuscript. We are left to imagine what James Boice might have said about the opening of the seventh seal, how he would have interpreted the two witnesses, or what warnings he would have given about the red dragon, the fearsome beasts, or "the great prostitute who is seated on many waters"—to say nothing of his explanation of the seven trumpets, the seven plagues, or the seven bowls full of the wrath of God. We can only wonder how he would have preached the "thousand years" of chapter 20, or the glorious beauties that follow in chapters 21 and 22, in which every tear is wiped away and night will be no more. Rather than proclaiming these mysteries from the pulpit, through death he was given the higher privilege of seeing them for himself!

Preaching through Revelation was an important part of Dr. Boice's preparation for glory. Evidently, studying the book had a profound spiritual influence on the man. This was apparent not only to those who knew him well—his friends, colleagues, and family members—but also to the congregation of Tenth Presbyterian Church. In the last year of his life, their pastor seemed to find even greater joy in the worship of God and to take even more delight in singing his praises. Now we know why: through his study of the glorious hymns in John's apocalypse, Dr. Boice was being spiritually prepared for the worship of heaven.

Studying Revelation can and should have the same influence on everyone. As Dr. Boice wrote in this commentary, the Bible's last book tells us "that because God is in control of all things, we and all the creation must make it our primary activity and duty to worship him." The more we read Revelation, and the more we get caught up in its worship, the more we fulfill the main purpose for which God made us, by giving him all the glory we can.

One tangible result of Revelation's influence on Dr. Boice was the hymn-writing that he did during the final months of his ministry. To share the joy that his soul was finding in the lyrics of heaven, he put some of its symbols, themes, and choruses into poetry. Sharing a few of these lines at the end of this commentary is a good way to give Dr. Boice the last word and God a little more of the glory that he alone deserves.

Inspired by his reading of Revelation 4 and 5—and trying to build a sense of overflowing praise through repetition, as those two chapters do—Dr. Boice wrote,

'Round the throne in radiant glory
All creation loudly sings
Praise to God, to God almighty—
Day and night the anthem rings:
"Holy, holy, holy, holy
Is our God, the King of kings."

Christ, the Lamb, is worthy, worthy—
Let the anthem loudly swell—
Jesus died for sin on Calv'ry,
Rescued us from death and hell:
"Holy, holy, holy, holy
Is our God, Immanuel."

All creation joins in praising
Christ, the Savior of our race,
Drawn from ev'ry tribe and nation,
People, language, time and place:

"Holy, holy, holy, holy
Is our God, the God of grace."[1]

Based on the gracious words of Revelation 21 and 22, Dr. Boice also paraphrased and repeated the loving invitations that God gives at the end of the Bible to every lost and weary soul. In his dying days, this hymn became his most beloved:

Come to the waters, whoever is thirsty;
Drink from the Fountain that never runs dry.
Jesus, the Living One, offers you mercy,
Life more abundant in boundless supply.

Come to the River that flows through the city,
Forth from the throne of the Father and Son.
Jesus the Savior says, "Come and drink deeply."
Drink from the pure, inexhaustible One.

Come to the Fountain without any money;
Buy what is given without any cost.
Jesus, the gracious One, welcomes the weary;
Jesus, the selfless One, died for the lost.[2]

Philip Graham Ryken
President
Wheaton College

1. Published in James Montgomery Boice and Paul Steven Jones, *Hymns for a Modern Reformation* (Philadelphia: Tenth Presbyterian Church, 2000), 19.
2. Published in Boice and Jones, 21.

INDEX OF SCRIPTURE

Index of Subjects and Names

images in the Bible
feet like bronze,
59–60
fire, 59
Jesus knocking, 148
manna, 99
morning star,
113–14
names written on
foreheads, 136
from Old Testa-
ment, 156, 227
open door, 131–32
refined gold, 145
soiled clothing, 119
stars, 69
sword, 60, 92
thief (*see* Jesus
Christ: coming
like a thief)
valuable stones, 155
imputed righteousness,
principle of, 182
Irenaeus, 16, 19, 22

James, 214
jasper, 155
Jehovah Sabaoth, 166
Jerome, 2
Jerusalem
destruction of, 21,
37
fall of, 7, 9
Jesse, 180
Jesus Christ
blood of, 215

as central figure in
Revelation, 24
coming like a thief,
124
"comings" of, 37
as conqueror, 181,
183; of death, 80,
181; of Satan,
181; of sin, 181
being in control,
209–10
death of, 33, 194–95
as "faithful witness,"
25
as firstborn, 26
as focal point of
history, 35
as framer of New
Testament
prophecy, 9
having freed his
people, 31–32
as "the holy one,"
129, 130
as Judge, 35, 105–6,
124, 201
kingdom of (*see*
kingdom of
Christ)
among the
lampstands,
58–59, 149
being "like a son of
man," 58
as Lion, 180, 181,
183

as "the living one,"
62
as Lord of history,
200
love of, 30–31, 147
ministry of, 34
"new name" of,
136
omnipotence of,
185
omniscience of, 185
his opposition to
false teachers,
98, 104
prayer of, 216
as priest, 59
as prophet, 59
as ransom, 190
as Redeemer, 191
his relationship to
the Father, 176
as Root of David,
180, 181
as ruler, 26–27
his self-description,
142
his self-designation,
69–70
having been slain,
190
as son of man, 186
as sovereign God,
189
suffering of, 183,
184
teaching of, 212–13

ALSO BY JAMES MONTGOMERY BOICE

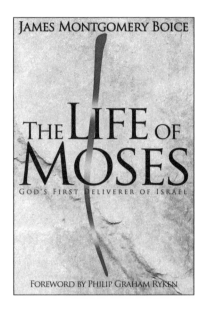

In this epic undertaking, James Montgomery Boice delves into the narrative of Moses's life to uncover its rich meaning and gospel application to us today. We can learn a lot from Moses about faithfulness, prayerfulness, meekness, and good leadership—we can even learn from his sins and failure! But Boice shows how we can also look beyond Moses and the Israelites to the awesome power of God and the promise of a much needed, much greater Deliverer.

"Here we find astounding moments and breathtaking scenes. Here we find ourselves standing on holy ground. Here we learn from Moses that we must trust God, obey God, and focus on God to the exclusion of all else. And here Dr. Boice continues to teach us of our ultimate calling: to worship God in the splendor of his glory."
—**Stephen J. Nichols**, President, Reformation Bible College